Praise for *Why Don't Students Like School*

"Brilliant analysis."

—Wall Street Journal

"A triumph of critical thinking."

—Washington Post

"Accessible, entertaining prose that knits together the cognitive science of learning with illuminating examples, to reveal students' challenges navigating school. A real gem is Willingham's convergence on clear implications for classroom improvement. The book is a masterpiece of style and content that every teacher will find indispensable."

—Mark McDaniel, professor,
Washington University in St. Louis, co-author of *Make It Stick*

"In these pages, Daniel Willingham lays out key ideas that have the power to improve education, borne from the study of cognitive science and evidence of how students learn, using accessible and thought-provoking examples that educators—and, indeed, everyone with an interest in schools—can find compelling. Since its initial publication, and through today, *Why Don't Students Like School?* represents a critical addition to the literature on teaching and learning. Daniel Willingham expertly examines cognition in multiple ways and then puts that knowledge to work with recommendations for practical actions that teachers can take in their classrooms to strengthen their instructional pedagogy. Amid a massive national shift to the increased use of distance learning, this second edition also focuses on what research currently tells us about the use of technology in education, and helps to provide educators with the essential questions they should ask about adopting new technologies and teaching tools. To be sure, this second edition of Daniel Willingham's pathbreaking work is right on time."

—John B. King Jr., 10th U.S. Secretary of Education and
President and CEO of The Education Trust

"A rare pairing of intelligible theoretical principles and practical strategies, crafted with teachers in mind. Willingham's book is one that educators can revisit and appreciate anew with every year of teaching."

—Jasmine Lane, high school English teacher, Minnesota

"Every school teacher and home-schooling caregiver should read this book. A distinguished cognitive scientist and brilliant explainer, Daniel Willingham brings us up to date on the latest science showing how critically important factual knowledge is for a person's competence and success. He shows us exactly how to cause youngsters to LOVE gaining it! A great contribution!"

—E.D. Hirsch Jr., author of *How to Educate a Citizen*, and founder of the Core Knowledge Foundation

"This second edition of *Why Don't Students Like School?* comes as COVID-19 has exacerbated longstanding inequities and schooling has become more foundational to helping keep students engaged and hopeful. Willingham's clear explanation of what it takes to learn and think well gives teachers and policymakers a strong blueprint for helping our youth not only tackle COVID's aftermath but thrive."

—Randi Weingarten, president, American Federation of Teachers

"Willingham's second edition takes us on a deeper dive into the knowledge of the mind; it takes what we now know and presents it in a way that encourages educators to hone their craft. Not only will education be better, students will also benefit with the retention of long-term learning."

—Patrice M. Bain, EdS, educator and author of *Powerful Teaching*

WHY DON'T
STUDENTS
Like
SCHOOL?

DANIEL T.
WILLINGHAM

Why Don't Students *Like* School?

A COGNITIVE SCIENTIST
ANSWERS QUESTIONS ABOUT HOW
THE MIND WORKS AND WHAT IT
MEANS FOR THE CLASSROOM

Second Edition

JB JOSSEY-BASS™
A Wiley Brand

Jossey-Bass

A Wiley Imprint

111 River St, Hoboken, NJ 07030 www.josseybass.com

Jossey-Bass books and products are available through most bookstores. To contact Jossey-Bass directly, call our Customer Care Department within the U.S. at 800-956-7739, outside the U.S. at +1 317 572 3986, or fax +1 317 572 4002.

Wiley also publishes its books in a variety of electronic formats and by print-on-demand. Some material included with standard print versions of this book may not be included in e-books or in print-on-demand. If this book refers to media such as a CD or DVD that is not included in the version you purchased, you may download this material at http://booksupport.wiley.com. For more information about Wiley products, visit www.wiley.com.

Library of Congress Cataloging-in-Publication Data is Available:

ISBN 9781119715665 (paperback)
ISBN 9781119715795 (epdf)
ISBN 9781119715801 (epub)

Cover image: School Desk: © CSA-Archive/Getty Images
                    Student: © A-Digit/Getty Images
Cover design: Wiley

Second Edition

SKY10074490_050324

For Trisha

Contents

Acknowledgments
to the First Edition

Esmond Harmsworth, my literary agent, has been an asset every step of the way, starting with the initial concept. Lesley Iura, Amy Reed, and the whole team at Jossey-Bass showed great expertise and professionalism during the editing and production processes. Anne Carlyle Lindsay was an exceptional help with the artwork in the book. Special thanks go to two anonymous reviewers who went far above and beyond the call of duty in providing extensive and helpful comments on the entire manuscript. Finally, I thank my many friends and colleagues who have generously shared thoughts and ideas and taught me so much about students and education, especially Judy Deloach, Jason Downer, Bridget Hamre, Lisa Hansel, Vikram Jaswal, Angel Lillard, Andy Mashburn, Susan Mintz, Bob Pianta, Trisha Thompson-Willingham, and Ruth Wattenberg.

Acknowledgments to the Second Edition

My thanks to the team at Wiley for their care in the editing and production process. Esmond Harmsworth, my literary agent, has been an asset every step of the way, and I thank Greg Culley for bringing his expertise to the artwork. This book owes much to teachers and researchers who have generously shared their expertise since the publication of the first edition.

The Author

Daniel T. Willingham earned his B.A. degree in psychology from Duke University in 1983 and his Ph.D. degree in cognitive psychology from Harvard University in 1990. He is currently professor of psychology at the University of Virginia, where he has taught since 1992. He is the author of several books, and his writing on education has appeared in 17 languages. In 2017 President Obama appointed him to the National Board for Education Sciences. His website is http://www.danielwillingham.com.

Introduction

Arguably the greatest mysteries in the universe lie in the three-pound mass of cells, approximately the consistency of oatmeal, that reside in the skull of each of us. It has even been suggested that the brain is so complex that our species is smart enough to fathom everything except what makes us so smart; that is, the brain is so cunningly designed for intelligence that it is too stupid to understand itself. We now know that is not true. The mind is at last yielding its secrets to persistent scientific investigation. We have learned more about how the mind works in the last 25 years than we did in the previous twenty-five hundred.

It would seem that greater knowledge of the mind would yield important benefits to education – after all, education is based on change in the minds of students, so surely understanding the student's cognitive equipment would make teaching easier or more effective. Yet the teachers I know don't believe they've seen much benefit from what psychologists call "the cognitive revolution." We all read stories in the newspaper about research breakthroughs in learning or problem solving, but it is not clear how each latest advance is supposed to change what a teacher does on Monday morning.

The gap between research and practice is understandable. When cognitive scientists study the mind, they intentionally isolate mental processes (for example, learning or attention) in the laboratory in order to make them easier to study. But mental processes are not isolated in the classroom. They all operate simultaneously, and they often interact in difficult-to-predict ways. To provide an obvious example, laboratory studies show that repetition helps learning, but any teacher knows that you can't take that finding and pop it into a classroom by, for example, having students repeat long-division problems until they've mastered the process. Repetition is good for learning but terrible for motivation. With too much repetition, motivation plummets, students stop paying attention, and no learning takes place. The classroom application would not duplicate the laboratory result.

Why Don't Students Like School? began as a list of nine principles that are so fundamental to the mind's operation that they do *not* change as circumstances change. They are as true in the classroom as they are in the laboratory* and therefore can reliably be applied to classroom situations. Many of these principles likely won't surprise you: factual knowledge is important, practice is necessary, and so on.

What may surprise you are the implications for teaching that follow. You'll learn why it's more useful to view the human species as *bad* at thinking rather than as cognitively gifted. You'll discover that authors routinely write only a fraction of what they mean, which I'll argue implies very little for reading instruction but a great deal for the factual knowledge your students must gain. You'll explore why you remember the plot of *Star Wars* without even trying, and you'll learn how to harness that ease of learning for your classroom. You'll follow the brilliant mind of television doctor Gregory House as he solves a case, and you'll discover why you should *not* try to get your students to think like real scientists. You'll see how people like American politician Julian Castro and actress Scarlett Johansson have helped psychologists analyze the obvious truth that kids inherit their intelligence from their parents – only to find that it's not true after all, and you'll understand why it is so important that you communicate that fact to your students.

Why Don't Students Like School? ranges over a variety of subjects in pursuit of two goals that are straightforward but far from simple: to tell you how your students' minds work and to clarify how to use that knowledge to be a better teacher.

Note

*There actually were three other criteria for inclusion: (i) using versus ignoring a principle had to have a big impact on student learning; (ii) there had to be an enormous amount of data, not just a few studies, to support the principle; and (iii) the principle had to suggest classroom applications that teachers might not already know. The first edition offered nine principles; in this second edition I've added a tenth chapter on technology and education.

1

Why Don't Students Like School?

Q *uestion:* Most of the teachers I know entered the profession because they loved school as children. They want to help their students feel the same excitement and passion for learning that they felt.

They are understandably dejected when they find that some of their pupils don't like school much, and that they, the teachers, have trouble inspiring them. Why is it difficult to make school enjoyable for students?

A *nswer:* Contrary to popular belief, the brain is not designed for thinking. It's designed to save you from having to think, because the brain is actually not very good at thinking. Thinking is slow and unreliable. Nevertheless, people enjoy mental work if it is successful. People like to solve problems but not to work on unsolvable problems. If schoolwork is always just a bit too difficult (or too easy) for a student, it should be no surprise that she doesn't like school much. The cognitive principle that guides this chapter is:

> People are naturally curious, but we are not naturally good thinkers; unless the cognitive conditions are right, we will avoid thinking.

The implication of this principle is that teachers should reconsider how they encourage their students to think, in order to maximize the likelihood that students will get the pleasurable rush that comes from successful thought.

The Mind Is Not Designed for Thinking

What is the essence of being human? What sets us apart from other species? Many people would answer that it is our ability to reason – birds fly, fish swim, and humans think. (By thinking I mean solving problems, reasoning, reading something complex, or doing any mental work that requires some effort.) Shakespeare extolled our cognitive ability in Hamlet: "What a piece of work is man! How noble in reason!" Some three hundred years later Henry Ford more cynically observed, "Thinking is the hardest work there is, which is the probable reason why so few people engage in it"* (Figure 1.1).

Both Shakespeare and Ford had a point. Humans are good at certain types of reasoning, particularly in comparison to other animals, but we exercise those abilities infrequently. A cognitive scientist would add another observation: Humans don't think very often because our brains are designed not for thought but for the avoidance of thought.

Your brain has many capabilities, and thinking is not the one it does best. Your brain also supports the ability to see and to move, for example, and these functions operate much more efficiently and reliably than your ability to think. It's no accident that most of your brain's real estate is devoted to these activities. The extra brain power is needed because seeing is actually more difficult than playing chess or solving calculus problems.

FIGURE 1.1: Kanye West is one the most successful and respected songwriters and performers, as well as a highly successful businessman. But he has said, "I actually don't like thinking. I think people think I like to think a lot. And I don't. I do not like to think at all."¹ Source: © Getty Images/ Brad Barket.

You can appreciate the power of your visual system by comparing human abilities to those of computers. When it comes to math, science, and other traditional "thinking" tasks, machines beat people, no contest. Calculators that can perform simple calculations faster and more accurately than any human have been cheaply available for 40 years. With $50 you can buy chess software that can defeat more than 99% of the world's population. But we're still struggling to get a computer to drive a truck as well as a human. That's because computers can't see, especially not in complex, ever-changing environments like the one you face every time you drive. And in fact, the self-driving vehicles in development typically use radar, lasers, and other sensors to supplement information from visible light.

Robots are similarly limited in how they move. Humans are excellent at configuring our bodies for tasks, even if the configuration is unusual, such as when you twist your torso and contort your arm in an effort to dust behind books on a shelf. Robots are not very good at figuring out novel ways to move and are most useful in repetitive work such as spray painting automotive parts or moving pallets or boxes at an Amazon fulfillment center – jobs in which the objects to be grasped and the locations to move them are predictable. Tasks that you take for granted – for example, walking on a rocky shore where the footing is uncertain – are much more difficult than playing top-level chess (Figure 1.2).

 FIGURE 1.2: Hollywood robots (left), like humans, can move in complex environments, but that's true only in the movies. Most real-life robots (right) move in predictable environments. Our ability to see and move is a remarkable cognitive feat. Source: Hollywood robots © Getty Images/Koichi Kamoshida; factory robots © Getty Images/Christopher Furlong.

Compared to your ability to see and move, thinking is slow, effortful, and uncertain. To get a feel for why I say this, try solving this problem:

> In an empty room are a candle, some matches, and a box of tacks. The goal is to have the lit candle about 5 ft off the ground. You've tried melting some of the wax on the bottom of the candle and sticking it to the wall, but that wasn't effective. How can you get the lit candle 5 ft off the ground without having to hold it there?[2]

Twenty minutes is the usual maximum time allowed, and few people are able to solve it by then, although once you hear the answer you will realize it's not especially tricky. You dump the tacks out of the box, tack the box to the wall, and use it as a platform for the candle.

This problem illustrates three properties of thinking. First, thinking is slow. Your visual system instantly takes in a complex scene. When you enter a friend's backyard you don't think to yourself, "Hmmm, there's some green stuff. Probably grass, but it could be some other ground cover – and what's that rough brown object sticking up there? A fence, perhaps?" You take in the whole scene – lawn, fence, flowerbeds, gazebo – at a glance. Your thinking system does not instantly calculate the answer to a problem the way your visual system immediately takes in a visual scene. Second, thinking is effortful; you don't have to try to see, but thinking takes concentration. You can perform other tasks while you are seeing, but you can't think about something else while you are working on a problem. Finally, thinking is uncertain. Your visual system seldom makes mistakes, and when it does you usually think you see something similar to what is actually out there – you're close, if not exactly right. Your thinking system might not even get you close. In fact, your thinking system may not produce an answer at all, which is what happens to most people when they try to solve the candle problem.

If we're all so bad at thinking, how does anyone get through the day? How do we find our way to work or spot a bargain at the grocery store? How does a teacher make the hundreds of decisions necessary to get through her day? The answer is that when we can get away with it, we don't think. Instead we rely on memory. Most of the problems we face are ones we've solved before, so we just do what we've done in the past. For example, suppose that next week a friend gives you the candle problem. You would immediately say, "Oh, right. I've heard this one. You tack the box to the wall." Just as your visual system takes in a scene and, without any effort on your part, tells you what is in the environment, so too your memory system immediately and effortlessly recognizes that you've heard the problem before and provides the answer. You may think you have a terrible memory, and it's true that your memory system is not as reliable as your visual or movement system – sometimes you forget, sometimes you think you remember when you don't – but your memory system is much more reliable than your thinking system, and it provides answers quickly and with little effort.

We normally think of memory as storing personal events (memories of my wedding) and facts (the seat of the Coptic Orthodox Church is in Egypt). Our memory also stores strategies to guide what we should do: where to turn when driving home, how to handle a minor dispute when monitoring recess, what to do when a pot on the stove starts to boil over (Figure 1.3). For the vast majority of decisions we make,

 FIGURE 1.3: Your memory system operates so quickly and effortlessly that you seldom notice it working. For example, your memory has stored away information about what things look like (Gandhi's face) and how to manipulate objects (turn the left faucet for hot water, the right for cold) and strategies for dealing with problems you've encountered before (such as a pot boiling over). Source: Gandhi © Getty Images/Dinodia Photos; faucet © Shutterstock/RVillalon; pot © Shutterstock/Andrey_Popov.

we don't stop to consider what we might do, reason about it, anticipate possible consequences, and so on. For example, when I decide
to make spaghetti for dinner, I don't scour the Internet for recipes,
weighing each for taste, nutritional value, ease of preparation, cost of
ingredients, visual appeal, and so on – I just make spaghetti sauce the
way I usually do. As two psychologists put it, "Most of the time what
we do is what we do most of the time."[3] When you feel as though you
are "on autopilot," even if you're doing something rather complex,
such as driving home from school, it's because you are using memory
to guide your behavior. Using memory doesn't require much of your
attention, so you are free to daydream, even as you're stopping at red
lights, passing cars, watching for pedestrians, and so on.

Of course you could make each decision with care and thought.
When someone encourages you to "think outside the box" that's
usually what he means – don't go on autopilot, don't do what you
(or others) have always done. Consider what life would be like if
you always strove to think outside the box. Suppose you approached
every task afresh and tried to see all of its possibilities, even daily
tasks like chopping an onion, entering your workplace, or sending
a text message. The novelty might be fun for a while, but life would
soon be exhausting (Figure 1.4).

You may have experienced something similar when traveling, especially if you've traveled where you don't speak the local language.
Everything is unfa-
miliar and even triv-
ial actions demand
lots of thought. For
example, buying a
soft drink from a ven-
dor requires figuring
out the flavors from
the exotic packaging,
trying to communi-
cate with the ven-
dor, working through
which coin or bill to
use, and so on. That's

FIGURE 1.4: "Thinking outside the box" for a
mundane task like selecting bread at the
supermarket would probably not be worth the
mental effort. Source: © Shutterstock/B Brown.

one reason that traveling is so tiring: all of the trivial actions that at home could be made on autopilot require your full attention.

So far I've described two ways in which your brain is set up to save you from having to think. First, some of the most important functions (for example, vision and movement) don't require thought: you don't have to reason about what you see; you just immediately know what's out in the world. Second, you are biased to use memory to guide your actions rather than to think. But your brain doesn't leave it there; it is capable of changing in order to save you from having to think. If you repeat the same thought-demanding task again and again, it will eventually become automatic; your brain will change so that you can complete the task without thinking about it. I discuss this process in more detail in Chapter 5, but a familiar example here will illustrate what I mean. You can probably recall that learning to drive a car was mentally very demanding. I remember focusing on how hard to depress the accelerator, when to apply the brake as I approached a red light, how far to turn the steering wheel to execute a turn, when to check my mirrors, and so forth. I didn't even listen to music while I drove, for fear of being distracted. With practice, however, the process of driving became automatic, and now I don't need to think about those small-scale bits of driving any more than I need to think about how to walk. I can drive while simultaneously chatting with friends, gesturing with one hand, and eating French fries – an impressive cognitive feat, if not very attractive to watch.[†] Thus a task that initially takes a great deal of thought becomes, with practice, a task that requires little thought.

The implications for education sound rather grim. If people are bad at thinking and try to avoid it, what does that say about students' attitudes toward school? Fortunately, the story doesn't end with people stubbornly refusing to think. Despite the fact that we're not that good at it, we actually like to think. We are naturally curious, and we look for opportunities to engage in certain types of thought. But because thinking is so hard, the conditions have to be right for this curiosity to thrive, or we quit thinking rather readily. The next section explains when we like to think and when we don't.

People Are Naturally Curious, But Curiosity Is Fragile

Even though the brain is not set up for very efficient thinking, people actually enjoy mental activity, at least in some circumstances. We have hobbies like solving crossword puzzles or scrutinizing maps. We watch information-packed documentaries. We pursue careers – such as teaching – that offer greater mental challenge than competing careers, even if the pay is lower. Not only are we willing to think, we intentionally seek out situations that demand thought.

Solving problems brings pleasure. When I say "problem solving" in this book, I mean any cognitive work that succeeds; it might be understanding a difficult passage of prose, planning a garden, or sizing up an investment opportunity. There is a sense of satisfaction, of fulfillment, in successful thinking. Neuroscientists have found overlap between the brain areas that are important in learning and those that are important in perception of pleasure, and many neuroscientists suspect that the two systems are related. Rats in a maze learn better when rewarded with cheese. When you solve a problem or satisfy your curiosity, your brain may reward itself with a small burst of a naturally occurring chemical in the brain's pleasure system. Even though the neurochemistry is not completely understood, it seems undeniable that people take pleasure in solving problems.

It's notable too that the pleasure is in the solving of the problem. Working on a problem with no sense that you're making progress is not pleasurable. In fact, it's frustrating. Then too, there's not great pleasure in simply knowing the answer. I told you the solution to the candle problem; did you get any fun out of it? Think how much more fun it would have been if you had solved it yourself – in fact, the problem would have seemed more clever, just as a joke that you get is funnier than a joke that has to be explained. Even if someone doesn't tell you the answer to a problem, once you've had too many hints you lose the sense that you've solved the problem, and getting the answer doesn't bring the same mental snap of satisfaction.

Mental work appeals to us because it offers the opportunity for that pleasant feeling when it succeeds. But not all types of thinking are equally attractive. People choose to work crossword puzzles but not algebra problems. A biography of Taylor Swift is more likely to sell well than a biography of Keats. What characterizes the mental activity that people enjoy (Figure 1.5)?

The answer that most people would give may seem obvious: "I think crossword puzzles are fun and Taytay is cool, but math is boring and so is Keats." In other words, it's the content that matters. We're curious about some stuff but not about other stuff. Certainly that's the way people describe our own interests – "I'm a stamp collector" or "I'm into medieval symphonic music." But I don't think content drives interest. We've all attended a lecture or watched a video (perhaps only after being prevailed upon to do so) about a subject we thought we weren't interested in, only to find ourselves fascinated. And it's easy to find yourself bored even when you usually like the topic. I'll never forget my eagerness for the day my middle school teacher was to talk about sex. As a teenage boy in a staid 1970s suburban culture, I fizzed with anticipation of any talk about sex, anytime, anywhere. But when the big day came, my friends and I were bored senseless. It's not that the teacher talked about flowers and pollination – he really did talk about human sexuality – but somehow it was still dull. I actually wish I could remember how he did it; boring a bunch of hormonal teenagers with a sex talk is quite a feat.

Hard Sudoku (Set 100)

	7	1				5		
6							7	
		7			3		4	
3			4			5	2	
	2		8		5		4	
	8	4			3			6
1		5			2			
	7						6	
	4				9	1		

4	9	7	1	3	8	6	5	2
2	6	3	9	5	4	8	7	1
8	5	1	7	2	6	3	9	4
3	1	9	4	6	7	5	2	8
7	2	6	8	1	5	9	4	3
5	8	4	2	9	3	7	1	6
1	3	5	6	7	2	4	8	9
9	7	8	3	4	1	2	6	5
6	4	2	5	8	9	1	3	7

Symmetric-fill with one unique solution

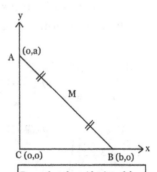

Prove that the midpoint of the hypotenuse of a right triangle is equidistant from the vertices of the triangle.

 FIGURE 1.5: Why are many people fascinated by problems like the one shown on the left, but very few people willingly work on problems like the one on the right? Source: Sudoku © Shutterstock/Heather Wallace; geometry © Anne Carlyle Lindsay.

I once made this point to a group of teachers when talking about motivation and cognition. About five minutes into the talk I presented a slide depicting the model of motivation shown in Figure 1.6. I didn't prepare the audience for the slide in any way; I just displayed it and started describing it. After about 15 seconds I stopped and said to the audience, "Anyone who is still listening to me, please raise your hand." One person did. The other 59 were also attending voluntarily; it was a topic in which they were presumably interested, and the talk had only just started – but in 15 seconds their minds were somewhere else. To be clear, I'm not blaming them; the content of a problem – whether it's about sex or human motivation – may be sufficient to prompt your interest, but it won't maintain it.

So, if content is not enough to keep your attention, when does curiosity have staying power? The answer seems to lie in our judgment of how much we are likely to learn. Curiosity is maintained when we think we'll learn a lot.

That judgment – will I learn? – is closely related to our perception of the difficulty of the problem. If it's that little burst of pleasure from solving a problem that we look forward to, then there's no point in working on a problem that is too easy – there'll be no pleasure when it's solved because it didn't feel like much of a problem in the first place. Then too, when you size up a problem as very difficult, you are judging that you're unlikely to solve it, and are therefore unlikely to get the satisfaction that comes with the solution. A crossword puzzle

 FIGURE 1.6: A difficult-to-understand figure that will bore most people unless it is adequately introduced. Source: © Anne Carlyle Lindsay.

that is too easy is just mindless work: you fill in the squares, scarcely thinking about it, and there's no gratification, even though you're getting all the answers. But you're unlikely to work long at a crossword puzzle that's too difficult. You know you'll solve very little of it, so it will just be frustrating. The slide in Figure 1.6 is too detailed to be absorbed with minimal introduction; my audience quickly concluded that it was overwhelming and mentally checked out of my talk.

To summarize, I've said that thinking is slow, effortful, and uncertain. Nevertheless, people like to think – or more properly, we like to think if we judge that the mental work will pay off with the pleasurable feeling we get when we learn something new. So there is no inconsistency in claiming that people avoid thought and in claiming that people are naturally curious – curiosity prompts people to explore new ideas and problems, but when we do, we quickly evaluate how much mental work it will take to solve the problem or understand what's described. If it's too much work or too little, we stop thinking about the problem if we can.

This analysis of the sorts of mental work that people seek out or avoid also provides one answer to why more students don't like school. Working on problems that are of the right level of difficulty is rewarding, but working on problems that are too easy or too difficult is unpleasant. Students can't opt out of these problems the way adults often can. If the student routinely gets work that is a bit too difficult, it's little wonder that he doesn't care much for school. I wouldn't want to work on the Sunday New York Times crossword puzzle for several hours each day.

So what's the solution? Give the student easier work? You could, but of course you'd have to be careful not to make it so easy that the student would be bored. And anyway, wouldn't it be better to boost the student's ability a little bit? Instead of making the work easier, is it possible to make thinking easier?

How Thinking Works

Understanding a bit about how thinking happens will help you understand what makes thinking hard. That will in turn help you understand how to make thinking easier for your students, and therefore help them enjoy school more.

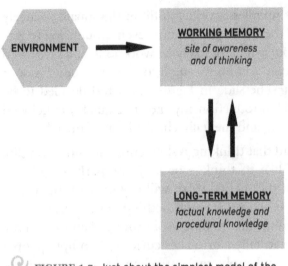

FIGURE 1.7: Just about the simplest model of the mind possible. Source: © Greg Culley.

Let's begin with a very simple model of the mind. On the left of Figure 1.7 is the environment, full of things to see and hear, problems to be solved, and so on. On the right is one component of your mind that scientists call working memory. For the moment, consider it to be synonymous with consciousness; it holds the stuff you're thinking about. The arrow from the environment to working memory shows that working memory is the part of your mind where you are aware of what is around you: the sight of a shaft of light falling onto a dusty table, the sound of a dog barking in the distance, and so forth. Of course you can also be aware of things that are not currently in the environment; for example, you can recall the sound of your mother's voice, even if she's not in the room (or indeed no longer living). Long-term memory is the vast storehouse in which you maintain your factual knowledge of the world: that leopards have spots, that your favorite flavor of ice cream is chocolate, that your three-year-old surprised you yesterday by mentioning kumquats, and so on. Factual knowledge can be abstract; for example, it would include the idea that triangles are closed figures with three sides and your knowledge of what a dog generally looks like. All of the information in long-term memory resides outside of awareness. It lies quietly until it is needed and then enters working memory and so enters consciousness. For example, if I asked you, "What color is a polar bear?" you would say, "white" almost immediately. That information was in long-term memory 30 seconds ago, but you weren't aware of it until I posed the question that made it relevant to ongoing thought, whereupon it entered working memory.

Thinking occurs when you combine information (from the environment and long-term memory) in new ways. That combining happens in working memory. To get a feel for this process, read the problem depicted in Figure 1.8 and try to solve it. (The point is not so much to solve it as to experience what is meant by thinking and working memory.)

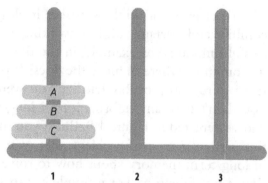

FIGURE 1.8: The figure depicts a playing board with three pegs. There are three rings of decreasing size on the leftmost peg. The goal is to move all three rings from the leftmost peg to the rightmost peg. There are just two rules about how you can move rings: you can move only one ring at a time, and you can't place a larger ring on top of a smaller ring. Source: © Greg Culley.

With some diligence you might be able to solve this problem,‡ but the real point is to feel what it's like to have working memory absorbed by the problem. You begin by taking information from the environment – the rules and the configuration of the game board – and then imagine moving the discs to try to reach the goal. Within working memory you must maintain your current state in the puzzle – where the discs are – and imagine and evaluate potential moves. At the same time you have to remember the rules regarding which moves are legal, as shown in Figure 1.9.

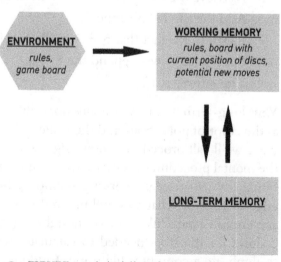

FIGURE 1.9: A depiction of your mind when you're working on the puzzle shown in Figure 1.8. Source: © Greg Culley.

The description of thinking makes it clear that knowing how to combine and rearrange ideas in working memory is essential to successful thinking. For example, in the discs and pegs problem, how do you know where to move the discs? If you hadn't seen the problem before, you probably felt like you were pretty much guessing. You didn't have any information in long-term memory to guide you, as depicted in Figure 1.9. But if you have had experience with this particular type of problem, then you likely have information in long-term memory about how to solve it, even if the information is not foolproof. For example, try to work this math problem in your head:

$$18 \times 7$$

You know just what to do for this problem. The sequence of your mental processes was likely something close to this:

1. Multiply 8 and 7.
2. Retrieve the fact that $8 \times 7 = 56$ from long-term memory.
3. Remember that the 6 is part of the solution, then carry the 5.
4. Multiply 7 and 1.
5. Retrieve the fact that $7 \times 1 = 7$ from long-term memory.
6. Add the carried 5 to the 7.
7. Retrieve the fact that $5 + 7 = 12$ from long-term memory.
8. Put the 12 down, append the 6.
9. The answer is 126.

Your long-term memory contains not only factual information, such as the color of polar bears and the value of 8×7, but it also contains what we'll call procedural knowledge, which is your knowledge of the mental procedures necessary to execute tasks. If thinking is combining information in working memory, then procedural knowledge is a list of what to combine and when — it's like a recipe to accomplish a particular type of thought. You might have stored procedures for the steps needed to calculate the area of a triangle, or to duplicate a computer file using Windows, or to drive from your home to your workplace.

It's pretty obvious that having the appropriate procedure stored in long-term memory helps a great deal when we're thinking. That's why it was easy to solve the math problem and hard to solve the discs-and-pegs problem. But how about factual knowledge? Does that help you think as well? It does, in several different ways, which are discussed in Chapter 2. For now, note that solving the math problem required the retrieval of factual information, such as the fact that $8 \times 7 = 56$. I've said that thinking entails combining information in working memory. Often the information provided in the environment is not sufficient to solve a problem, and you need to supplement it with information from long-term memory.

There's a final necessity for thinking, which is best understood through an example. Have a look at this problem:

In the inns of certain Himalayan villages is practiced a refined tea ceremony. The ceremony involves a host and exactly two guests, neither more nor less. When his guests have arrived and seated themselves at his table, the host performs three services for them. These services are listed in the order of the nobility the Himalayans attribute to them: stoking the fire, fanning the flames, and pouring the tea. During the ceremony, any of those present may ask another, "Honored Sir, may I perform this onerous task for you?" However, a person may request of another only the least noble of the tasks that the other is performing. Furthermore, if a person is performing any tasks, then he may not request a task that is nobler than the least noble task he is already performing. Custom requires that by the time the tea ceremony is over, all the tasks will have been transferred from the host to the most senior of the guests. How can this be accomplished?[4]

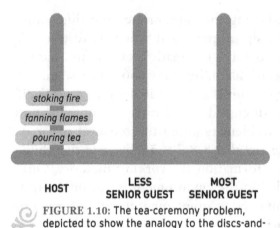

FIGURE 1.10: The tea-ceremony problem, depicted to show the analogy to the discs-and-pegs problem. Source: © Greg Culley.

Your first thought upon reading this problem was likely "Huh?" You could probably tell that you'd have to read it several times just to understand it, let alone begin working on the solution. It seemed overwhelming because you did not have sufficient space in working memory to hold all of the aspects of the problem. Working memory has limited space, so thinking becomes increasingly difficult as working memory gets crowded.

The tea-ceremony problem is actually the same as the discs-and-pegs problem presented in Figure 1.8. The host and two guests are like the three pegs, and the tasks are the three discs to be moved among them, as shown in Figure 1.10. (The fact that very few people see this analogy and its importance for education is taken up in Chapter 4.)

This version of the problem seems much harder because some parts of the problem that are laid out in Figure 1.8 must be juggled in your head in this new version. For example, Figure 1.8 provides a picture of the pegs that you can use to help maintain a mental image of the discs as you consider moves, whereas the tea ceremony version provides no such support. And in the tea version, the description of the rules that govern moves is longer and therefore occupies so much space in working memory that it's difficult to plan a solution.

Aristotle said, "The pleasures arising from thinking and learning will make us think and learn all the more."[5] You've seen that this view is too optimistic. It's *successful* learning that's pleasurable and that will keep students coming back for more. We've seen that one of the factors in successful learning is having the right information in long-term memory. In the next chapter, we examine that need more closely.

Summary

People's minds are not especially well suited to thinking; thinking is slow, effortful, and uncertain. For this reason, deliberate thinking does not guide people's behavior in most situations. Rather, we rely on our memories, following courses of action that we have taken before. Nevertheless, we find successful thinking pleasurable. We like solving problems, understanding new ideas, and so forth. Thus, we will seek out opportunities to think, but we are selective in doing so; we choose problems that pose some challenge but that seem likely to be solvable, because these are the problems that lead to feelings of pleasure and satisfaction. For problems to be solved, the thinker needs adequate information from the environment, room in working memory, and the required facts and procedures in long-term memory.

Implications for the Classroom

Let's turn now to the question that opened this chapter: Why don't students like school, or more accurately, why don't more of them like it? Any teacher knows that there are lots of reasons that a student might or might not enjoy school. (My wife loved it, but primarily for social reasons.) From a cognitive perspective, an important factor is whether or not a student consistently experiences the pleasurable rush of learning something new, of solving a problem. What can teachers do to ensure that each student gets that pleasure?

Be Sure That There Are Problems to Be Solved

By problem I don't necessarily mean a question addressed to the class by the teacher, or a mathematical puzzle. I mean cognitive work that poses moderate challenge, including such activities as understanding a poem or thinking of novel uses for recyclable materials. This sort of cognitive work is of course the main stuff of teaching – we want our students to think. But without some attention, a lesson plan can become a long string of teacher explanations, with little opportunity for students to solve problems. So scan each lesson plan with an eye toward the cognitive work that students will be doing. How often does such work occur? Is it intermixed with cognitive breaks? Is it real cognitive work that can lead to the feeling of discovery and not just retrieval from memory? (Think especially about questions posed during whole-class instruction – research shows it's easy for teachers to slip into a pattern of asking lots of fact-retrieval questions.) When you have identified the challenges, consider whether they are open to negative outcomes such as students failing to understand what they are to do, or students being unlikely to solve the problem, or students simply trying to guess what you would like them to say or do.

Respect Students' Cognitive Limits

When trying to develop effective mental challenges for your students, bear in mind the cognitive limitations discussed in this chapter. For example, suppose you began a history lesson with a question: "You've read that 35 nations united to expel Iraq from Kuwait in the First Gulf War, the largest coalition since World War II. Why do you suppose so many nations joined?" Do your students have the necessary background knowledge in memory to consider this question? What do they know about the relationship of Iraq and neighboring countries that ended up joining the coalition prior to the war? Do they know about how Iraq brought their dispute with Kuwait to the Arab League before the invasion? Do they know about the significance of oil to the world economy and the forecast economic consequences of the invasion? Could they generate reasonable alternative courses of action for those countries leading the invasion? If they lack the appropriate background knowledge, the question you pose will quickly be judged as "boring." If students lack the background knowledge to engage with a problem, save it for another time when they have that knowledge.

Equally important is the limit on working memory. Remember that people can keep only so much information in mind at once, as you experienced when you read the tea-ceremony version of the discs-and-pegs problem. Overloads of working memory are caused by such things as multistep instructions, lists of unconnected facts, chains of logic more than two or three steps long, and the application of a just-learned concept to new material (unless the concept is quite simple). The solution to working memory overloads is straightforward: slow the pace, and use memory aids such as writing on the whiteboard to save students from keeping too much information in working memory.

Clarifying the Problems to Be Solved

How can you make the problem interesting? A common strategy is to try to make the material "relevant" to students. This strategy sometimes works well, but it's hard to use for some material, and your struggle to make it relevant to students is usually obvious. Another difficulty is that a teacher's class may include two football fans, a doll collector, a NASCAR enthusiast, a horseback riding competitor – you get the idea. Mentioning a popular singer in the course of a history lesson may give the class a giggle, but it won't do much more than that. I have emphasized that our curiosity is provoked when we perceive a problem that we believe we can solve. What is the question that will engage students and make them want to know the answer?

One way to view schoolwork is as a series of answers. We want students to know Boyle's law, or three causes of World War I, or why Poe's raven kept saying, "Nevermore." Sometimes I think that we, as teachers, are so eager to get to the answers that we do not devote sufficient time to developing the question. That probably happens because the question is obvious to us. But of course it's not obvious to students, and as the information in this chapter indicates, it's the question that piques people's interest. Being told an answer doesn't do anything for you. You may have noted that I could have organized this book around principles of cognitive psychology. Instead I organized it around questions that I thought teachers would find interesting.

When you plan a lesson, you start with the information you want students to know by its end. As a next step, consider what the key question for that lesson might be and how you can frame that question so it will have the right level of difficulty to engage your students and so you will respect your students' cognitive limitations.

Reconsider When to Puzzle Students

Teachers often seek to draw students into a lesson by presenting a problem that we believe will interest the students. For example, asking, "Why is there a law that you have to go to school?" could introduce the process by which laws are passed. Another strategy is to conduct a demonstration or present a fact that we think students will find surprising. In either case, the goal is to puzzle students, to make them curious. This is a useful technique, but it's worth considering whether these strategies might be used not only at the beginning of a lesson but also after the basic concepts have been learned. For example, a classic science demonstration is to put a burning piece of paper in a milk bottle and then put a boiled egg over the bottle's opening. After the paper burns, the egg appears to be sucked into the bottle. Students will no doubt be astonished, but if they don't know the principle behind it, the demonstration is like a magic trick – it's a momentary thrill, but their curiosity to understand may not be long-lasting. Another strategy would be to conduct the demonstration after students know that warm air expands and cooling air contracts, potentially forming a vacuum. Every fact or demonstration that would puzzle students before they have the right background knowledge has the potential to be an experience that will puzzle students momentarily and then lead to the pleasure of problem solving. It is worth thinking about when to use a marvelous device like the egg-in-the-bottle trick.

Accept and Act on Variation in Student Preparation

As I describe in Chapter 8, I don't accept that some students are "just not very bright" and ought to be tracked into less demanding classes. But it's naïve to pretend that all students come to your class equally prepared to excel; they have had different preparations, as well as different levels of support at home, and they will therefore differ in their abilities, as well as their perception of themselves as students. Those factors, in turn, affect therefore their persistence and resilience to failure. If that's true, and if what I've said in this chapter is true, it is self-defeating to give all of your students the same work. The less capable students will find it too difficult and will struggle against their brain's bias to mentally walk away from schoolwork. To the extent that you can, it's smart, I think, to assign work to individuals or groups of students that is appropriate to their current level of competence. Naturally, you will want to do this in a sensitive way, minimizing the extent to which some students will perceive themselves as behind others. But the fact is that they are behind the others, and giving them work that is beyond them is unlikely to help them catch up and is likely to make them fall still further behind.

Change the Pace

We all inevitably lose the attention of our students, and as this chapter has described, it's likely to happen if they feel somewhat confused. They will mentally check out. The good news is that it's relatively easy to get them back. Change grabs attention, as you no doubt know. When there's a bang outside your classroom, every head turns to the windows. When you change topics, start a new activity, or in some other way show that you are shifting gears, virtually every student's attention will come back to you, and you will have a new chance to engage them. So plan shifts and monitor your class's attention to see whether you need to make them more often or less frequently.

Keep a Diary

The core idea presented in this chapter is that solving a problem gives people pleasure, but the problem must be easy enough to be solved yet difficult enough to take some mental effort. Finding this sweet spot of difficulty is not easy. Your experience in the classroom is your best guide – whatever works, do again; whatever doesn't, discard. But don't expect that you will really remember how well a lesson plan worked a year later. Whether a lesson goes brilliantly well or down in flames, it feels at the time that we'll never forget what happened; but the ravages of memory can surprise us, so write it down. Even if it's just a quick scratch on a sticky note, try to make a habit of recording your success in gauging the level of difficulty in the problems you pose for your students.

One of the factors that contributes to successful thought is the amount and quality of information in long-term memory. In Chapter 2 I elaborate on the importance of background knowledge to effective thinking.

Notes

*A more eloquent version comes from eighteenth-century British painter Sir Joshua Reynolds: "There is no expedient to which a man will not resort to avoid the real labor of thinking."
†And in fact people's driving is more impaired than they realize when they multitask. Don't try this at home!
‡If you couldn't solve it, here's a solution. As you can see, the rings are marked A, B, and C, and the pegs are marked 1, 2, and 3. The solution is A3, B2, A2, C3, A1, B3, A3.

Further Reading

Less Technical

Coalition for Psychology in Schools and Education. (2015). Top 20 principles from psychology for preK-12 teaching and learning. https://www.apa.org/ed/schools/teaching-learning/top-twenty-principles.pdf (accessed 13 July 2020). A brief, easy introduction to applying knowledge from psychology to classrooms, and a free download.

Csikszentmihalyi, M. (1990). *Flow: The Psychology of Optimal Experience.* New York: Harper Perennial. The author describes the ultimate state of interest, when one is completely absorbed in what one is doing, to the point that time itself stops. The book does not tell you how to enter this state, but it is an interesting read in its own right.

Didau, D., & Rose, N. (2016). *What Every Teacher Needs to Know About Psychology.* Melton, UK: John Catt. Brief chapters on a broad sweep of topics, including evolution, creativity, motivation, and more, very much from a teacher's perspective.

National Academies of Sciences, Engineering, and Medicine. (2018). *How People Learn II: Learners, Contexts, and Cultures.* National Academies Press. https://www.nap.edu/catalog/24783/how-people-learn-ii-learners-contexts-and-cultures (accessed 13 July 2020). Intended as an overview of cognition applied to education, this book sometimes overreaches, moving into peripheral topics, but it's worth the read, and it's a free download.

Willingham, D. T. (2019a). The high price of multitasking. *New York Times* (15 July), p. A21. https://www.nytimes.com/2019/07/14/opinion/multitasking-brain.html. A quick review of evidence that we cannot cope with working memory overload as well as we think we can.

Willingham, D. T. (2019b). Why aren't we curious about the things we want to be curious about? *New York Times* (20 October), p. SR9. https://www.nytimes.com/2019/10/18/opinion/sunday/curiosity-brain.html. This op-ed considers what triggers curiosity and how we might make ourselves curious about things that align with our long-term interests.

More Technical

Baddeley, A. (2018). *Exploring Working Memory: Selected Works of Alan Baddely*. Oxford, UK: Routledge. A retrospective of the most important articles by Alan Baddeley, commonly considered the central figure in the development of working memory theory over the last 50 years.

Berridge, K. C., & Kringelbach, M. L. (2015). Pleasure systems in the brain. *Neuron*, 86(3), 646–664. Reviews evidence that various types of pleasure we feel—from using addictive drugs, listening to music, experiencing romantic love, or eating delicious food—all have a common anatomic basis in the brain.

Kidd, C., & Hayden, B. Y. (2015). The psychology and neuroscience of curiosity. *Neuron*, 88(3), 449–460. An overview of contemporary theories of curiosity, focusing on the idea that curiosity evolved to ensure that animals, including humans, learn about their environment. We are maximally curious when we think the environment offers the greatest opportunity to learn.

Long, N. M., Kuhl, B. A., & Chun, M. M. (2018). Memory and attention. *Stevens' Handbook of Experimental Psychology and Cognitive Neuroscience*, 1–37. Hoboken, NJ: Wiley. You probably didn't need to be convinced that paying attention is a prerequisite for learning. This chapter offers much more detail and, as you'd expect, some caveats and complications.

Willingham, D. T., & Riener, C. (2019). *Cognition: The Thinking Animal*, 4. Cambridge, UK: Cambridge University Press. This is a college-level textbook on cognitive psychology that can serve as an introduction to the field. It assumes no background, but it is a textbook, so although it is thorough, it might be a bit more detailed than you want.

Discussion Questions

1. We like to think only when we believe we'll be successful. If you want to engage in thinking more often, how then might you change your environment so that you more often encounter the right sort of mental challenge? Or what might you say to yourself to get you to try more often?

2. When are your students on autopilot? It's easy to say there's value in trying to go off autopilot and *think* more often, but what are the obstacles to doing so? Can you think of ways of picking problems that they currently solve on autopilot that actually seem promising to think about?

3. Just how much reward does a student need for the work of thinking? There's no firm answer to this question, and we'd certainly guess that it would vary by age and would vary within a classroom, probably based on students' concept of themselves as students and some inherent aspect of each student's persistence. Nevertheless it's worth considering: on average, how often would you like students to feel the pleasure of success? Equally important, how do you know when they do? If they solve a problem, are you sure they feel success? If not, is there anything you can do to prompt that feeling?

4. Think of some assignments that your students consistently enjoy, and view them through the cognitive-work-that-succeeds lens. Does that work share any common characteristics?

5. I suggested that students don't fully understand or appreciate the question that the to-be-learned content is meant to answer. How often do you think that applies to your context? How easy or difficulty might it be to get students to both understand the question at stake and to engage with it?

6. I was a little casual in the implications section when I said that it's straightforward to deal with working memory overload. I said you should slow down and break things into smaller chunks, which is true, as far as it goes. What's trickier to deal with are the differences among students in what makes them feel overloaded. What can be done about that?

2

How Can I Teach Students the Skills They Need When Standardized Tests Require Only Facts?

Question: Much has been written about fact learning, and much of it has been negative. The narrow-minded schoolmaster demanding that students parrot facts they do not understand has become a cliché of American education, although the stereotype is neither new nor especially American – Dickens used it in *Hard Times*, published in 1854. Concern has increased since the early 2000s as the importance of standardized tests have increased; they typically offer little opportunity for students to analyze, synthesize, or critique and instead demand the recall of isolated facts. Many teachers feel that time for teaching skills is crowded out by preparation for standardized tests. Just how useful or useless is fact learning?

Answer: There is no doubt that having students memorize lists of isolated facts is not enriching. It is also true (though less often appreciated) that trying to teach students skills such as analysis or synthesis in the absence of factual knowledge is impossible. Research from cognitive science has shown that the sorts of skills that teachers want for students – such as the ability to analyze and to think critically – require extensive factual knowledge. The cognitive principle that guides this chapter is:

> Thinking skills depend on factual knowledge.

The implication is that students must have the opportunity to learn factual knowledge. That should be done in the context of practicing thinking skills and will ideally start in preschool and even before.

> There is a great danger in the present day lest science-teaching should degenerate into the accumulation of disconnected facts and unexplained formulae, which burden the memory without cultivating the understanding.[1]
>
> –J. D. Everett, writing in 1873

When I was a freshman in college a guy down the hall from me had a poster depicting Einstein and a quotation from the brilliant, frowsy-haired physicist: "Imagination is more important than knowledge." I thought this was very deep. Perhaps I was anticipating what I might say to my parents if my grades were poor: "Sure, I got Cs, but I have imagination! And according to Einstein . . ."

Some 40 years later teachers have a different reason to be wary and weary of "knowledge." Governments seek some assurance of quality in their schools. That usually means that children will be tested, and those tests are often heavy on multiple-choice questions that require straightforward recall of facts because those questions are the easiest to score. Here are two examples from my home state of Virginia, one from the eighth-grade science test and one from the third-grade history test.[2]

Sea anemones are poisonous. However, the clownfish has developed an outer layer of mucus that provides protection from the stinging cells of the sea anemone. The mucus is best described as

    A. *an adaptation*

    B. a relationship

    C. an energy requirement

    D. a social hierarchy

George Washington Carver invented new ways to use

    A. paper

    B. electricity

C. *peanuts*

D. bananas

It's easy to see why a teacher, parent, or student would protest that knowing the answer to a lot of these questions doesn't prove that one really *knows* science or history. We want our students to think, not simply to memorize. When someone shows evidence of thinking critically, we consider her smart and well educated. When someone spouts facts without context, we consider her boring and a show-off.

That said, there are obvious cases in which everyone would agree that factual knowledge is necessary. When a speaker uses unfamiliar vocabulary, you may not understand what he means. For example, if a friend texted you that she thought your daughter was dating a "yegg," you'd certainly want to know the definition of the word (Figure 2.1). Similarly, you may know all of the vocabulary words but lack the conceptual knowledge to knit the words together into something comprehensible. For example, a recent copy of the technical journal *Science* contained an article titled "Measuring magnetic field texture in correlated electron systems under extreme conditions."[3] I know what each of these words means, but I don't know enough about magnetic fields to understand what's meant by their texture, let alone why one might want to measure it.

 FIGURE 2.1: If someone said your daughter is dating a *yegg*, you'd certainly want to know whether the word meant "nice-looking fellow," "Internet addict," or "burglar." Source: Nice fellow © Shutterstock/G-Stock Studio; addict © Shutterstock/Kopytin Georgy; burglar © Shutterstock/Lisa_S.

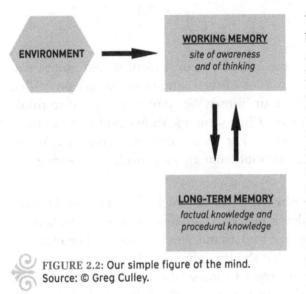

FIGURE 2.2: Our simple figure of the mind.
Source: © Greg Culley.

The necessity of background knowledge for comprehension is pretty obvious, at least as I've described it so far. You could summarize this view by noting that *to think* is a transitive verb. You need something to think *about*. But you could counter (and I've heard the argument often) that you don't need to have this information memorized – you can always look it up. Recall the figure of the mind in Chapter 1 (Figure 2.2).

I defined *thinking* as combining information in new ways. The information can come from long-term memory – facts you've memorized – or from the environment. In today's world, why memorize anything? You can find any factual information you need in seconds via the Internet – including the definition of *yegg*. Then too, things change so quickly that half of the information you commit to memory will be out of date in five years – or so the argument goes. Perhaps instead of learning facts, it's better to practice critical thinking, to have students work at *evaluating* all the information available on the Internet rather than trying to commit some small part of it to memory.

In this chapter I show that this argument is false. (In Chapter 9 we'll examine looking things up.) Data from the last 40 years lead to a conclusion that is not scientifically challengeable: thinking well requires knowing facts, and that's true not simply because you need something to think *about*. The very processes that teachers care about most – critical thinking processes such as reasoning and problem solving – are intimately intertwined with factual knowledge that is stored in long-term memory (not just found in the environment).

It's hard for many people to conceive of thinking processes as intertwined with knowledge. Most people believe that thinking processes are akin to the functions of a calculator. A calculator has available a set of procedures (addition, multiplication, and so on) that can manipulate numbers, and these procedures can be applied to *any set of numbers*. The data (the numbers) and the operations that manipulate the data are separate. Thus, if you learn a new thinking operation (for example, how to critically analyze historical documents), that operation should be applicable to all historical documents, just as a fancier calculator that computes sines can do so for all numbers.

But the human mind does not work that way. When we learn to think critically about, say, the geopolitics of Europe resulting from World War II, it does not mean we can also think critically about a chess game or about the current situation in the Middle East or even about geopolitics of Europe resulting from the French revolution. Critical thinking processes are tied to background knowledge (although they become less so when we gain significant experience, as I describe in Chapter 6). The conclusion from this work in cognitive science is straightforward: we must ensure that students acquire background knowledge in parallel with practicing critical thinking skills (Figure 2.3).

In this chapter I describe how cognitive scientists know that thinking skills and knowledge are bound together.

FIGURE 2.3: The human mind is more like this astrolabe than like a calculator. Among other functions, it can be used to measure the altitude of a celestial body above the horizon, but that function is *not* independent of knowledge. An astrolabe's knowledge representations – the numbers you see engraved, and the way the parts move in relation to one another – are part of its construction. Of course, you need processing – you need to know *how* to use the astrolabe – but the knowledge representations are also essential.
Source: © Getty Images/Science & Society Picture Library.

Knowledge Is Essential to Reading Comprehension

Background knowledge helps you understand what someone is saying or writing. In the last section I gave a couple of rather obvious examples: if a vocabulary word (for example, *yegg*) or a concept (for example, *magnetic field texture*) is missing from your long-term memory, you'll likely be confused. But the need for background knowledge is deeper than the need for definitions.

Suppose a sentence contains two ideas – call them A and B. Even if you know the vocabulary and you understand both A and B, you still might need background knowledge to understand the sentence. For example, suppose you read the following sentence in a novel:

> *"I shouldn't use my new barbecue when the boss comes to dinner,"*
> *Mark said.*

You could say that idea A is Mark using his new barbecue, and idea B is that he shouldn't do it when his boss comes to dinner. Obviously, you're meant to understand more than just A and B; the writer expects you to understand the relationship of these two ideas, that B (boss coming) is the cause of A (shouldn't use new barbecue). But the writer has omitted two pieces of information that would help you bridge A and B: that people often make mistakes the first time they use a new appliance and that Mark would like to impress his boss. Putting these facts together would help you understand that Mark is afraid he'll ruin the food the first time he uses his new barbecue, and he doesn't want that to be the meal he serves to his boss.

Reading comprehension depends on combining the ideas in a passage, not just comprehending each idea on its own. But writers seldom provide the reader all of the information needed to bridge ideas. Writers assume the reader has that knowledge in long-term memory. In the example just given, the writer assumed that the reader would know the relevant facts about new appliances and about bosses.

Why do writers leave gaps? Don't they run the risk that the reader *won't* have the right background knowledge and so will be confused? That's a risk, but writers can't include all the factual details. If they did, prose would be impossibly long and tedious. For example, imagine reading this:

> *"I shouldn't use my new barbecue when the boss comes to dinner,"* Mark said. *Then he added, "Let me make clear that by* boss *I mean my immediate supervisor. Not the president of the company, nor any of the other supervisors intervening. And I'm using* dinner *in the local vernacular, not to mean 'noontime meal,' as it is used in some parts of the United States. And when I said* barbecue, *I was speaking imprecisely, because I really meant grill, because* barbecue *generally refers to slower roasting, whereas I plan to cook over high heat. Anyway, my concern, of course, is that my inexperience with the barbecue (that is, grill) will lead to inferior food, and I hope to impress the boss. Because I believe impressing my boss will improve my standing at the company. And bad food is not impressive."*

We've all known someone who talks that way (and we try to avoid him or her), but not many; most writers and speakers feel safe omitting some information.

How do writers and speakers decide what to omit? It depends on their audience. Suppose you were sitting in your office, working at your laptop, when someone came in and asked, "What are you doing?" How would you respond?

It depends on who asked. If it was bring-your-child-to-work day and the questioner were a colleague's two-year-old you might say, "I'm typing on a computer." But that would be a ridiculous answer for an adult. Why? Because you should assume that the adult knows you're typing. A more appropriate response might be, "I'm filling out a form."

Thus, we calibrate our answers, providing more or less (or different) information depending on our judgment of what the other person knows, thereby deciding what we can safely leave out and what needs to be explained (Figure 2.4).*

What happens when the knowledge is missing? Suppose you read the following sentence:

> *I believed him when he said he had a lake house, until he said it's only 40 feet from the water at high tide.*

If you're like me, you're confused. When I read a similar passage, my mother-in-law later explained to me that lakes don't have appreciable tides. I didn't have that bit of background knowledge that the author

FIGURE 2.4: Consider the difference in how you would describe a planned lesson to your spouse or friend, versus a fellow teacher. Source: © Shutterstock/Monkey Business Images.

assumed I had, so I didn't understand the passage.

So, background knowledge in the form of vocabulary helps us understand a single idea (call it A), but background knowledge is also often necessary to understand the connection between two ideas (A and B). In fact, writers often present multiple ideas in rapid succession – A, B, C, D, E, and F – expecting that the reader will knit them together into a coherent whole. Have a look at this sentence from chapter 35 of *Moby-Dick*:

> *Now, it was plainly a labor of love for Captain Sleet to describe, as he does, all the little detailed conveniences of his crow's-nest; but though he so enlarges upon many of these, and though he treats us to a very scientific account of his experiments in this crow's-nest, with a small compass he kept there for the purpose of counteracting the errors resulting from what is called the "local attraction" of all binnacle magnets; an error ascribable to the horizontal vicinity of the iron in the ship's planks, and in the Glacier's case, perhaps, to there having been so many broken-down blacksmiths among her crew; I say, that though the Captain is very discreet and scientific here, yet, for all his learned "binnacle deviations," "azimuth compass observations," and "approximate errors," he knows very well, Captain Sleet, that he was not so much immersed in those profound magnetic meditations, as to fail being attracted occasionally towards that well replenished little case-bottle, so nicely tucked in on one side of his crow's-nest, within easy reach of his hand.*[4]

Why is this sentence so hard to understand? You run out of mental room. It has a lot of ideas in it, and because it's one sentence, you try to keep them all in mind at once and to relate them to one another. But there are so many ideas, you can't keep them all in mind simultaneously. To use the terminology from Chapter 1, you don't have sufficient capacity in working memory. In some situations, background knowledge can help with this problem.

To understand why, let's start with a demonstration. Read the following list of letters once, then cover the list and see how many letters you can remember.

X C N

N P H

D L O

L G M

T FA

Q X

Okay, how many could you remember? If you're like most people, the answer would perhaps be seven. Now try the same task with this list:

X

C N N

P H D

L O L

G MT

FA Q

X

You probably got many more letters correct with this second list, and you no doubt noticed that it's easier because the letters form acronyms that are familiar. But did you notice that the first and second lists are the same? I just changed the spacing to make the acronyms more apparent in the second list.

This is a working memory task. You'll remember from Chapter 1 that working memory is the part of your mind in which you combine and manipulate information – think of it as synonymous with consciousness. Working memory has a limited capacity, so you can't maintain in your working memory all of the letters from list one. But you can for list two. Why? Because the amount of space in working memory doesn't depend on the number of letters; it depends on the number of meaningful objects. If you can remember seven individual letters, you can remember seven (or just about seven) meaningful acronyms or words. The letters *F, A,* and *Q* together count as only one object because combined they are meaningful to you.

The phenomenon of mentally tying together separate pieces of information from the environment is called *chunking.* The advantage is obvious: you can keep more stuff in working memory if it can be chunked. The trick, however, is that chunking works only when you have applicable factual knowledge in long-term memory. You will see *CNN* as meaningful only if you already know what CNN is. In the first list, one of the three-letter groups was *NPH.* If you're a neurologist you may have treated this group as a chunk, because *NPH* stands for a brain disorder, normal pressure hydrocephalus. If you don't have that knowledge in your long-term memory, you would not treat *NPH* as a chunk. This basic effect – using background knowledge to group things in working memory – doesn't work only for letters. It works for anything. Bridge players do it with hands of cards, dancing experts do it with dance moves, and so forth.

So factual knowledge in long-term memory allows chunking, and chunking increases space in working memory. What does the ability to chunk have to do with reading comprehension? Well, I was saying before that if you read ideas A, B, C, D, E, and F, you would need to relate them to one another in order to comprehend their meaning. That's a lot of stuff to keep in working memory. But suppose you could *chunk* A through F into a single idea? Comprehension would be much easier. For example, consider this passage:

> *Ashburn hit a ground ball to Wirtz, the shortstop, who threw it to Dark, the second baseman. Dark stepped on the bag, forcing out Cremin, who was running from first, and then threw it to Anderson, the first baseman. Ashburn failed to beat the throw.*

If you're like me this passage is hard to comprehend. There are a number of individual actions, and they are hard to tie together. But for someone who knows about baseball, it's a familiar pattern, like *CNN.* The sentences describe a frequently encountered sequence of events called a double play.

A number of studies have shown that people understand what they read much better if they already have some background knowledge about the subject. Part of the reason is chunking. A clever study on this point was conducted with junior high school students.[5] Half were good readers and half were poor readers, according to standard reading tests. The researchers asked the students to read a story that described half an inning of a baseball game. As they read, the students were periodically stopped and asked to show that they understood what was happening in the story by using a model of a baseball field and players. The interesting thing about this study was that some of the students knew a lot about baseball and some knew just a little. (The researchers made sure that everyone could comprehend individual actions, for example, what happened when a player got a double.) The dramatic finding, shown in Figure 2.5, was

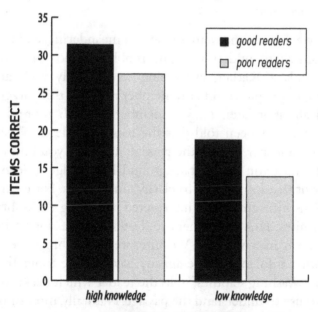

BASEBALL KNOWLEDGE

FIGURE 2.5: Results from a study of reading. As you would predict, the good readers (shaded bars) understood more than the poor readers (unshaded bars), but this effect is modest compared to the effect of knowledge. The people who knew a lot about baseball (leftmost columns) understood the passage much better than the people who didn't know a lot, regardless of whether they were "good" or "poor" readers, as measured by standard reading tests. Source: Based on data from "Effect of prior knowledge on good and poor readers' memory of text" by D. R. Recht and L. Leslie in *Journal of Educational Psychology* 80: 16-20. Copyright © 1988 by the American Psychological Association.

that the students' knowledge of baseball determined how much they understood of the story. Whether they were "good readers" or "bad readers" didn't matter nearly as much as what they knew.

Thus, background knowledge allows chunking, which makes more room in working memory, which makes it easier to relate ideas, and therefore to comprehend.

Background knowledge also clarifies details that would otherwise be ambiguous and confusing. In one experiment illustrating this effect,[6] subjects read the following passage:

> *The procedure is actually quite simple. First, you arrange items into different groups. Of course one pile may be sufficient depending on how much there is to do. If you have to go somewhere else due to lack of facilities, that is the next step; otherwise, you are pretty well set. It is important not to overdo things. That is, it is better to do too few things at once than too many.*

The passage went on in this vein, vague and meandering, and therefore very difficult to understand. The problem is not that you're missing vocabulary. Rather, everything seems really ambiguous. Not surprisingly, people couldn't remember much of this paragraph when asked about it later. They remembered much more, however, if they had first been told that the passage's title is "Washing Clothes." Have another look at the passage now that you know the title. The title tells you which background knowledge is relevant, and you recruit that knowledge to clarify ambiguities. For example, "Arrange items into groups" is interpreted as sorting darks, bright colors, and whites. This experiment indicates that we don't take in new information in a vacuum. We interpret new things we read in light of other information we already have on the topic. In this case, the title, "Washing Clothes," tells the reader which background knowledge to use to understand the passage. Naturally, most of what we read is not so vague, and we usually know which background information is relevant. Thus, when we read an ambiguous sentence, we seamlessly use background knowledge to interpret it, and likely don't even notice the potential ambiguities (Figure 2.6).

I've listed four ways that background knowledge is important to reading comprehension: (i) it provides vocabulary; (ii) it allows you

FIGURE 2.6: Most people would not even notice that the word "it" is ambiguous because background knowledge tells you what ought to be picked up and what need not be. Source: Man holding dog @istock/Aleksandr Zotov; dog waste station © Daniel Willingham; Photoshop © nyretouch/Nihal Organ.

to bridge logical gaps that writers leave; (iii) it allows chunking, which increases room in working memory and thereby makes it easier to tie ideas together; and (iv) it guides the interpretation of ambiguous sentences. There are in fact other ways that background knowledge helps reading, but these are some of the highlights.

Some observers believe that the importance of knowledge to reading is the main driver of the fourth-grade slump. If you're unfamiliar with that term, it refers to the fact that students from underprivileged homes often read at grade level through the third grade, but then suddenly in the fourth grade they fall behind. The interpretation is that reading instruction through third grade focuses mostly on decoding – figuring out how to sound out words using the printed symbols – so that's what reading tests emphasize. By the time the fourth grade rolls around, most students are good decoders, so reading tests start to emphasize *comprehension*. As described here, comprehension depends on background knowledge, and that's where kids from privileged homes have an edge. They come to school with a bigger vocabulary and more knowledge about the world than underprivileged kids. And because knowing things makes it easier to learn new things (as described in the next section), the gap between privileged and underprivileged kids widens.

Background Knowledge Is Necessary for Cognitive Skills

Not only does background knowledge make you a better reader, it also is necessary to be a good thinker. The processes we most hope to engender in our students – thinking critically and logically – are not possible without background knowledge.

First, you should know that much of the time when we see someone apparently engaged in logical thinking, he or she is actually engaged in memory retrieval. As I described in Chapter 1, memory is the cognitive process of *first* resort. When faced with a problem, you will first search for a solution in memory, and if you find one, you will very likely use it. Doing so is easy and fairly likely to be effective; you probably remember the solution to a problem because it worked the last time, not because it failed. To appreciate this effect, first try a problem for which you *don't* have relevant background knowledge, such as the one shown in Figure 2.7.[7]

The problem depicted in Figure 2.7 is more difficult than it first appears. In fact, only about 15% or 20% of college students get it right. The correct answer is to turn over the A card and the 3 card. Most people get A – it's clear that if there is not an even number on the other side, the rule has been violated. Many people incorrectly think they need to turn over the 2 card. The rule does not, however, say what must be

FIGURE 2.7: Each card has a letter on one side and a digit on the other. There is a rule: If there is a vowel on one side, there must be an even number on the other side. Your job is to verify whether this rule is met for this set of four cards and to turn over the minimum number of cards necessary to do so. Which cards would you turn over? Source: © Greg Culley.

on the other side of a card with an even number. The 3 card must be flipped because if there is a vowel on the other side, the rule has been violated.

BEER **31** **COKE** **17**

FIGURE 2.8: You are to imagine that you are a doorman in a bar. Each card represents a patron, with the person's age on one side and their drink on the other. You are to enforce this rule: If you're drinking beer, then you must be 21 or over. Your job is to verify whether this rule is met for this set of four people. You should turn over the minimum number of cards necessary to do so. Which cards would you turn over? Source: © Greg Culley.

Now let's look at another version of the problem, shown in Figure 2.8.[8]

If you're like most people, this problem is relatively easy: you flip the beer card (to be sure this patron is over 21) and you flip the 17 card (to be sure this kid isn't drinking beer). Yet logically the 17 card has the same role in the problem that the 3 card did in the previous version, and it was the 3 card that everyone missed. Why is it so much easier this time? One reason (but not the only one) is that the topic is familiar. You have background knowledge about the idea of a drinking age, and you know what's involved in enforcing that rule. Thus you don't need to reason logically. You have experience with the problem and you remember what to do rather than needing to reason it out.

In fact, people draw on memory to solve problems more often than you might expect. For example, it appears that much of the difference among the world's best chess players is *not* their ability to reason about the game or to plan the best move; rather, it is their memory for game positions. Here's a key finding that led to that conclusion. Chess matches are timed, with each player getting an hour to complete his or her moves in the game. There are also so-called blitz tournaments in which players get just five minutes to make all of their moves in a match (Figure 2.9). It's no surprise that everyone plays a little bit worse in a blitz tournament. What's surprising is that the best players are still the best, the nearly best are still nearly best, and so on.[†] This finding indicates that whatever makes the best players better than everyone else is still present in blitz tournaments;

FIGURE 2.9: A device used to time a chess match. The black hand on each clock counts down the minutes remaining. After making a move, the player pushes the button above his clock, which stops it and causes his opponent's clock to restart. Players set identical amounts of time to elapse on each clock - just five minutes in a blitz tournament - representing the total time the player can take for all moves in the game. The flag near the 12 on each clock is pushed aside by the black hand as it approaches 12. When the flag falls, the player has exceeded his allotted time, and so forfeits the match. Source: © Shutterstock/Gavran333.

whatever gives them their edge is *not* a process that takes a lot of time, because if it were they would have lost their edge in blitz tournaments.

It seems that it is memory that creates the differences among the best players. When tournament-level chess players select a move, they first size up the game, deciding which part of the board is the most critical, the location of weak spots in their defense and that of their opponents, and so on. This process relies on the player's memory for similar board positions and, because it's a memory process, it takes very little time, perhaps a few seconds. This assessment greatly narrows the possible moves the player might make. Only then does the player engage slower reasoning processes to select the best among several candidate moves. This is why top players are still quite good even in a blitz tournament. Most of the heavy lifting is done by memory, a process that takes very little time. On the basis of this and other research, psychologists estimate that top chess players may have fifty thousand board positions in long-term memory. Thus background knowledge is decisive even in chess, which we might think is the prototypical game of reasoning.

That's not to say that all problems are solved by comparing them to cases you've seen in the past. You do, of course, sometimes reason, but even then background knowledge can help. Earlier in this chapter I discussed chunking, the process that allows us to think of individual items as a single unit (for example, when *C, N,* and *N* become *CNN*), thereby creating more room in working memory. I emphasized that in reading, the extra mental space afforded by chunking can be used to relate the meaning of sentences to one another. This extra space is also useful when reasoning.

Here's an example. Do you have a friend who can walk into someone else's kitchen and rapidly produce a nice dinner from whatever food is around, usually to the astonishment of whoever's kitchen it is? When your friend looks in a cupboard, she doesn't see ingredients, she sees recipes. She draws on extensive background knowledge about food and cooking. For example, have a look at the pantry in Figure 2.10.

A food expert will have the background knowledge to see many possibilities here, for example, crushing pecans with the Stove Top stuffing to bread the chicken, or using the tea to scent the rice. The necessary ingredients will then become a chunk in working memory, so the expert will have room in working memory to devote to other aspects of planning, for example, to consider other dishes that might complement this one, or to begin to plan the steps of cooking.

Chunking applies to classroom activities as well. For example, take two algebra students. One is still a little shaky on the distributive property, the other knows it cold. When the first student is trying to solve a problem and sees a(b + c), he's unsure whether that's the same as ab + c, or

FIGURE 2.10: Suppose you were at a friend's house and she asked you to make dinner with some chicken and whatever else you could find. What would you do? Source: © Shutterstock/ Darryl Brooks.

b + ac, or ab + ac. So he stops working on the problem and substitutes small numbers into a(b + c) to be sure he's got it right. The second student recognizes a(b + c) as a chunk and doesn't need to stop and occupy working memory with this subcomponent of the problem. Clearly the second student is more likely to complete the problem successfully.

There is a final point to be made about knowledge and thinking skills. Much of what experts tell us they do in the course of thinking about their field *requires* background knowledge, even if it's not described that way. Let's take science as an example. We could tell students a lot about how scientists think, and they could memorize those bits of advice. For example, we could tell students that when interpreting the results of an experiment, scientists are especially interested in anomalous (that is, unexpected) outcomes. Unexpected outcomes indicate that their knowledge is incomplete and that this experiment contains hidden seeds of new knowledge. But for results to be unexpected, you must have an expectation! An expectation about the outcome would be based on your knowledge of the field. Most or all of what we tell students about scientific thinking strategies is impossible to use without appropriate background knowledge. Or as the well-known geologist, Herbert Harold Read, said, "The best geologist is the one who has seen the most rocks" (Figure 2.11).

The same holds true for history, language arts, music, and so on. Generalizations that we can offer to students about how to think

FIGURE 2.11: Judge Sharon Newcomb shown here inspecting a Miniature Pinscher at the Westminster Kennel Club Dog Show has acquired expertise, in part, through experience with thousands of dogs. To become a American Kennel Club show judge requires not just straightforward demonstration of knowledge (passing tests on dog anatomy and show ring procedure) and relevant experience (assistant-judging at local events); prospective judges must have been around a great many dogs, evidenced by at least 12 years experience with the breed they hope to judge. Source: © Getty Images/Sarah Stier.

and reason successfully in the field may *look* like they don't require background knowledge, but when you consider how to apply them, they often do.

Factual Knowledge Improves Your Memory

When it comes to knowledge, those who have more gain more. Many experiments have confirmed the benefit of background knowledge to memory using the same basic method. The researchers bring into the laboratory some people who have some expertise in a field (for example, football or dance or electronic circuitry) and some who do not. Everyone reads a story or a brief article. The material is simple enough that the people without expertise have no difficulty understanding it; that is, they can tell you what each sentence means. But the next day the people with background knowledge remember substantially more of the material than the people who do not have background knowledge.

You might think this effect is really due to attention. If I'm a basketball fan, I'll enjoy reading about basketball and will pay close attention, whereas if I'm not a fan, reading about basketball will bore me. But other studies have actually *created* experts. The researchers had people learn either a lot or just a little about subjects that were new to them (for example, Broadway musicals). Then they had them read other, new facts about the subject, and they found that the "experts" (those who had earlier learned a lot of facts about the subject) learned new facts more quickly and easily than the "novices" (who had earlier learned just a few facts about the subject).[9]

Why is it easier to remember material if you already know something about the topic? I've already said that if you know more about a particular topic, you can better understand new information about that topic; for example, people who know about baseball *understand* a baseball story better than people who don't. We remember much better if something has meaning. That generalization is discussed and refined in the next chapter, but to get a sense of this effect, read each of the following two brief paragraphs:

Motor learning is the change in capacity to perform skilled movements that achieve behavioral goals in the environment. A fundamental and unresolved question in neuroscience is whether there is a separate neural system for representing learned sequential motor responses. Defining that system with brain imaging and other methods requires a careful description of what specifically is being learned for a given sequencing task.	A chiffon cake replaces butter – the traditional fat in cakes – with oil. A fundamental and unresolved question in entertaining is when to make a butter cake and when to make a chiffon cake. Answering this question with expert tasting panels and other methods requires a careful description of what characteristics are desired for a cake.

The paragraph on the left is taken from a technical research article.[10] Each sentence is likely comprehensible, and if you take your time, you can see how they are connected: The first sentence provides a definition, the second sentence poses a problem, and the third states that a description of the thing under study (skills) is necessary before the problem can be addressed. I wrote the paragraph on the right to parallel the motor-skill paragraph. Sentence by sentence, the structure is the same. Which do you think you will remember better tomorrow?

The paragraph on the right is easier to understand (and therefore will be better remembered) because you can tie it to things you already know. Your experience tells you that a good cake tastes buttery, not oily, so the interest value of the fact that some are made with oil is apparent. Similarly, when the final sentence refers to "what characteristics are desired for a cake," you can imagine what those characteristics might be – fluffiness, moistness, and so on. Note that these effects aren't about comprehension; you can comprehend the paragraph on the left pretty well despite a lack of background knowledge. But some richness, some feeling of depth to the comprehension is missing. That's because when you have background knowledge your mind connects the material you're reading with what you already know about the topic, even if you're not aware that it's happening.

It's those connections that will help you remember the paragraph tomorrow. Remembering things is all about *cues* to memory. We dredge up memories when we think of things that are related to what we're trying to remember. Thus, if I said, "Try to remember that paragraph you read yesterday," you'd say to yourself, "Right, it was about cakes," and automatically (and perhaps outside of awareness) information about cakes would start to flit through your mind – they are baked . . . they are frosted . . . you have them at birthday parties . . . they are made with flour and eggs and butter . . . and suddenly, that background knowledge (that cakes are made with butter) provides a toehold for remembering the paragraph: "Right, it was about a cake that uses oil instead of butter." It's adding these lines from the paragraph to your background knowledge that makes the paragraph seem both better understood and easier to remember. The motor-skills paragraph, alas, is marooned, removed from any background knowledge, and so is more difficult to remember later.

This final effect of background knowledge – that having factual knowledge in long-term memory makes it easier to acquire still more factual knowledge – is worth contemplating for a moment. It means that the amount of information you retain depends on what you already have. So, if you have more than I do, you retain more than I do, which means you gain more than me. To make the idea concrete (but the numbers manageable), suppose you have ten thousand facts in your memory but I have only nine thousand. Let's say we each remember a percentage of new stuff, and that percentage is based on what's already in our memories. You remember 10% of the new facts you hear, but because I have less knowledge in long-term memory, I remember only 9% of new facts. Table 2.1 shows how many facts each of us has in long-term memory over the course of 10 months, assuming we're each exposed to five hundred new facts each month.

By the end of 10 months, the gap between us has widened from 1000 facts to 1043 facts. Because people who have more in long-term memory learn more easily, the gap is only going to get wider. The only way I could catch up is to make sure I am exposed to more facts than you are. In a school context, I have some catching up to do, but it's very difficult because you are pulling away from me at an ever-increasing speed.

TABLE 2.1: A demonstration that, when it comes to knowledge, the rich get richer.

Months	Facts in your memory	% of new facts you remember	Facts in my memory	% of new facts I remember
1	10000	10.000	9000	9.000
2	10050	10.050	9045	9.045
3	10100	10.100	9090	9.090
4	10151	10.151	9135	9.135
5	10202	10.202	9181	9.181
6	10253	10.253	9227	9.227
7	10304	10.304	9273	9.273
8	10356	10.356	9319	9.319
9	10408	10.408	9366	9.366
10	10460	10.460	9413	9.413

I have of course made up all of the numbers in the foregoing example, but we know that the basics are correct – the rich get richer. We also know where the riches lie. If you want to be exposed to new vocabulary and new ideas, the places to go are books, magazines, and newspapers. Videos, gaming, social media, and texting friends offer less exposure to new ideas and vocabulary.

I began this chapter with a quotation from Einstein: "Imagination is more important than knowledge." I hope you are now persuaded that Einstein was wrong. Knowledge is more important, because it's a prerequisite for imagination, or at least for the sort of imagination that leads to problem solving, decision making, and creativity. Other great minds have made similar comments that denigrate the importance of knowledge, as shown in Table 2.2.

I don't know why some great thinkers (who undoubtedly knew many facts) took delight in denigrating schools, often depicting them as factories for the useless memorization of information. I suppose we are to take these remarks as ironic, or at least as interesting, but I for one don't need brilliant, highly capable minds telling me (and my children) that it's useless to know things. As I've shown

TABLE 2.2: Quotations from great thinkers denigrating the importance of factual knowledge.

Education is what survives when what has been learned has been forgotten.	Psychologist B. F. Skinner
I have never let my schooling interfere with my education.	Writer Mark Twain
Nothing in education is so astonishing as the amount of ignorance it accumulates in the form of inert facts.	Writer Henry Brooks Adams
Your learning is useless to you till you have lost your textbooks, burned your lecture notes, and forgotten the minutiae you learned by heart for the examination.	Philosopher Alfred North Whitehead
We are shut up in schools and college recitation rooms for 10 or 15 years, and come out at last with a bellyful of words and do not know a thing.	Poet Ralph Waldo Emerson

in this chapter, the cognitive processes that are most esteemed – logical thinking, problem solving, and the like – are intertwined with knowledge. It is certainly true that facts without the skills to use them are of little value. It is equally true that one cannot deploy thinking skills effectively without factual knowledge.

As an alternative to the quotations in Table 2.2, I offer a Spanish proverb that emphasizes the importance of experience and, by inference, knowledge: *Mas sabe El Diablo por viejo que por Diablo.* Roughly translated: "The Devil is not wise because he's the Devil. The Devil is wise because he's *old*."

Summary

Few today set as a goal for schooling that students should acquire knowledge simply for the sake of knowing things. Our goal is that students learn to think. In addition, it's natural to describe thinking as a *process* and therefore to conclude that knowledge doesn't matter much. But we've seen many ways that thinking well relies on knowledge. Knowledge allows you to bridge the gaps writers leave in prose and guides your interpretation when sentences are ambiguous. Knowledge is essential for chunking, the process that saves room in working memory, and so facilitates reasoning. Sometimes knowledge *substitutes* for reasoning, when you simply recall a previous problem solution, and other times, knowledge is required to deploy a thinking skill, as when a scientist judges that an experimental result is anomalous. Rather than thinking of knowledge as data that might be plugged into thinking processes, it's better to think of knowledge and thinking as intertwined.

Implications for the Classroom

If factual knowledge makes cognitive processes work better, the obvious implication is that we must help children learn background knowledge. How can we ensure that this happens?

Which Knowledge Should They Learn?

We might well ask ourselves, *Which knowledge should students learn?* This question often becomes politically charged rather quickly. When we start to specify what must be taught and what can be omitted, it appears that we are grading information on its importance. The inclusion or omission of historical events and figures, playwrights, scientific achievements, and so on leads to charges of cultural bias. A cognitive scientist sees this issue differently. The question, *What should students be taught?* is equivalent not to *What knowledge is important?* but rather to *What do you want students to be able to do?* This question has two answers.

For reading, students must know whatever information writers assume they know and hence leave out. So the key question is, what do you want students to be able to read? A common answer – but certainly not the only answer – is "a daily newspaper, and books and periodicals written for the intelligent layperson." To read the *Washington Post* with good comprehension, one must have in long-term memory the information that the writers and editors of that newspaper assume their readers have. What they assume is very broad, because the *Post* publishes articles on politics, visual arts, literature, civics, history, drama, dance, science, architecture, and so on. But the writers and editors of the *Post* don't expect great depth of knowledge. They might assume you know that Picasso was a painter but not that he was a cubist.

It's important to add that you might have other goals for what you'd like students to read. I mentioned the "educated layperson" goal because I think it's common among parents. If you want students to be able to read other sorts of material, you should target the information that *those* writers assume in their readership. Students will most successfully read texts on topics they know something about.

The second answer to the question "What knowledge matters?" applies to core subject matter courses. *What should students know of science, of history, of mathematics?* This question is different than the first because the uses of knowledge in these subject areas are different than the uses of knowledge for general reading. A *Washington Post* article may not define the word nebula, but the author won't count on my having a deeper definition than "astronomical object." If I'm studying astrophysics, I need to know much more.

Students can't learn everything, so what should they know? Cognitive science leads to the rather obvious conclusion that students must learn the concepts that come up again and again – the unifying ideas of each discipline. Some educational thinkers have suggested that a limited number of ideas should be taught in great depth, beginning in the early grades and carrying through the curriculum for years as different topics are taken up and viewed through the lens of one or more of these ideas. From the cognitive perspective, that makes sense.

When You Require Critical Thinking, Be Sure Students Have Enough Relevant Knowledge to Succeed

Our goal is not simply to have students know a lot of stuff – it's to have them know stuff in service of being able to think effectively. As emphasized in this chapter, thinking critically requires background knowledge. Critical thinking is not a set of procedures that can be practiced and perfected while divorced from background knowledge. Thus it makes sense to consider whether students have the necessary background knowledge to carry out a critical thinking task you might assign. For example, I once observed a teacher ask her fourth-grade class what they thought it would be like to live in a rain forest. Although the students had spent a couple of days talking about rain forests, they didn't have the background knowledge to give anything beyond rather shallow responses (such as "It would be rainy"). She asked the same question at the end of the unit, and the student's answers were much richer. One student immediately said she wouldn't want to live there because the poor soil and constant shade would mean she would probably have to include meat in her diet – and she was a vegetarian.

Note, this doesn't mean "just teach knowledge until they have a ton of it, and *only then* encourage thinking!" Naturally, you still want children to think, even as they are acquiring knowledge. Recognizing that critical thinking requires knowledge might prompt you to change those critical thinking questions and tasks to better reflect what students know.

Thinking About Thinking Is Valuable . . . But It's Not Enough

Because we want students to think critically, it's natural that we should try to provide direct instruction in critical thinking. If you're thinking about how you ought to think, that's *metacognition*, and there's good evidence that teaching students metacognitive strategies is helpful. What's great about metacognitive strategies is their simplicity, the speed with which they can be taught, and the hope that they will be applicable across a range of content. But they can appear to achieve more than they really do.

Reading comprehension strategies provide a familiar example. You tell students things like "When you come to unfamiliar word, see if the context helps you figure out the meaning." Or "before you read a text, use the title to make predictions about the content." These are strategies to control thinking in a manner that will boost comprehension.

But you've seen that a key factor in reading comprehension is providing knowledge from memory that the author omitted, as in the example of Mark and his barbecue. Fitting together "shouldn't use his new barbecue" and "boss coming to dinner" requires missing knowledge and that missing knowledge *is unique to that sentence.*

It's how the two ideas fit together. The whole point of strategies is that they are general, because they are supposed to be all-purpose. Thus, strategies *can't* tell you how ideas fit together – each "fitting" is unique to the sentence you're reading.

Elsewhere, I offered this analogy.[11] Suppose you bought a piece of furniture at IKEA, got home, dumped the pieces on the floor, and saw that the directions merely said, "Before you start, think about other pieces of furniture you've seen in the past. Then put stuff together. Take it slow and don't force anything. Also, as you're build-ing, stop every now and then, look at your progress, and see if it is starting to look like a piece of furniture."

This is actually helpful advice! But it's not enough – you need to know which pieces are supposed to be bolted together. Likewise, reading requires the specifics of how ideas are supposed to connect. But general strategies like "pay attention to whether you're under-standing as you go" are still useful.

I think this characterization holds for most, if not all, metacognitive strategies. It's good to memorize "when judging whether a scien-tific experiment is sound, evaluate whether the control condition matches the experimental condition." Knowing you're supposed to do that helps, even though memorizing the strategy doesn't tell you *how* to do it. For that, you need background knowledge.

Shallow Knowledge Is Better Than No Knowledge
Some of the benefits of factual knowledge require that the knowl-edge be fairly deep – for example, reasoning often requires under-standing many roles that the thing you're reasoning about might play. But other benefits accrue from shallow knowledge. We often don't need deep knowledge of a concept to be able to understand its meaning in context when we're reading. For example, I know almost nothing about baseball, but for general reading, a shallow definition such as "a sport played with a bat and ball, in which two teams oppose one another" will often do. Of course deep knowl-edge is better than shallow knowledge. But we're not going to have deep knowledge of everything, and shallow knowledge is certainly better than no knowledge.

Do Whatever You Can to Get Kids to Read . . . But It's Not Enough

The effects of knowledge described in this chapter also highlight why reading is so important. Reading exposes children to more facts and to a broader vocabulary than virtually any other activity, and persuasive data indicate that people who read for pleasure enjoy cognitive benefits throughout their lifetime.

People sometimes ask whether graphic novels "count," or whether audiobooks do. The answer is an emphatic "yes!" Graphic novels can be very sophisticated in terms of plotting, vocabulary, and so on. And listening to an audiobook has considerable overlap with reading print. Sure, a child is not getting practice in decoding or developing fluency, but the process of comprehension is similar whether one is reading or listening, so when we're talking about building vocabulary and background knowledge, audiobooks are great. They are especially great because you can listen at times when it's hard to read print, for example, when exercising or commuting.

That said, I don't believe it is quite the case that any book is fine "as long as they're reading." Naturally, if a child has a history of resisting reading, I'd be happy if she picked up any book at all. But once she is over that hump, if I feel that a bit of challenge won't dampen her reading motivation, I'd start trying to nudge her toward books at the appropriate reading level. That doesn't mean kids should never reread books. A child just may not have really understood everything the first time through, or she may return to a much-loved book for an emotional lift at a tough time. That said, it's rather obvious that a student doesn't gain as much from reading books significantly below her reading level and there are fun, fascinating books at every reading level, so why not nudge her toward a book that meets her where she is? It's just as obvious that a too difficult book is a bad idea. The student won't understand it and will just end up frustrated. The school librarian should be a tremendous resource and ally in helping children learn to love reading, and she is arguably the most important person in any school when it comes to reading.

As much as I'm an advocate of leisure reading, for most long-term goals we would set for students, leisure reading won't be enough.

The background knowledge students acquire in their leisure reading will be particular to their interests; the child who loves historical fiction may learn a lot about British monarchs whereas the child who loves fantasy will learn about mythical creatures. That's as it should be, but if we want children to be strong general readers, both need to learn about, for example, the solar system. Leisure reading is wonderful for building background knowledge, but students still need a strong curriculum.

Knowledge Acquisition Can Be Incidental

It's very important to keep in mind that the learning of factual knowledge can be incidental – that is, it can happen simply by exposure rather than only by concentrated study or memorization. Think about all you have learned by reading books and magazines for pleasure, or by watching video documentaries and the news, or through conversation with friends, or by spiraling down Internet rabbit holes. School offers many of the same opportunities. Students can learn information from math problems, or through sample sentences when they are learning grammar, or from the vocabulary you use when you select a classroom monitor. Every teacher knows so much that students don't. There are opportunities to fold this knowledge into each school day.

Start Early

At the end of the last section I noted that a child who starts behind in terms of knowledge will fall even further behind unless there is some intervention. There seems to be little doubt that this is a major factor in why some children fare poorly in school. Home environments vary a great deal. What sort of vocabulary do parents use? Do the parents ask the children questions and listen to the children's answers? Do they take their child to the museum or aquarium? Do they make books available to their children? Do the children observe their parents reading? All of these factors (and others) play a role in what children know on their first day of school. In other words, before a child meets her first teacher, she may be quite far behind the child sitting next to her in terms of how easy it is going to be for her to learn. Trying to level this playing field is a teacher's greatest challenge. There are no shortcuts and no alternatives to trying to increase the factual knowledge that the child has not picked up at home.

To be clear, I'm not blaming parents who do not do all of these things; people have limits of time and other resources to provides this sort of environment for their children. I think every teacher would happy if every student could access similar resources at school.

Knowledge Must Be Meaningful

Teachers should not take the importance of knowledge to mean that they should create lists of facts – whether shallow or detailed – for students to learn. Sure, some benefit might accrue, but it would be small. Knowledge pays off when it is conceptual and when the facts are related to one another, and that is not true of list learning. Also, as any teacher knows, learning a list is difficult and boring and so would do more harm than good; it would encourage the belief that school is a place of drudgery, not excitement and discovery. But what is a better way to ensure that students acquire factual knowledge, now that we've concluded it's so important? In other words, why do some things stick in our memory whereas other things slip away? That is the topic of the next chapter.

Notes

*One of the pleasures of the experiences shared with a close friend is the "inside joke," a reference that only the two of you understand. Hence, if her best friend asked what she was doing, the typist might say, "I'm painting a gravel road" – their personal code, based on a shared experience, for a long, pointless task. That's one extreme of assuming information on the part of your audience.

†Tournament-level chess players all have rankings – a number representing their skill level – based on whom they have beaten and who has beaten them.

Further Reading

Less Technical

Goodwin, B. (2011). Research says . . . don't wait until 4th grade to address the slump. *Educational Leadership*, 68(7), 88–89. Brief review of the idea that the dip in reading scores for disadvantaged children is due in part to a lack of background knowledge, and what to do about it.

Lareau, A. (2003). *Unequal Childhoods*. Berkeley: University of California Press. Fascinating ethnographic study of childhood in homes of different socioeconomic status.

Shing, Y. L., & Brod, G. (2016). Effects of prior knowledge on memory: implications for education. *Mind, Brain, and Education*, 10(3), 153–161. Reasonably user-friendly review of the role of memory in new learning, with an eye toward educational applications.

Willingham, D. T. (2017). How to get your mind to read. *New York Times* (25 November), p. SR6. https://www.nytimes.com/2017/11/25/opinion/sunday/how-to-get-your-mind-to-read.html. Op-ed on the importance of background knowledge to reading comprehension. Useful to send to someone for a quick introduction to the ideas covered here.

More Technical

Best, R. M., Floyd, R. G., & McNamara, D. S. (2008). Differential competencies contributing to children's comprehension of narrative and expository texts. *Reading Psychology*, 29(2), 137–164. Article examining the role of background knowledge in reading comprehension and how the lack of knowledge contributes to the fourth-grade slump.

Cromley, J. G., & Kunze, A. J. (2020). Metacognition in education: translational research. *Translational Issues in Psychological Science* 6(1), 15–20. A review of research showing that metacognitive strategies are useful in classroom contexts.

Fernández, G., & Morris, R. G. (2018). Memory, novelty and prior knowledge. *Trends in Neurosciences*, 41(10), 654–659. Brief article summarizing some key findings in the role of prior knowledge in new learning.

Gobet, F., & Charness, N. (2018). Expertise in chess. In *The Cambridge Handbook of Expertise and Expert Performance, 2* (eds. K. Ericsson, R. Hoffman, A. Kozbelt, & A. Williams) 597–615. Cambridge, UK: Cambridge University Press. This chapter summarizes much of the important research showing that knowledge is fundamental to chess skill.

Mol, S. E., & Bus, A. G. (2011). To read or not to read: a meta-analysis of print exposure from infancy to early adulthood. *Psychological Bulletin*, 137(2), 267–296. A review of 99 studies showing that reading produces a virtuous cycle: Reading during leisure time leads to improvement in components of reading (knowledge and others) that makes reading easier and therefore makes people more likely to read.

Pfost, M., Hattie, J., Dörfler, T., & Artelt, C. (2014). Individual differences in reading development: a review of 25 years of empirical research on Matthew effects in reading. *Review of Educational Research*, 84(2), 203–244. A review of many studies showing that students who know more learn more from reading.

Discussion Questions

1. It's important to remember that the knowledge that supports thinking skills can come from *outside* of school, as well as within the school curriculum. But simply telling parents to "make sure your children acquire knowledge outside of school" is too vague to do much. What might educators say or do that would be more effective?

2. Consider the very long sentence from *Moby-Dick* in this chapter. As noted, you run out of mental room while reading it and so are likely not to comprehend it. Are

there comparable materials or moments in your classroom that confuse students? One solution, noted in the last chapter, is to break up complex material into smaller bits. Another solution, noted in this chapter, is to acquire enough knowledge to enable chunking. Could that solution apply to any complex situations in your classroom?

3. The baseball study shows the striking effect that knowledge can have on comprehension. It also leads me to think about how a reader who usually struggles experiences reading that passage. Is it striking to him or her that they are so successful? We know that reader confidence is an important predictor of whether they read during leisure time, and struggling readers of course have many experiences telling them they should not be confident. How could we use findings like the baseball study to inspire methods of building confidence in struggling readers?

4. The "Washing Clothes" passage shows how effective background knowledge can be in clarifying ambiguous communication. You could imagine that there are times you sometimes speak in an analogous way – you say something that's actually quite vague, but, because you have the right background knowledge, it's quite clear to *you* what you mean. Can you think of an example of a misunderstanding between you and someone you were teaching? Is there a reliable way to help you bear in mind the difference between what you know and what your students know?

5. The more you know, the easier it is to learn new things. That indicates that children who begin school with less knowledge will fall further and further behind. What does this fact imply for early education? How about elementary school and beyond?

6. We live in an age where expertise is sometimes viewed with suspicion. Politicians appeal to the idea that you don't need to be knowledgeable about a topic, and that with common sense and smarts you'll actually make better decisions than so-called experts. What silent (or overt) messages do you think your society's culture sends to students about the value of knowing things? How about your local school?

3

Why Do Students Remember Everything That's on Television and Forget Everything I Say?

Question: Memory is mysterious. You may lose a memory created 15 seconds earlier, such as when you find yourself standing in your kitchen trying to remember what you came there to fetch. Other seemingly trivial memories (for example, advertisements) may last a lifetime. What makes something stick in memory, and what is likely to slip away?

Answer: We can't store everything we experience in memory. Too much happens. So what should the memory system tuck away? Things that are repeated again and again? But what about a really important one-time event such as a wedding? Things that cause emotion? But then you wouldn't remember important yet neutral things (for example, most schoolwork). How can the memory system know what you'll need to remember later? Your memory system lays its bets this way: if you think about something carefully, you'll probably have to think about it again, so it should be stored. Thus your memory is not a product of what you want to remember or what you try to remember; it's a product of what you think about. A teacher once told me that for a fourth-grade unit on the Underground Railroad he had his students bake biscuits, because this was a staple food for enslaved people seeking escape. He asked what I thought about the assignment. I pointed out that his students probably thought for 40 seconds about the relationship of biscuits to the Underground Railroad, and for 40 minutes about measuring flour, mixing shortening, and so on. Whatever students think about is what they will remember. The cognitive principle that guides this chapter is:

> ## Memory is the residue of thought.

To teach well, you should pay careful attention to what an assignment will actually make students think about (not what you hope they will think about), because that is what they will remember.

The Importance of Memory

Every teacher has had the following experience: you teach what you think is a terrific lesson, full of lively examples, deep content, engaging problems to solve, and a clear message, but the next day students remember nothing of it except a joke you told and an off-the-subject aside about your family[1] – or worse, when you say, "The point of yesterday's lesson was that one plus one equals two," they look at you incredulously and say, "Wait, one plus one equals *two?*" Obviously, if the message of Chapter 2 is "background knowledge matters," then we must closely consider how we can make sure that students acquire this background knowledge. So why do students remember some things and forget others?

Let's start by considering why you fail to remember something. Suppose I said to you, "Can you summarize the last professional development session you attended?" Let's further suppose that you brightly answer, "Nope, I sure can't." Why don't you remember?

One of four things has happened, all of which are illustrated in Figure 3.1, a slightly elaborated version of the diagram of the mind that we've used before. You will recall that working memory is where you keep things "in mind," the location of consciousness. There is lots of information in the environment, most of which we are not aware of. For example, as I write this, the refrigerator is humming, birds are chirping outside, and there is pressure on my backside from the chair I'm sitting on – but none of that was in my working memory (that is, my awareness) until I paid attention to it. As you can see in Figure 3.1, things can't get into long-term memory unless

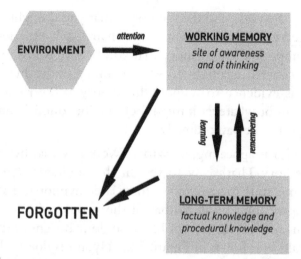

FIGURE 3.1: A slightly modified version of our simple diagram of the mind. Source: © Greg Culley.

they have first been in working memory. So this is a somewhat complex way of explaining the familiar phenomenon: *If you don't pay attention to something, you can't learn it!* You won't remember much of the professional development session if you were thinking about something else.

Information can enter working memory not only from the environment but also from long-term memory; that's what I mean when I refer to remembering, as shown by the labeled arrow. So another possible reason you don't remember is that the process by which things are drawn from long-term memory has failed. I discuss why that happens in Chapter 4.

A third possibility is that the information no longer resides in long-term memory – that it has been forgotten. I'm not going to discuss forgetting, but it's worth taking a moment to dispel a common myth. You sometimes hear that the mind records in exquisite detail everything that happens to you, like a video camera, but you just can't get at most of it – that is, memory failures are a problem of access. If you were given the right cue, the theory goes, anything that ever happened to you would be recoverable. For example, you may think you remember almost nothing of a childhood home you left at age five, but when you revisit it the smell of the camellia blooms in the yard wipes away the years, and the memories that you thought were lost can be pulled out, like charms on a fine chain. Such experiences raise the possibility that *any* memory that you believe is lost can in principle be recovered again. Successful memory under hypnosis is often raised as evidence to support this theory. If the right cue (camellia blossoms or whatever it might be) can't be found, hypnosis allows you to probe the vault directly.

Although this idea is appealing, it's wrong. We know that hypnosis doesn't aid memory. That's easy to test in the laboratory. Simply give people some stuff to remember, then later hypnotize half of them and compare their recall to that of the people who are not hypnotized. This sort of experiment has been done dozens of times, and typical results are shown in Figure 3.2.[2] Hypnosis doesn't help.

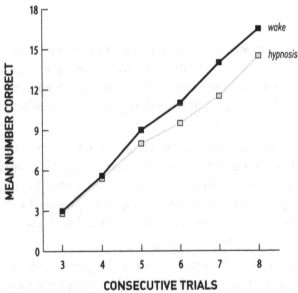

FIGURE 3.2: Subjects were shown 40 drawings of common objects and then had to try to recall them. Session 1 happened right away; sessions 2 through 8 occurred a week later. Naturally there was significant forgetting during the week, and with each attempt to remember, subjects on average did recall more. Also, the hypnotized subjects didn't remember any more than the nonhypnotized subjects. Source: From "Evaluating hypnotic memory enhancement (Hypermnesia and Reminiscence) using multitrial forced recall" by David F. Dinges, Wayne G. Whitehouse, Emily C. Orne, John W. Powell, Martin T. Orne, and M. H. Erdelyi in *Journal of Experimental Psychology: Learning, Memory and Cognition* 18, figure 1, p. 1142. Copyright © 1992 by the American Psychological Association.

It does make you more confident that your memory is right, but it doesn't actually make your memory more accurate.

The other bit of evidence – that a good cue such as the odor of camellia can bring back long-lost memories – is much more difficult to test in a laboratory experiment, although most memory researchers believe that such recoveries are possible. But even if we allow that lost memories can be recovered in this way, it doesn't mean that *all* seemingly forgotten memories are recoverable – it just means that some are. In sum, memory researchers see no reason to believe that all memories are recorded forever.

Now, let's return to our discussion of forgetting. Sometimes you *do* pay attention, so the material rattles around working memory for a while, but it never makes it to long-term memory. An example of a few such bits of information from my own experience are shown in Figure 3.3. *Lateral line* is a term I have looked up more

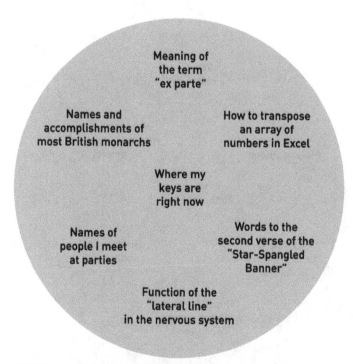

FIGURE 3.3: Bits of information that I am certain I have paid attention to and that thus have resided in my working memory but that have never made it into my long-term memory. Source: © Greg Culley.

than once, but I couldn't tell you now what it means. You doubt-less have your own examples of things you are certain you *ought* to know, because you've looked them up or heard them (and thus they have been in working memory), yet they have never stuck in long-term memory.

Just as odd is that some things have remained in your long-term memory for years although you had no intention of learning them; indeed, they held no special interest for you. For example, why do I know the jingle from the 1970s Bumble Bee tuna advertisement (Figure 3.4)?

You could make a good argument that understanding the differ-ence between Figures 3.3 and 3.4 is one of the core problems in education. We all know that students won't learn if they aren't pay-ing attention. What's more mysterious is why, when they *are* paying attention, they sometimes learn and sometimes don't. What else is needed besides attention?

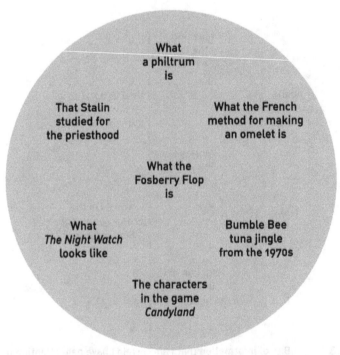

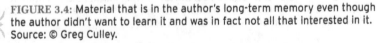

FIGURE 3.4: Material that is in the author's long-term memory even though the author didn't want to learn it and was in fact not all that interested in it. Source: © Greg Culley.

A reasonable guess is that we remember things that bring about some emotional reaction. Aren't you likely to remember really happy moments, such as a wedding, or really sad ones, such as hearing that a beloved relative has passed away? You are, and in fact if you ask people to name their most vivid memories, they often relate events that probably had some emotional content, such as a first date or a birthday celebration (Figure 3.5).

Naturally, we pay more attention to emotional events, and we are likely to talk about them later, so scientists have had to conduct very careful studies to show that it's really the emotion and not the repeated thought about these events that provides the boost to memory. The effect of emotion on memory is indeed real, and researchers have actually worked out some of the biochemistry behind it, but the emotion needs to be reasonably strong to have much impact. If memory *depended* on emotion, we would remember little of what we encounter in school. So the answer *Things go into long-term memory if they create an emotional reaction* is not quite right. It's more accurate to say, *Things that create an emotional reaction will be better remembered, but emotion is not necessary for learning.*

Repetition is another obvious candidate for what makes learning work. Maybe the reason I remember the Bumble Bee tuna jingle (Figure 3.4) from 40 years ago is that I heard it a lot. Repetition is very important, and I discuss it in Chapter 5, but it turns out that not just any repetition will do. Material may be repeated almost indefinitely and still not stick in your memory. For example, have a look at Figure 3.6. Can you spot the real penny among the counterfeits?

FIGURE 3.5: Emotional events tend to be well remembered, whether they are happy, such as this woman winning the Miss Philippines title, or anguished, as this Bosnian man mourning a relative who had died. Source: Miss Philippines © Getty Images/Majority World; mourning © Getty Images /DIMITAR DILKOFF.

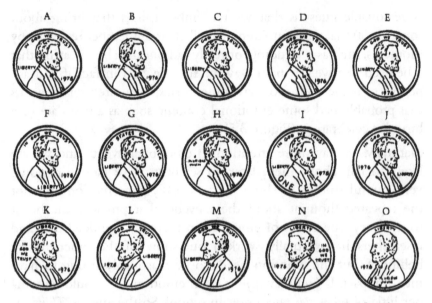

FIGURE 3.6: Can you find the real penny among the counterfeits? People are terrible at this task even though they have seen a penny thousands of times. Source: From "Long term memory for a common object" by R. S. Nickerson and M. J. Adams in *Cognitive Psychology* 11: 287-307. Copyright © 1979. Reprinted with permission from Elsevier.

If you've spent time in the United States you've seen hundreds or thousands of pennies – a huge number of repetitions. Yet, if you're like most people, you don't know much about what a penny looks like.[3] (The real penny is choice *A*, by the way.)

So repetition alone won't do it. It's equally clear that *wanting* to remember something is not the magic ingredient. How marvelous it would be if memory did work that way. Students would sit down with a book, say to themselves, "I want to remember this," and they would! You'd remember the names of people you've met, and you'd always know where your car keys are. Sadly, memory doesn't work that way, as demonstrated in a classic laboratory experiment.[4] Subjects were shown words on a screen one at a time and were asked to make a simple judgment about each word. (Some subjects had to say whether the word contained either an *A* or a *Q*; others had to say whether the word made them think of pleasant things or unpleasant things.) An important part of the experiment was that half of the subjects were told that their memory for the words would be tested later, after they had seen the whole list. The other subjects were not warned about the test. One of the remarkable findings was that knowing about the future test didn't improve subjects' memories. Other experiments have shown that telling subjects they'll be paid for each remembered word doesn't help much. So *wanting* to remember has little or no effect.

But there's another finding from this experiment that's still more important. Remember that when subjects saw each word they had to make a judgment about it – either about whether it contained an *A* or a *Q* or about whether it made them think of pleasant or unpleasant things. The people who made the second type of judgment remembered nearly twice as many words as the people who made the first judgment. Now we seem to be getting somewhere. We've found a situation in which memory gets a big boost. But why would it help to think about whether a word is pleasant or not?

In this case it matters because judging pleasantness makes you think about what the word *means* and about other words that are related to that meaning. Thus, if you saw the word *oven*, you might think about cakes and roasts and about your kitchen oven, which doesn't work well, and so on. But if you were asked to judge whether *oven* contained an *A* or a *Q*, you wouldn't have to think about the meaning at all.

So it seems we're poised to say that *thinking about meaning is good for memory*. That's close, but not quite right. The penny example doesn't fit that generalization. In fact, the penny example shows just the opposite. I said that you've been exposed to a penny thousands of times (at least), and most of those times you were thinking about the penny's meaning – that is, you were thinking about its function, about the fact that it has monetary value, even if that value is modest. But having thought about the meaning of a penny doesn't help when you're trying to remember what the penny looks like, which is what the test in Figure 3.6 requires.

Here's another way to think about it. Suppose you are walking the halls of your school and you see a student muttering to himself in front of his open locker. You can't hear what he's saying, but you can tell from his tone that he's angry. There are several things you could focus on. You could think about the *sound* of the student's voice, you could focus on how he *looks,* or you could think about the *meaning* of the incident (why the student might be angry, whether you should speak to him, and so on). These thoughts will lead to different memories of the event the next day. If you thought only about the sound of the student's voice, the next day you'd probably remember that sound quite well but not his appearance. If you focused on visual details, then that's what you'd remember the next day, not what the student's voice sounded like. In the same way, if you think about the meaning of a penny but never about the visual details, you won't remember the visual details, even if they have been in front of your eyes ten thousand times.

Whatever you think about, that's what you remember. *Memory is the residue of thought.* Once stated, this conclusion seems impossibly obvious. Indeed, it's a very sensible way to set up a memory system. Given that you can't store everything away, how should you pick what to store and what to drop? Your brain lays its bets this way: If you don't think about something very much, then you probably won't want to think about it again, so it need not be stored. If you do think about something, then it's likely that you'll want to think about it *in the same way* in the future. If I think about what the student looks like when I see him, then his appearance is probably what I'll want to know about when I think about that student later.

There are a couple of subtleties to this obvious conclusion that we need to draw out. First, when we're talking about school, we usually want students to remember what things mean. Sometimes what things look like is important – for example, the beautiful facade of the Parthenon, or the shape of Benin – but much more often we want students to think about meaning. Ninety-five percent of what students learn in school concerns meaning, not what things look like or what they sound like.* Therefore, a teacher's goal should almost always be to get students to think about meaning.

The second subtlety (again, obvious once it's made explicit) is that there can be different aspects of meaning for the same material. For example, the word *piano* has lots of meaning-based characteristics (Figure 3.7). You could think about the fact that it makes music, or about the fact that it's expensive, or that it's really heavy, or that it's made from fine-quality wood, and so on. In one of my all-time favorite experiments, the researchers led subjects to think of one or another characteristic of words by placing them in sentences – for example, "The moving men lugged the PIANO up the flight of stairs" or "The professional played the PIANO with a lush, rich sound."[5] The subjects knew that they needed to remember only the word in capitals. Later, experimenters administered a memory test for the words, with some hints. For *piano,* the hint was either "something heavy" or "something that makes music." The results showed that the subjects' memories were really good if the hint matched the way they had thought about *piano,* but poor if it didn't. That is, if the subjects read the moving men version of the sentence, hearing the cue "something that makes music" didn't help them remember *piano.* So it's not even enough to say, "You should think about meaning." You have to think about the right aspect of meaning.

Let me summarize what I've said about learning so far. For material to be learned (that is, to end up in long-term memory), it must reside for some period in working memory – that is, a student must pay attention to it. Further, *how* the student thinks of the experience completely determines what will end up in long-term memory.

FIGURE 3.7: We seldom think about it, but the context in which we think about even a simple word influences which aspect of meaning we focus on: that pianos produce music, that they can serve as a seat, that they are very heavy. Source: Playing piano © Getty Images/Frank Hoensch; sitting © Getty Images/Harry Dempster; moving © Shutterstock/Volodymyr TVERDOKHLIB.

The obvious implication for teachers is that they must design lessons that will ensure that students are thinking about the meaning of the material. A striking example of an assignment that didn't work for this reason came from my nephew's sixth-grade teacher. He was to draw a plot diagram of a book he had recently finished. The point of the plot diagram was to get him to think about the story elements and how they related to one another. The teacher's goal, I believe, was to encourage her students to think of novels as having *structure,* but the teacher thought that it would be useful to integrate art into this project, so she asked her students to draw pictures to represent the plot elements. That meant that my nephew thought very little about the relation between different plot elements and a great deal about how to draw a good castle. My daughter had completed a similar assignment some years earlier, but her teacher had asked students to use words or phrases rather than pictures. I think that assignment more effectively fulfilled the intended goal because my daughter thought more about how ideas in the book were related.

Now you may be thinking, "OK, so cognitive psychologists can explain why students have to think about what material means – but I really already knew they should think about that. Can you tell me *how* to make sure that students think about meaning?" Glad you asked.

What Good Teachers Have in Common

If you read Chapter 1, you can easily guess a common technique that I would *not* recommend for getting students to think about meaning: trying to make the subject matter relevant to the students' interests. I know that sounds odd, so let me elaborate.

Trying to make the material relevant to students' interests doesn't work. As I noted in Chapter 1, content is seldom the decisive factor in whether or not our interest is maintained. For example, I love cognitive psychology, so you might think, "Well, to get Willingham to pay attention to this math problem, we'll wrap it up in a cognitive psychology example." But Willingham is quite capable of being bored by cognitive psychology, as has been proved repeatedly at professional conferences I've attended. Another problem with trying to use content to engage students is that it's sometimes very difficult to do and the whole enterprise comes off as artificial. How would a math instructor make algebra relevant to my 13-year-old daughter? With a "real-world" example using numbers of Instagram likes? I just finished pointing out that any material has different aspects of meaning. If the instructor used a math problem with Instagram likes, isn't there some chance that my daughter would think about Instagram rather than about the problem? And that thoughts about Instagram would lead to thoughts about the instant message she received earlier, which would make her think of how sick she is of Jasmine's drama, which would make her wonder whether she should even invite Jasmine to her birthday dinner . . . ?

So if content won't do it, how about style? Students often refer to good teachers as those who "make the stuff interesting." It's not that the teacher relates the material to students' interests – rather, the teacher has a way of interacting with students that they find engaging. Let me give a few examples from my own experience with fellow college-level teachers who are consistently able to get students to think about meaning.

Teacher A is the comedian. She tells jokes frequently. She never misses an opportunity to use a silly example.

Teacher B is the den mother. She is very caring, very directive, and almost patronizing, but so warm that she gets away with it. Students call her "Mom" behind her back.

Teacher C is the storyteller. He illustrates almost everything with a story from his life. Class is slow paced and low key, and he is personally quiet and unassuming.

Teacher D is the showman. If he could set off fireworks inside, he would do it. The material he teaches does not lend itself easily to demonstrations, but he puts a good deal of time and energy into thinking up interesting applications, many of them involving devices he's made at home.

Each of these teachers is one to whom students refer as making boring material interesting, and each is able to get students to think about meaning. Each style works well for the person using it, although obviously not everyone would feel comfortable taking on some of these styles. It's a question of personality.

Style is what the students notice, but it is only a part of what makes these teachers so effective. College professors typically get written student evaluations of their teaching at the end of every course. Most schools have a form for students to fill out that includes such items as "The professor was respectful of student opinions," "The professor was an effective discussion leader," and so on, and students indicate whether or not they agree with each statement. Researchers have examined these sorts of surveys to figure out which professors get good ratings and why. One of the interesting findings is that most of the items are redundant. A two-item survey would be almost as useful as a 30-item survey, because many questions are variations on these two: Does the professor seem like a nice person, and is the class well organized? (Figure 3.8.) Although they don't realize they are doing so, students treat each of the 30 items as rephrasings of one of these two questions. What matters is cognition and connection.

Although K–12 students don't complete questionnaires about their teachers, we know that more or less the same thing is true for them. The emotional bond between students and teacher – for better or worse – accounts for whether students learn. The brilliantly well-organized teacher whom fourth graders see as mean will not be very effective. But the funny teacher, or the gentle storytelling teacher, whose lessons are poorly organized won't be much good either. Effective teachers have both qualities. They are able to connect personally with students, and they organize the material in a way that makes it interesting and easy to understand.

That's my real point in presenting these different types of teachers. When we think of a good teacher, we tend to focus on personality and on the way the teacher presents himself or herself. But that's only half of good teaching. The jokes, the stories, and the warm manner all generate goodwill and get students to pay attention. But then how do we make sure they think about meaning? That is where the second property of being a good teacher comes in – organizing the

FIGURE 3.8: How would each of these men be as a teacher? In *Game of Thrones*, Tywin Lannister (played by actor Charles Dance) is intelligent but cold and remote. The character Joey Tribbiani from *Friends* (played by actor Matt LeBlanc) is warm and friendly but not terribly smart. Teachers need to be both well organized and approachable. Source: LeBlanc © Getty Images/NBCUniversal; Dance © Getty Images/WireImage.

ideas in a lesson plan in a coherent way so that students will understand and remember. Cognitive psychology cannot tell us how to be personable and likable to our students, but I can tell you about one set of principles that cognitive psychologists know about to help students think about the meaning of a lesson.

The Power of Stories

The human mind seems exquisitely tuned to understand and remember stories – so much so that psychologists sometimes refer to stories as "psychologically privileged," meaning that they are treated differently in memory than other types of material. I'm going to suggest that organizing a lesson plan like a story is an effective way to help students comprehend and remember. It also happens to be the organizing principle used by the four teachers I described. The way in which each of them related emotionally to their students was very different, but the way they got their students to think about the meaning of material was identical.

Before we can talk about how a story structure could apply to a classroom, we must go over what a story structure is. There is not universal agreement over what makes a story, but most sources point to the following four principles, often summarized as *the four Cs*. The first C is *causality*, which means that events are causally related to one another. For example, "I saw Jane; I left the house" is just a chronological telling of events. But if you read, "I saw Jane, my hopeless old love; I left the house," you would understand that the two events are linked causally. The second C is *conflict*. A story has a main character pursuing a goal, but he or she is unable to reach that goal. In *Star Wars* the main character is Luke Skywalker, and his goal is to deliver the stolen plans and help destroy the Death Star. Conflict occurs because there is an obstacle to the goal. If Luke didn't have a worthy adversary – Darth Vader – it would make for a rather short movie. In any story the protagonist must struggle to meet his goal. The third C is *complications*. If Luke simply hammered away for 90 minutes at his goal of delivering the plans, that would be rather dull. Complications are subproblems that arise from the main goal. Thus, if Luke wants to deliver the plans, he must first get off his home planet, Tatooine – but he has no transportation. That's a complication that leads to his meeting another major character, Han Solo, and leaving the planet amid a hail of gunfire – always a movie bonus. The final C is *character*. A good story is built around strong, interesting characters, and the key to those qualities is *action*. A skillful storyteller shows rather than tells the audience what a character is like. For example, the first time the *Star Wars* audience sees Princess Leia she is shooting at storm troopers. Hence we don't need to be told that she is brave and ready to take action.

If we're trying to communicate with others, using a story structure brings several important advantages. First, stories are easy to comprehend, because the audience knows the structure, which helps to interpret the action. For example, the audience knows that events don't happen randomly in stories. There must be a causal connection, so if the cause is not immediately apparent, the audience will think carefully about the previous action to try to connect it to present events. For example, at one point in *Star Wars* Luke, Chewbacca, and Han are hiding on an Empire ship. They need to get to another part of the ship, and Luke suggests putting handcuffs on Chewbacca. That suggestion is mildly puzzling because Luke and Chewbacca are allies. The audience must figure out that Luke intends to pretend that Chewbacca is a prisoner and that he and Han are guards. The audience will do that bit of mental work because they know there must be a reason for this puzzling action.

Second, stories are interesting. Reading researchers have conducted experiments in which people read lots of different types of material and rate each for how interesting it is. Stories are consistently rated as more interesting than other formats (for example, expository prose), even if the same information is presented. Stories may be interesting because they demand the kind of inferences I discussed in Chapter 1. Recall that problems (such as crossword puzzles) are interesting if they are neither too difficult nor too easy. Stories demand these medium-difficulty inferences, as in the handcuff example.

Formal work in laboratory settings has shown that people rate stories as less interesting if they include too much information, thus leaving no inferences for the listener to make. But formal research is hardly necessary to confirm this phenomenon. We all have one or two friends who kill every story they tell with too much information. (See Figure 3.9.) An acquaintance of mine once spent 10 minutes relating that she hadn't visited her favorite Chinese restaurant for a year because they stopped accepting checks, only to bump into the owner who told her that he would happily make an exception for her. Delivered in 15 seconds with cheeky pride, this story would have been cute. But with the details packed in (and no inferences for me to make) over the course of 10 full minutes, it was all I could do not to scream.

Third, stories are easy to remember. There are at least two contributing factors here. Because comprehending stories requires lots of medium-difficulty inferences, you must think about the story's meaning throughout. As described earlier in the chapter, thinking about meaning is excellent for memory because it is usually meaning that you want to remember. Your memory for stories is also aided by their causal structure. If you remember one part of the plot, it's a good guess that the next thing that happened was caused

Senators Crapo, Risch (catching a few minutes), and Blunt. 1-21-20
while House manager Val Demings addresses Senators

FIGURE 3.9: Senators listening to evidence during President Trump's 2020 impeachment trial found it difficult to pay attention; some even appeared to fall asleep, as an artist captured Senator Risch doing. (Cameras are not permitted in the Senate.) Part of the reason it was so boring was that listeners already knew all of the evidence, both from news reports and briefings. In explaining to reporters why they seemed so bored Senator Mike Braun of Indiana said, "The subject matter is something we've all heard."[6] Source: © Art Lien.

by what you remember. For example, if you're trying to remember what happened after Luke put handcuffs on Chewbacca, you'll be helped by remembering that they were on an Empire ship (hence the ruse), which might help you remember that they went to rescue Princess Leia from the detention area.

Putting Story Structure to Work

Now, all this about movies has been a diverting interlude (at least I hope it has), but what does it have to do with the classroom? My intention here is not to suggest that you simply tell stories, although there's nothing wrong with doing so. Rather, I'm suggesting something one step removed from that. Structure your lessons the way stories are structured, using the four Cs: causality, conflict, complications, and character. This doesn't mean you must do most of the talking. Small group work or projects or any other method may be used. The story structure applies to the way you *organize* the material that you encourage your students to think about, not to the methods you use to teach the material.

In some cases, the way to structure a lesson plan as a story is rather obvious. For example, history can be viewed as a set of stories. Events are caused by other events; there is often conflict involved; and so on. Still, thinking carefully about the four Cs as you consider a lesson plan can be helpful. It might encourage you to think about a different perspective from which to tell the story. For example, suppose you are an American teacher planning a lesson on Pearl Harbor. You might first think of the organization shown in Figure 3.10. It's chronological and it makes the United States the main character – that is, events are taken from the US point of view. Your goal is to get students to think about three points: US isolationism before Pearl Harbor, the attack, and the subsequent "Germany first" decision and the putting of the United States on a war footing.

Suppose, however, you thought of the four Cs when you were telling this story. From that perspective, the United States is not the strong character. Japan is, because that country had the goal that propelled events forward – regional domination – and had significant obstacles to this goal – Japan lacked natural resources and was embroiled in a protracted war with China. This situation set up a subgoal: to sweep up the European colonies in the South Pacific. Meeting that goal would raise Japan's standing as a world power and help obtain crucial raw materials for finishing the war with China. But that subgoal brought with it another complication. The United States was the other major naval power in the Pacific. How was Japan to deal with that problem? Rather than plundering the European colonies and daring the United States to intervene across five thousand miles of ocean (which the United States probably would not have done), Japan chose to try to eliminate the threat in one surprise attack. If one seeks to organize a lesson plan as a story, the one in Figure 3.10 is less compelling than the one in Figure 3.11.

My suggestion to use the Japanese point of view of Pearl Harbor doesn't mean that the American point of view should be ignored or deemed less important. Indeed, I could imagine a teacher in the United States electing not to use this story structure precisely because it takes a Japanese point of view in a US history class. My point here is that using a story structure may lead you to organize a lesson in ways that you hadn't considered before. And the story structure does bring cognitive advantages.

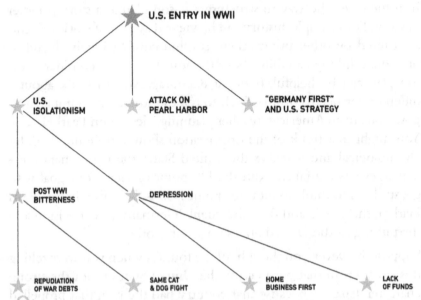

FIGURE 3.10: A tree diagram showing the typical structure of a lesson plan on Pearl Harbor. The organization is chronological. Source: © Greg Culley.

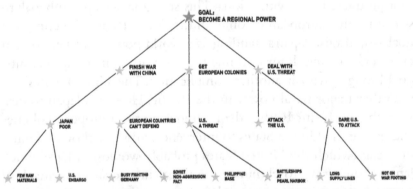

FIGURE 3.11: Alternative organization for a lesson plan on Pearl Harbor. From a storytelling point of view, Japan is the strong character because she takes actions that move the story forward. Source: © Greg Culley.

Using storytelling to teach history seems easy, but can you really use a story structure in a math class? Absolutely. Here's an example of how I introduced the concept of a Z-score – a common way to transform data – when I taught introductory statistics. Begin with the simplest and most familiar example of probability – the coin flip. Suppose I have a coin that I claim is loaded – it always comes up heads. To prove it to you, I flip the coin and it does indeed come up heads. Are you convinced? College students understand that the answer should be no because there is a 50-50 chance that a fair coin would have come up heads. How about 100 heads in a row? Clearly the odds are really small that a fair coin will come up heads 100 times in a row, so you'd conclude that the coin isn't fair.

That logic – how we decide whether a coin is fishy or fair – is used to evaluate the outcome of many scientific experiments. When we see headlines in the newspaper saying "New drug for Alzheimer's found effective" or "Older drivers less safe than younger" or "Babies who watch videos have smaller vocabularies," these conclusions rest on the same logic as the coin flip. How?

Suppose we want to know whether an advertisement is effective. We ask 200 people, "Does Colgate toothpaste give you sex appeal?" One hundred of these people have seen an advertisement for Colgate and 100 have not. We want to know if the percentage of people in the saw-the-ad group who say it gives you sex appeal is higher than the percentage in the didn't-see-the-ad group who say it gives you sex appeal. The problem here is just like the problem with the coin-flip example. The odds of the saw-the-ad group being higher are around 50%. One of the two groups *has* to be higher. (If they happened to tie, we'd assume that the ad didn't work.)

The logic for getting around this problem is the same as it was for the coin-flip example. For the coin flip, we judged 100 heads in a row as a highly improbable event *assuming that the coin was fair*. The odds of a fair coin coming up heads 100 times in a row are very small. So if we observe that event – 100 heads in a row – we conclude that our assumption must have been wrong. It's *not* a fair coin. So the saw-the-ad group being higher than the other group may also not be improbable – but what if that group was *much* more likely to answer yes? Just as we judged that there was something funny about the coin, so too we should judge that there is something funny about people who have seen the ad – at least funny when it comes to answering our question.

Of course *funny* in this context means "improbable." In the case of the coin, we knew how to calculate the "funniness," or improbability, of events because we knew the number of possible outcomes (two) and the probability of each individual outcome (.5), so it was easy to calculate the odds of successive events, as shown in Table 3.1. But here's our next problem: How do we calculate the "funniness," or probability, of other types of events? How much worse does the vocabulary of kids who watched videos have to be compared to that of kids who didn't watch videos before we're prompted to say, "Hey, these two groups of kids are not equal. If they were equal, their vocabularies would be equal. But their vocabularies are *very* unequal."

All of this description of coins, advertisements, and experiments is really a prelude to the lesson. I'm trying to get students to understand and care about the goal of the lesson, which is to explain how we can determine the probability of an event occurring by chance. That is the conflict for this lesson. Our worthy adversary in pursuit of this goal is not Darth Vader but the fact that most events we care about are not like coin flips – they don't have a limited number of outcomes (heads or tails) for which we know the probabilities (50%). That's a complication, which we address with a particular type of graph called a histogram; but implementing this approach leads to a further complication: we need to calculate the area under the curve of the histogram, which is a complex computation. The

TABLE 3.1: The odds, out of 10 tosses, of tossing a successively greater number of heads.

Number of tosses	Approximate probability of all heads
1	0.5
2	0.25
3	0.125
4	0.063
5	0.031
6	0.016
7	0.008
8	0.004
9	0.002
10	0.001

problem is solved by the Z-score, which is the point of the lesson (Figure 3.12).

A couple of things are worth noticing. A good deal of time – often 10 or 15 minutes of a 75-minute class – is spent setting up the goal, or to put it another way, persuading students that it's important to know how to determine the probability of a chance event. The material covered during this setup is only peripherally related to the lesson. Talking about coin flips and advertising campaigns doesn't have much to do with Z-scores. It's all about elucidating the central conflict of the story.

Spending a lot of time clarifying the conflict follows a formula for storytelling from, of all places, Hollywood. The central conflict in a Hollywood film typically starts about 20 minutes into the standard 100-minute movie. The screenwriter uses that 20 minutes to acquaint you with the characters and their situation so that when

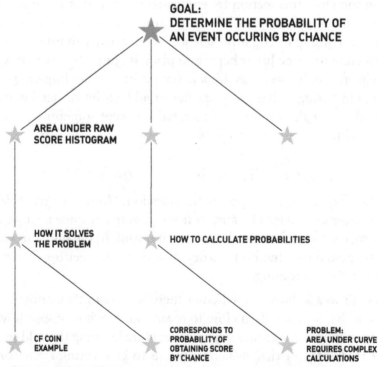

FIGURE 3.12: Part of the organizational scheme for a lesson plan on the Z-score transformation for a statistics class. Source: © Greg Culley.

the main conflict arises, you're already involved and you care what happens to the characters. A film may start with an action sequence, but that sequence is seldom related to what will be the main story line of the movie. James Bond movies often start with a chase scene, but it's always part of some other case, not the case that Bond will work on for the bulk of the movie. The conflict for that case is introduced about 20 minutes into the film.

When it comes to teaching, I think of it this way: The material I want students to learn is actually the answer to a question. *On its own, the answer is almost never interesting.* But if you know the question, the answer may be quite interesting. That's why making the question clear is so important. But as I said in Chapter 1, I sometimes feel that we, as teachers, are so focused on getting to the answer, we spend insufficient time making sure that students understand the question and appreciate its significance. To us, the question and its importance are obvious. To them, they aren't.

Let me close this section by emphasizing again that there are many ways in which one can be a good teacher. I don't mean to imply that, according to cognitive science, every teacher should use a story structure to shape his or her lesson plans. It's just one way that we can help ensure that students think about meaning. I am implying – well, no, I'm stating – that every teacher should get his or her students to think about the meaning of material – except sometimes, which is the subject of the next section.

But What If There Is No Meaning?

This chapter began by posing the question, *How can we get students to remember something?* The answer from cognitive science is straightforward: get them to think about what it means. In the previous section I suggested one method – story structure – for getting students to think about meaning.

It's fair to ask, however, whether there is content that students must learn that is pretty darn close to meaningless. For example, how can you emphasize meaning when students are learning the odd spelling of *Wednesday*, or that *enfranchise* means to give voting rights, or that *travailler* is the French verb for *work*? Some material just doesn't seem to have much meaning, or if it does – Wednesday's origins are to do with the Germanic god Wodan – you're not sure it's worth going into it. Such material seems especially prevalent when one is entering a new field or domain of knowledge (Figure 3.13).

Memorizing meaningless material is commonly called *rote memorization*. I will say more about rote memory in Chapter 4, but for the moment let's just acknowledge that a student who has memorized, say, the first nine elements of the periodic table has little or no idea why she has done so or what the ordering might mean. There are times when a teacher may deem it important for a student to have such knowledge ready in long-term memory as a stepping-stone to understanding something deeper. How can a teacher help the student get that material into long-term memory?

There is a group of memory tricks, commonly called *mnemonics*, that help people memorize content when it is not meaningful. Some examples are listed in Table 3.2.

I'm not a big fan of the peg-word and method-of-loci methods because they are hard to use for different sets of material. If I use my mental walk (back porch, dying pear tree, gravel driveway, and so on) to learn some elements of the periodic table, can I use the same

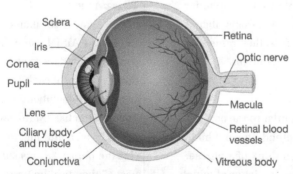

FIGURE 3.13: A biology teacher may be most interested in students appreciating physiology and function of the eye . . . but it's hard to talk about function without being able to name the parts of the eye. So at the beginning of the unit, the teacher may choose to have the students commit some of the anatomic names to memory. Source: © Shutterstock/solar22.

TABLE 3.2: Common mnemonic methods.

Mnemonic	How it works	Example
Peg word	Memorize a series of peg words by using a rhyme – for example, one is a bun, two is a shoe, three is a tree, and so on. Then memorize new material by associating it via visual imagery with the pegs.	To learn the list "radio, shell, nurse," you might imagine a radio sandwiched in a bun, a shoe on a beach with a conch in it, and a tree growing nurses' hats like fruit.
Method of loci	Memorize a series of locations on a familiar walk – for example, the back porch of your house, a dying pear tree, your gravel driveway, and so on. Then visualize new material at each "station" of the walk.	To learn the list "radio, shell, nurse," you might visualize a radio hanging by its cord on the banister of your back porch, someone grinding shells to use as fertilizer to revitalize the dying tree, and a nurse shoveling fresh gravel onto your driveway.
Link method	Visualize each of the items connected to one another in some way.	To learn the list "radio, shell, nurse," you might imagine a nurse listening intently to a radio while wearing large conch shells on her feet instead of shoes.
Acronym method	Create an acronym for the to-be-remembered words, then remember the acronym.	To learn the list "radio, shell, nurse," you might memorize the word RAiSiN using the capitalized letters as cues for the first letter of each word you are to remember.
First-letter method	Similar to the acronym method, this method has you think of a phrase, the first letter of which corresponds to the first letter of the to-be-remembered material.	To learn the list "radio, shell, nurse," you could memorize the phrase "Roses smell nasty," then use the first letter of each word as a cue for the words on the list.

TABLE 3.2: Continued

Mnemonic	How it works	Example
Songs	Think of a familiar tune to which you can sing the words.	To learn the list "radio, shell, nurse," you could sing the words to the tune of "Happy Birthday to You."

Mnemonics help you to memorize meaningless material.

walk to learn the conjugations for some French verbs? The problem is that there might be interference between the two lists; when I get to the gravel driveway, I get confused about what's there because I've associated two things with it.

The other methods are more flexible because students can create a unique mnemonic for each thing they learn. The acronym method and the first-letter method are effective, but students do need to have some familiarity with the material to be learned. I always think of the sentence "Dear Kate, Please Come Over For Great Spaghetti" for the order of taxonomy in biology. If I didn't already know the names, these first-letter cues wouldn't do me much good, but the first letter of each pushes me over the edge from tip-of-the-tongue to ready recall. The acronym method works in much the same way and has the same limitation.

Setting to-be-learned information to music or chanting it to a rhythm also works quite well. Most English speakers learned the letters of the alphabet by singing the ABC song, and I've heard the periodic table of elements set to Offenbach's "Can-Can Music." Music and rhythm do make words remarkably memorable. I (and millions of other kids) grew up seeing School House Rocks cartoons on Saturday mornings, which offered snippets of geography, civics, math, or grammar. I remember being in middle school and subvocally singing "Conjunction Junction" to myself in English class.[†]

Conjunction Junction, what's your function?
Hooking up words and phrases and clauses.

The difficulty with songs is that they are more difficult to generate than the other mnemonic devices.

Why do mnemonics work? Primarily by giving you cues. The acronym ROY G. BIV gives you the first letter of each color in the spectrum of visible light. The first letter is quite a good cue to memory. As I discuss in the next chapter, memory works on the basis of cues. If you don't know anything about a topic, or if the things you're trying to remember are confusing because they are arbitrary (there's nothing about red that makes it obvious that its wavelength is longer than green), mnemonics help because they impose some order on what you are trying to remember.

Summary

If we agree that background knowledge is important, then we must think carefully about how students can acquire that background knowledge – that is, how learning works. Learning is influenced by many factors, but one factor trumps the others: students remember what they think about. That principle highlights the importance of getting students to think about the right thing at the right time. We usually want students to understand what things *mean*, which sets the agenda for a lesson plan. How can we ensure that students think about meaning? I offered one suggestion, which is to use the structure of a story. Stories are easily comprehended and remembered, and they are interesting; but one can't get students to think about meaning if the material *has* no meaning. In that case, it may be appropriate to use a mnemonic device.

Implications for the Classroom

Thinking about meaning helps memory. How can teachers ensure that students think about meaning in the classroom? Here are some practical suggestions.

Review Each Lesson Plan in Terms of What the Student Is Likely to Think About

This sentence may represent the most general and useful idea that cognitive psychology can offer teachers. The most important thing about schooling is what students will remember after the school day is over, and there is a direct relationship between what they think during the day and their later memory. So it's a useful double-check for every lesson plan to try to anticipate what the lesson will *actually* make students think about (rather than what you hope it will make them think about). Doing so may make it clear that students are unlikely to get what the teacher intended out of the lesson.

For example, I once observed a high school social studies class work in groups of three on projects about the Spanish Civil War. Each group was to examine a different aspect of the conflict (for example, compare it to the US Civil War, or consider its impact on today's Spain) and then teach the remainder of the class what they had learned, using the method of their choice. Students in one group noticed that PowerPoint was loaded on the computers, and they were very enthusiastic about using it to teach their bit to the other groups. (This was a while ago, when PowerPoint was not in common use in high schools.) The teacher was impressed by their initiative and gave his permission. Soon all of the groups were using PowerPoint. Many students had some familiarity with the basics of the program, so it could have been used effectively. The problem was that the students changed the assignment from "learn about the Spanish Civil War" to "learn esoteric features of PowerPoint." There was still a lot of enthusiasm in the room, but it was directed toward using animations, integrating videos, finding unusual fonts, and so on. At that point the teacher felt it was far too late to ask all of the groups to switch, so he spent much of the rest of the week badgering students to be sure their presentation had content, not just flash.

This story illustrates one of the reasons that experienced teachers are so good. This teacher clearly didn't let students use PowerPoint the next year, or he thought of a way to keep them on task. Before you have accumulated these experiences, the next best thing is to think carefully about how your students will react to an assignment and what it will make them think about.

Think Carefully About Attention Grabbers
Almost every teacher I have met likes, at least on occasion, to start class with an attention grabber. If you hook students early in the

lesson, they should be curious to know what is behind whatever surprised or awed them. But attention grabbers may not always work. Here's a conversation I had with my oldest daughter when she was in sixth grade.

DAD: What did you do in school today?

REBECCA: We had a guest in science. He taught us about chemicals.

DAD: Oh yeah? What did you learn about chemicals?

REBECCA: He had this glass? That looked like water? But when he put this little metal thingy in it, it boiled. It was so cool. We all screamed.

DAD: Uh-huh. Why did he show you that?

REBECCA: I don't know.

The guest surely planned this demonstration to pique the class's interest, and that goal was met. I'm willing to bet that the guest followed the demonstration with an age-appropriate explanation of the phenomenon but that information was not retained. Rebecca didn't remember it because she was still thinking about how cool the demonstration was. You remember what you think about.

Another teacher once told me she wore a toga to class on the first day she began a unit on ancient Rome. I am sure that got her students' attention. I am also sure it continued to get their attention – that is, to distract them – once the teacher was ready for them to think about something else.

Here's one more example. A guest in a biology class asked the students to think of the very first thing they had ever seen. The students mulled that question over and generated such guesses as "the doctor who pulled me out," "Mom," and so forth. The guest then said, "Actually, the first thing each of you saw was the same. It was pinkish, diffuse light coming through your mother's belly. Today we're going to talk about how that first experience affected how your visual system developed, and how it continues to influence the way you see today." I love that example because it grabbed the students' attention and left them eager to hear more about the subject of the lesson.

As I alluded to earlier in the chapter, I think it is very useful to use the beginning of class to build student interest in the material by understanding the question the underlies the lesson for the day – or as the story framing puts it, to develop the conflict. You might consider, however, whether the beginning of the class is really when they need an attention grabber. In my experience, the transition from one subject to another (or for older students, from one classroom and teacher to another) is enough to buy at least a few minutes of attention from students. It's usually the middle of the lesson that needs a little drama to draw students back from whatever reverie they might be in. But regardless of when it's used, think hard about how you will draw a connection between the attention grabber and the point it's designed to make. Will students understand the connection, and will they be able to set aside the excitement of the attention grabber and move on? If not, is there a way to change the attention grabber to help students make that transition? Perhaps the toga could be worn over street clothes and removed after the first few minutes of class. Perhaps the "metal thingy" demonstration would have been better *after* the basic principle was explained and students were prompted to predict what might happen.

Use Discovery Learning with Care

Discovery learning refers to students learning by exploring objects, discussing problems with classmates, designing experiments, or any of a number of other techniques that use student inquiry rather than teacher telling students things. Indeed, the teacher ideally serves more as a resource than as the director of the class. Discovery learning has much to recommend it, when it comes to memory. If students have a strong voice in deciding which problems they want to work on, they will likely be engaged in the problems they select, and will likely think deeply about the material, with attendant benefits. An important downside, however, is that what students will think about is less predictable. If students are left to explore ideas on their own, they may well explore mental paths that are not profitable. If memory is the residue of thought, then students will remember incorrect "discoveries" as much as they will remember the correct ones. (There are other pluses and minuses to discovery learning, but here I'm focusing on memory.)

Now this doesn't mean that discovery learning should never be used, but it does suggest a principle for when to use it. Discovery learning is probably most useful when the environment gives prompt feedback about whether the student is thinking about a problem in a useful way. One of the best examples of discovery learning is when kids learn to use a computer, whether they are learning an operating system, a complex game, or a Web application. Students show wonderful ingenuity and daring under these circumstances. They are not afraid to try new things, and they shrug off failure. They learn by discovery! Note, however, that computer applications have an important property: when you make a mistake, it is immediately obvious. The computer does something other than what you intended. This immediate feedback makes for a great environment in which "messing around" can pay off. (Other environments aren't like that. Imagine a student left to "mess around" with frog dissection in a biology class.) If the teacher does not direct a lesson to provide constraints on the mental paths that students will explore, the environment itself can do so effectively in a discovery learning context, and that will help memory.

Design Assignments So That Students Will Unavoidably Think About Meaning

If the goal of a lesson plan is to get students to think about the meaning of some material, then it's pretty clear that the best approach is one in which thinking about meaning is unavoidable. One of the things that has always amazed me as a memory researcher is the degree to which people do not know how their own memory system works. It doesn't do any good to tell people, "Hey, I'm going to test your memory for this list of words later," because people don't know what to do to make the words memorable. But if you give people a simple task in which they *must* think of the meaning – for example, rating how much they like each word – they will remember the words quite well.

This idea can be used in the classroom as well as in the laboratory. At the start of this chapter I said that asking fourth graders to bake biscuits was not a good way to get them to appreciate what life on the

Underground Railroad may have been like because they spend too much time thinking about measuring flour and milk. The goal was to get students thinking about the perilous experience of enslaved people seeking escape. So a more effective lesson would be to lead students to consider that experience by, for example, asking them where they supposed people on the underground railroad obtained food, how they were able to prepare it, how they were able to pay for it, and so forth.

Don't Be Afraid to Use Mnemonics

Many teachers I have met shudder at the use of mnemonics. They conjure up images of nineteenth-century schoolrooms with children chanting rhymes of the state capitals. But as bad as a classroom would be if a teacher used *only* mnemonics, they do have their time and place, and I don't think teachers should have this instructional technique taken away from them.

When is it appropriate to ask students to memorize something before it has much meaning? Probably not often, but there will be times when a teacher feels that some material – meaningless though it may be now – must be learned for the student to move forward. Typical examples would be learning letter-sound associations prior to reading and learning foreign language vocabulary.

It might also be appropriate to memorize some material using mnemonics in parallel with other work that emphasizes meaning. When I was in elementary school, I was not required to memorize the multiplication table. Instead I practiced using different materials and techniques that emphasized what multiplication actually means. These techniques were effective, and I readily grasped the concept. But by about fifth grade, not knowing the multiplication table by heart really slowed me down because the new things I was trying to learn had multiplication embedded in them. So every time I saw 8 × 7 within a problem I had to stop and figure out the product. In the sixth grade I moved to a new school, where my teacher quickly figured out what was going on and made me memorize the multiplication table. It made math a lot easier for me, although it took a few weeks before I would admit it.

Try Organizing a Lesson Plan Around the Conflict

There is a conflict in almost any lesson plan, if you look for it. This is another way of saying that the material we want students to know is the answer to a question – and the question is the conflict. The advantage of being very clear about the conflict is that it yields a natural progression for topics. In a movie, trying to resolve a conflict leads to new complications. That's often true of school material too.

Start with the content you want your students to learn, and think backward to the intellectual question it poses. For example, the state may mandate that sixth graders will learn the models of the atom that were competing at the turn of the twentieth century. These are the answers. What is the question? In this story, the goal is to understand the nature of matter. The obstacle is that the results of different experiments appear to conflict with one another. Each new model that is proposed (Rutherford, cloud, Bohr) seems to resolve the conflict but then generates a new complication – that is, experiments to test the model seem to conflict with other experiments. If this organization seems useful to you, you might spend a good bit of time thinking about how to illustrate and explain to students the question, "What is the nature of matter?" How could that question intrigue sixth graders?

As I've emphasized, structuring a lesson plan around conflict can be a real aid to student learning. Another feature I like is that, if you succeed, you are engaging students with the actual substance of the discipline. I've always been bothered by the advice "make it relevant to the students" for two reasons. First, it often feels to me that it doesn't apply. Is the Epic of Gilgamesh relevant to students in a way they can immediately understand? Is trigonometry? Making these topics relevant to students' daily lives will be a strain, and students will probably think it's phony. Second, if I can't convince students that something is relevant to them, does that mean I shouldn't teach it? If I'm continually trying to build bridges between students' daily lives and their school subjects, the students may get the message that school is always about them, whereas I think there is value, interest, and beauty in learning about things that don't have much to do with me. I'm not saying it never makes sense to talk about things students are interested in. What I'm suggesting is that student interests should not be the main driving force of lesson planning. Rather, they might be used as initial points of contact that help students understand the main ideas you want them to consider, rather than as the reason or motivation for them to consider these ideas.

In the previous chapter I argued that students must have background knowledge in order to think critically. In this chapter I discussed how memory works, in the hope that by understanding this we can maximize the likelihood that students will learn this background knowledge; much of the answer to how we can do this was concerned with thinking about meaning. But what if students don't understand the meaning? In the next chapter I discuss why it is hard for students to comprehend the meaning of complex material, and what you can do to help.

Notes

*I made up this statistic.
†Search "Schoolhouse Rock: conjunction junction" on YouTube.

Further Reading

Less Technical

Baddeley, A., Eyesenck, M. W., & Anderson, M. C. (2015). *Memory*, 2. Hove, UK: Psychology Press. A textbook, but quite lucid, covering all the basic science of human memory.

Brown, P. C., Roediger, H. L. III, McDaniel, M. A. (2014). *Make It Stick*. Cambridge, MA: Belknap. Highly readable, this book includes information about the basic science of memory and useful applications of that science.

Dunlosky, J., Rawson, K. A., Marsh, E. J., Nathan, M. J., & Willingham, D. T. (2013). What works, what doesn't? *Scientific American Mind* (September–October), 47–53. A brief, reader-friendly version of a much longer technical article that reviews techniques for committing things to memory.

McKee, R. (1997). *Story*. New York: Harper Collins. There are many instruction manuals meant to help you tell stories effectively. This is one of the best known, based on McKee's legendary screenwriting workshops.

More Technical

Arya, D. J., & Maul, A. (2012). The role of the scientific discovery narrative in middle school science education: an experimental study. *Journal of Educational Psychology*, 104(4),

1022–1032. Experiment showing that middle schoolers remember science content better when it's framed in a discovery narrative, compared to a traditional, nonnarrative format.

Chang-Kredl, S., & Colannino, D. (2017). Constructing the image of the teacher on Reddit: best and worst teachers. *Teaching and Teacher Education*, 64, 43–51. Researchers examined 600 responses to queries for memories of "best" and "worst" teacher on the popular discussion website, Reddit. Common themes related to knowledge/organization of subject matter, and personal qualities of the teachers.

Kim, S-i. (1999). Causal bridging inference: a cause of story interestingness. *British Journal of Psychology*, 90, 57–71. In this study the experimenter varied the difficulty of the inference that readers had to make to understand the text and found that texts were rated as most interesting when the inferences were of medium-level difficulty.

Kleemans, M., Schaap, G., & Suijkerbuijk, M. (2018). Getting youngsters hooked on news. *Journalism Studies*, 19, 2108–2125. A study showing that adults of all ages remember news stories better when they are communicated in a narrative, as opposed to the traditional "inverted pyramid" format for news stories.

Markman, A. B. (2012). Knowledge representation. In: *The Oxford Handbook of Thinking and Reasoning* (eds. K. Holyoak & R. Morrison), pp. 36–51. New York: Oxford University Press. How memories are represented in the mind, and what representation actually means.

Roediger, H. L. (1980). The effectiveness of four mnemonics in ordering recall. *Journal of Experimental Psychology: Human Learning and Memory*, 6(5), 558–567. An article evaluating four different mnemonics (three of which are mentioned in this chapter) showing that all enhance memory.

Seiver, J. G., Pires, M., Awan, F., & Thompson, W. (2019). Retention of word pairs as a function of level of processing, instruction to remember, and delay. *Journal of Cognitive Psychology*, 31(7), 665–682. A recent example of a study showing that deeper (meaning-based) processing leads to better memory than shallow processing and that intention to learn has no impact.

Discussion Questions

1. Emotion leads to better memory, but intentionally inducing emotions in students to help them remember feels manipulative. Is there a way to use emotion in the classroom?

2. Intention to learn doesn't influence memory. But surely that can't mean that it doesn't matter whether or not students care about school. What's the resolution to this apparent paradox?

3. I suggested that trying to tie school content to student interests runs a risk; exactly because Instagram is so interesting to my daughter, she's more likely to go off on her own stream of thought. What are some solutions to this problem?

4. I've suggested it's useful to think of one's teaching on two very broad dimensions: organization/knowledge and emotional warmth. Self-reflect a bit . . . What do you see as your strengths and weaknesses on each of these? What do you want to work on? What resources are available to you for support?

5. I've suggested that using a story structure to organize a lesson plan might help maintain student interest. But for that to happen, students must understand and care about the conflict that drives the narrative. Consider the next class you are to teach. (Or pick another, if you like.) If the content of that lesson plan is the answer, do you think your students know the question? How easy is it to articulate the question in an age-appropriate manner? What might lead them to care about the question? Perhaps a parallel with their own concerns? Or maybe a puzzle that will entice them in the moment, and will lead to the next part of the question?

6. Do you ask students to learn content that is relatively devoid of meaning? As I've said, I think the practice sometimes makes sense, but I understand why people are critical of it, so I think it's worthwhile to be reflective about it. If you do ask students to engage in this sort of memorization, you can make it much easier for them if you create mnemonics. I'm usually a big fan of letting students do the creating whenever they can, and you might give that a go, but be forewarned that there is research showing people are not very good at writing their own mnemonics. One solution might be to see if students come up with good ones and share the best. And if none of them are very good, have ready one that you've prepared.

7. How do you think your students spend their leisure time? Are any of the common activities enriching for the sort of cognitive work discussed in this chapter? Are there closely related activities that might be more enriching? If so, what avenues are open to teachers to encourage them?

8. I've suggested anticipating what a lesson will *actually* make students think about. How hard is that to do? Would it be easier to do with someone else's lesson? Or if you hadn't thought about the lesson for a week, and so could bring a fresh eye to it?

4

Why Is It So Hard for Students to Understand Abstract Ideas?

Question: I once observed a teacher helping a student with geometry problems on the calculation of area. After a few false starts, the student accurately solved a word problem calling for the calculation of the area of a tabletop. A problem came up shortly thereafter that required the student to calculate the area of a soccer field. He looked blank and, even with prompting, did not see how this problem was related to the one he had just solved. In his mind, he had solved a problem about tabletops, and this problem was about soccer fields – completely different. Why are abstract ideas – for example, the calculation of area – so difficult to comprehend in the first place and, once comprehended, so difficult to apply when they are expressed in new ways?

Answer: Abstraction is the goal of schooling. The teacher wants students to be able to apply classroom learning in new contexts, including those outside of school. The challenge is that the mind seems not to care for abstractions. The mind seems to prefer the concrete. That's why, when we encounter an abstract principle – for example, a law in physics such as force = mass × acceleration – we ask for a concrete example to help us understand. The cognitive principle that guides this chapter is:

> We understand new things in the context of things we already know, and most of what we know is concrete.

Thus it is difficult to comprehend abstract ideas and difficult to apply them in new situations. The surest way to help students understand an abstraction is to expose them to many different versions of the abstraction – that is, to have them solve area calculation problems about tabletops, soccer fields, envelopes, doors, and so on. There are some techniques that may hurry this process.

Understanding Is Disguised Remembering

In Chapter 2 I emphasized that factual knowledge is important to schooling. In Chapter 3 I described how to make sure that students acquire those facts – that is, I described how things get into memory. But I've also assumed that students understand what you're trying to teach them. As you know, you can't bank on that. It's often difficult for students to understand new ideas, especially ones that are *really* novel, meaning they aren't related to other things they have already learned. What do cognitive scientists know about how students understand things?

The answer is that they understand new ideas (things they don't know) by relating them to old ideas (things they do know). That sounds fairly straightforward. It's a little like the process you go through when you encounter an unfamiliar word. If you don't know, for example, what *ab ovo* means, you look it up in a dictionary. There you see the definition "from the beginning." You already know those words, so now you have some idea of what *ab ovo* means.*

The fact that we understand new ideas by relating them to things we already know helps us understand some principles that are familiar to every teacher. One principle is the usefulness of analogies; they help us understand something new by relating it to something we already know about. For example, suppose I'm trying to explain Ohm's law to a student who knows nothing about electricity. I tell her that electricity is power created by the flow of electrons and that Ohm's law describes some influences on that flow. I tell her that Ohm's law is defined this way:

$$I = V / R$$

I is a measure of electrical current, that is, how fast the electrons are moving. *V,* or voltage, is the potential difference, which causes electrons to move. Potential will "even out," so if you have a difference in electrical potential at two points, that difference causes movement of electrons. *R* is a measure of resistance. Some materials are very effective conduits for electron movement (low resistance) whereas others are poor conduits (high resistance).

Although it's accurate, this description is hard to understand, and textbooks usually offer an analogy to the movement of water. Electrons moving along a wire are like water moving through a pipe. If there is high pressure at one end of the pipe (for example, created by a pump) and lower pressure at the other end, the water will move, right? But the movement is slowed by friction from the inside of the pipe, and it can be slowed even more if we partially block the pipe. We can describe how fast the water moves with a measure such as gallons per minute. So, in terms of the water analogy, Ohm's law says that how fast water flows depends on the amount of water pressure and the amount of resistance in the pipes. That analogy is helpful because we are used to thinking about water moving in pipes. We call on this prior knowledge to help us understand new information, just as we call on our knowledge of the word *beginning* to help us understand *ab ovo*.

So new things are understood by relating them to things we already understand. That's why analogies help (Figure 4.1).

FIGURE 4.1: "force = mass × acceleration" is difficult to understand because it is abstract. It's easier to understand with a concrete example. Use the same force (a woman swinging a bat) to hit different masses - a baseball or an automobile. We understand that the acceleration of the ball and the acceleration of the car will be quite different. Source: Game © Getty Images/SAMURAI JAPAN; car © Getty Images/FilmMagic.

Another consequence of our dependence on prior knowledge is our need for concrete examples. As you know, abstractions – for example, force = mass × acceleration, or a description of the poetical meter iambic pentameter – are hard for students to understand, even if all of the terms are defined. They need concrete examples to illustrate what abstractions mean. They need to actually hear:

> Is *this* the *face* that *launched* a *thou*sand *ships*?
> And *burnt* the *top*less *tow*ers of *Il*ium?

and

> Rough *winds* do *shake* the *dar*ling *buds* of *May*
> And *summer's lease* hath *all* too *short* a *date*

and other examples before they can feel they understand iambic pentameter.

Examples help not only because they make abstractions concrete. Concrete examples don't help much if they're not familiar. Suppose you and I had the following conversation:

ME Different scales of measurement provide different types of information. Ordinal scales provide ranks, whereas on an interval scale the differences between measurements are meaningful.

YOU That was utter gobbledygook.

ME OK, here are some concrete examples. The Mohs scale of mineral hardness is an ordinal scale, whereas a successful Rasch model provides an interval measurement. See?

YOU I think I'll go get a coffee now.

So it's not simply that giving concrete examples helps. (A better explanation of scales of measurement appears in Figure 4.2.) They must also be *familiar* examples, and the Mohs scale and the

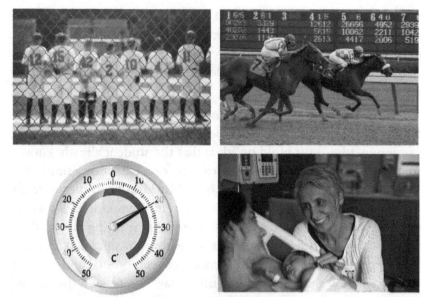

FIGURE 4.2: There are four, and only four, ways that numbers on a scale relate to one another. In a nominal scale, each number refers to one thing but the numbers are arbitrary - for example, the number on a baseball jersey tells you nothing about the player. On an ordinal scale, the numbers are meaningful, but they tell you nothing about the distance between them. In a horse race, for example, you know that the first place horse was ahead of the second place finisher, but you don't know by how much. On an interval scale, not only are the numbers ordered but also the intervals are meaningful - for example, the difference between 10° and 20° is the same as the interval between 80° and 90°. "Zero" on an interval scale is arbitrary; that is, zero degrees Celsius doesn't mean there is no temperature. A ratio scale, such as age, has a true zero point: that is, zero years means the absence of any years. Source: Baseball © Shutterstock/ Suzanne Tucker; horserace © Shutterstock/Don Blaise; thermometer © Shutter- stock/Flipser; generations © Getty Images/MNPhotoStudios.

Rasch model are not familiar to most people. It's not the concrete- ness, it's the familiarity that's important; but most of what students are familiar with is concrete, because abstract ideas are so hard to understand.

Ludwig Wittgenstein speculated that "The problems are solved, not by giving new information, but by arranging what we have always known." He was right. Understanding new ideas is mostly a mat- ter of getting the right old ideas into working memory and then rearranging them – making comparisons we hadn't made before, or thinking about a feature we had previously ignored. Consider the explanation of force in Figure 4.1. You know what happens when you hit a ball with a bat, and you know what happens when you hit a car with a bat, but have you ever before held those two ideas in mind at the same time and considered that the different outcome is due to the difference in mass?

Now you see why I claim that understanding is disguised remembering. No one can pour new ideas into a student's head directly. Every new idea must build on ideas that the student already knows. To get a student to understand, a teacher (or a parent or a book or a video or a peer) must ensure that the right ideas from the student's long-term memory are pulled up and put into working memory. In addition, the right features of these memories must be attended to, that is, compared or combined or somehow manipulated. For me to help you understand the difference between ordinal and interval measurement, it's not enough for me to say, "Think of a thermometer and think of a horse race." Doing so will get those concepts into working memory, but I also have to make sure they are compared in the right way.

We all know, however, that it's not really this simple. When we give students one explanation and one set of examples, do they understand? Usually not. Now that you have looked at Figure 4.2, would you say you "understand" scales of measurement? You know more than you did before, but your knowledge probably doesn't feel very deep, and you may not feel confident that you could identify the scale of measurement for a new example, say, centimeters on a ruler (Figure 4.3).

To dig deeper into what helps students understand, we need to address these two issues. First, even when students "understand," there are really degrees of comprehension. One student's understanding can be shallow while another's is deep. Second, even if students understand in the classroom, this knowledge may not transfer well to the world outside the classroom. That is, when students see a new version of what is at heart an old problem, they may think they are stumped, even though they recently solved the same problem. They don't know that they know the answer! In the next two sections I elaborate on each issue, that is, on shallow knowledge and on lack of transfer.

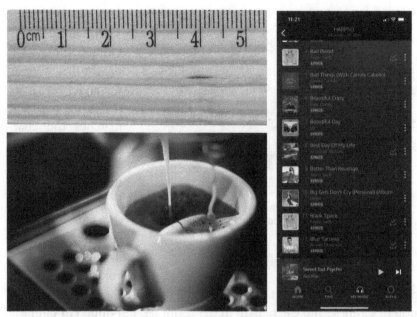

FIGURE 4.3: Here are three other examples of scales of measurement: centimeters (as measured by a ruler), people's ratings from 1 to 7 of how much they like espresso, and the numbered tracks on a playlist. Which scale of measurement does each of these examples use? Source: Ruler © Shutterstock/Olga Kovalenko; espresso © Getty Images/Guido Mieth; playlist © Daniel Willingham.

Why Is Knowledge Shallow?

Every teacher has had the following experience: You ask a student a question (in class or perhaps on a test), and the student responds using the exact words you used when you explained the idea or with the exact words from the textbook. Although his answer is certainly correct, you can't help but wonder whether the student has simply memorized the definition by rote and doesn't understand what he's saying (Figure 4.4).

This scenario brings to mind a famous problem posed by the philosopher John Searle.[1] Searle wanted to argue that a computer might display intelligent behavior without really *understanding* what it is doing. He posed this thought problem: Suppose a person is alone in a room. We can slip pieces of paper with Chinese writing on them under the door. The person in the room speaks no Chinese but responds to each message. She has an enormous book, each page of which is divided

FIGURE 4.4: The fear that students merely parrot ideas that they don't understand is not new; this image is from mid-nineteenth century France. (It's not very complimentary of teachers, either.) Source: © Getty Images/DEA/ICAS94.

into two columns. There are strings of Chinese characters on the left and on the right. She scans the book until she matches the character string on the slip of paper to a string in the left-hand column. Then she carefully copies the characters in the right-hand column onto the piece of paper and slips it back under the door. We have posed a question in Chinese and the person in the room has responded in Chinese. Does the person in the room understand Chinese?

Almost everyone says no. She's giving sensible responses, but she's just copying them from a book. Searle provided this example to argue that computers, even if they display sophisticated behavior such as comprehending Chinese, aren't thinking in the way in which we understand the term. We might say the same thing about students. Rote knowledge might lead to giving the right response, but it doesn't mean the student is thinking.[†]

We can see examples of "sophisticated answers" that don't have understanding behind them in "student bloopers," which are regular forwards in my e-mail inbox. Some of them are good examples of rote knowledge; for example, "Three kinds of blood vessels are arteries, vanes, and caterpillars," and "I would always read the works of the Cavalier poets, whose works always reflected the sentiment 'Cease the day!'" In addition to giving us a chuckle, these examples show that the student has simply memorized the "answer" without comprehension.

The fear that students will end up with no more than rote knowledge has been almost a phobia among some educators, but the truth is that rote knowledge is probably relatively rare. *Rote knowledge* (as I'm using the term) means you have *no* understanding of the material. You've just memorized words, so it doesn't seem odd to you that Cavalier poets, best known for light lyrics of love and their romantic view of life, would have the philosophy "Cease the day!"

Much more common than rote knowledge is what I call *shallow knowledge,* meaning that students have some understanding of the material but their understanding is limited. We've said that students come to understand new ideas by relating them to old ideas. If their knowledge is shallow, the process stops there. Their knowledge is tied to the analogy or explanation that has been provided. They can understand the concept only in the context that was provided. For example, you know that "Seize the day!" means "Enjoy the moment without worrying about the future," and you remember that the teacher said that "Gather ye rosebuds while ye may" (from Herrick's *To the Virgins, to Make Much of Time*) is an example of this sentiment. But you don't know much more. If the teacher provided a new poem, you would be hard put to say whether it was in the style of a Cavalier poet (Figure 4.5)

FIGURE 4.5: Title page to Sir John Suckling's "Fragmenta Aurea." Even if a student was unfamiliar with this particular work, if she had deep knowledge of Cavalier poetry, she would not be surprised to see terms like "wonder and delight" and "new spirit" applied to his work. Source: © Getty Images/Culture Club.

We can contrast shallow knowledge with deep knowledge. A student with deep knowledge knows more about the subject, and the pieces of knowledge are more richly interconnected. The student understands not just the parts but also the *whole*. This understanding allows the student to apply the knowledge in many different contexts, to talk about it in different ways, to imagine how the system as a whole would change if one part of it changed, and so forth. A student with deep knowledge of Cavalier poetry would be able to recognize elements of Cavalier ideals in other literatures, such as ancient Chinese poetry, even though the two forms seem very different on the surface. In addition, the student would be able to consider what-if questions, such as "What might Cavalier poetry have been like if the political situation in England had changed?" They can think through this sort of question because the pieces of their knowledge are so densely interconnected. They are interrelated like the parts of a machine, and the what-if question suggests the replacement of one part with another. Students with deep knowledge can predict how the machine would operate if one part were to be changed.

Obviously teachers want their students to have deep knowledge, and most teachers try to instill it. Why then would students end up with shallow knowledge? One obvious reason is that a student just might not be paying attention to the lesson. The mention of "rosebuds" makes a student think about the time she fell off her skateboard into the neighbor's rose bush, and the rest of the poem is lost on her. There are other, less obvious reasons that students might end up with shallow knowledge.

Here's one way to think about it. Suppose you plan to introduce the idea of government to a first-grade class. The main point you want students to understand is that people living or working together set up rules to make things easier for everyone. You will use two familiar examples – the classroom and students' homes – and then introduce the idea that there are other rules that larger groups of people agree to live by. Your plan is to ask your students to list some of the rules of the classroom and consider why each rule exists. Then you'll ask them to list some rules their families have at home and consider why those rules exist. Finally, you'll ask them to name some rules that exist outside of their families and classroom, which you know will take a lot more prompting. You hope your students will see that the rules for each group of people – family, classroom, and larger community – serve similar functions (Figure 4.6).

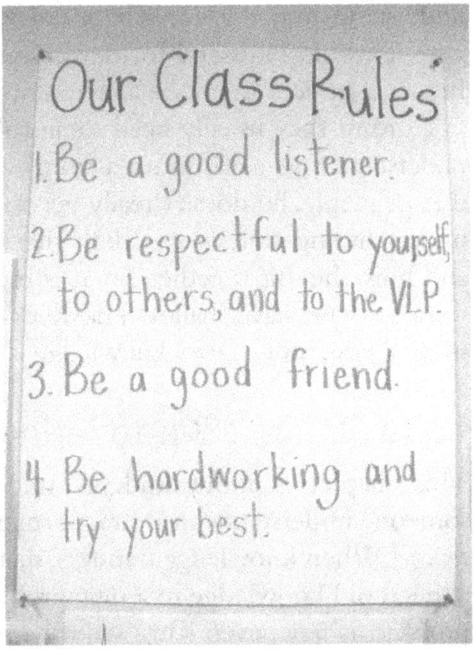

A student with rote knowledge might later report, "Government is like a classroom because both have rules." The student has no understanding of what properties the two groups have in common. The student with shallow knowledge understands that a government is like a classroom because both groups are a community of people who need to

FIGURE 4.6: Most classrooms have rules, sometimes made public in a list like this one. Understanding the need for rules in a classroom may be a stepping-stone to understanding why a group of people working or playing together benefits from a set of rules. Source: © Frank Hebbert Creative Commons CC BY 2.0.

agree on a set of rules in order for things to run smoothly and to be safe. The student understands the parallel but can't go beyond it. So for example, if asked, "How is government *different* from our school?" the student would be stumped. A student with deep knowledge would be able to answer that question and might successfully extend the principle to consider other groups of people who might need to form rules, for example, his group of friends playing pickup basketball.

This example can help us understand why all students might not get deep knowledge. The target knowledge – that groups of people need rules – is pretty abstract. It would appear, then, that the right strategy would be to teach the abstract concept directly; after all, that's what you want them to learn. But I said before that students don't understand abstractions easily or quickly. They need examples. That's why it would be useful to use the example of the classroom rules. In fact, a student might be able to say, "When people come together in a group, they usually need some rules," but if the student doesn't understand how a classroom, a family, and a community all exemplify that principle, he doesn't really get it. Thus deep knowledge means understanding *everything* – both the abstraction and the examples, and how they fit together. So, it is much easier to understand why most students have shallow knowledge, at least when they begin to study a new topic. Deep knowledge is harder to obtain than shallow.

Why Doesn't Knowledge Transfer?

This chapter is about students' understanding of abstractions. If someone understands an abstract principle, we expect they will show *transfer*. When knowledge transfers, that means they have successfully applied old knowledge to a new problem. Now, in some sense *every* problem is new; even if we see the same problem twice, we might see it in a different setting, and because some time has passed, we could say we have changed, even if only a little bit. Most often when psychologists talk about transfer they mean the new problem looks different from the old one, but we do have applicable knowledge to help us solve it. For example, consider the following two problems:

Jayden bought three jars of cocktail sauce and a tray of jumbo shrimp for a total of $40. If the price of a tray of jumbo shrimp is $25, what is the price of a jar of cocktail sauce?

Last week Julia drove her car to work and back three times and made one trip to see her friend, putting a total of 80 miles on her car. Her friend lives 50 miles away, round trip. How far does Julia live from work?

Each problem requires subtracting part of the total (shrimp tray or trip to friend) then dividing the result to get a unit value (price of cocktail sauce or number of miles to work). The two problems differ in what psychologists call their *surface structure* – that is, the first problem is framed in terms of buying food and the second in terms of putting miles on a car. The problems have the same *deep structure* because they require the same steps for solution. The surface structure of each problem is a way to make the abstraction concrete.

Obviously the surface structure of a problem is unimportant to its solution. We would expect that a student who can solve the first problem should be able to solve the second problem, because it's the deep structure that matters. Nevertheless, people seem to be much more influenced by surface structure than they ought to be. In a classic laboratory experiment showing the influence of surface structure,[2] the experimenters asked college students to solve the following problem:

Suppose you are a doctor faced with a patient who has a malignant tumor in his stomach. It is impossible to operate on the patient, but unless the tumor is destroyed, the patient will die. There is a kind of ray that can be used to destroy the tumor. If the rays reach the tumor all at once at a sufficiently high intensity, the tumor will be destroyed. Unfortunately, at this intensity the healthy tissue the rays pass through on the way to the tumor will also be destroyed. At lower intensities the rays are harmless to healthy tissue, but they will not affect the tumor either. What type of procedure might be used to destroy the tumor with the rays and at the same time avoid destroying the healthy tissue?

If a participant didn't solve it – and most couldn't – the experimenter told him or her the solution: send a number of rays of low intensity from different directions and have them all converge on the tumor; that way each weak ray can safely pass through the healthy tissue, but all of the rays will meet at the tumor, so it will be destroyed. The experimenter made sure the participant understood the solution, then presented them with the following problem:

A dictator ruled a small country from a fortress. The fortress was situated in the middle of the country, and many roads radiated outward from it, like spokes on a wheel. A great general vowed to capture the fortress and free the country of the dictator. The general knew that if his entire army could attack the fortress at once, it could be captured. But a spy reported that the dictator had planted mines on each of the roads. The mines were set so that small bodies of men could pass over them safely, because the dictator needed to be able to move troops and workers about; however, any large force would detonate the mines. Not only would this activity blow up the road, but the dictator would destroy many villages in retaliation. How could the general attack the fortress?

The two problems have the same deep structure: when combined forces will cause collateral damage, scatter your forces and have them converge on the point of attack from different directions. That solution may seem obvious, but it wasn't obvious to the participants. Only 30% solved the second problem, even though they had *just heard* the conceptually identical problem and its solution (Figure 4.7).

You experienced a similar phenomenon in Chapter 1. I described the disk-and-pegs problem and then introduced a problem with the same deep structure but a different surface structure – a tea ceremony, where tasks were to be transferred from the host to the most senior guest. If you're like most people, you didn't perceive that the two problems shared the same deep structure.

Why? The answer goes back to how we understand things. When we read or when we listen to someone talking, we are interpreting what is written or said in light of what we already know about similar topics. For example, suppose you read this passage: "Felix, the second named storm of the season to become a hurricane, gained strength with astonishing speed overnight, with wind speeds of 150 miles per hour and stronger gusts. Forecasters predict that the storm's path may take it to the coast of Belize within the next 12

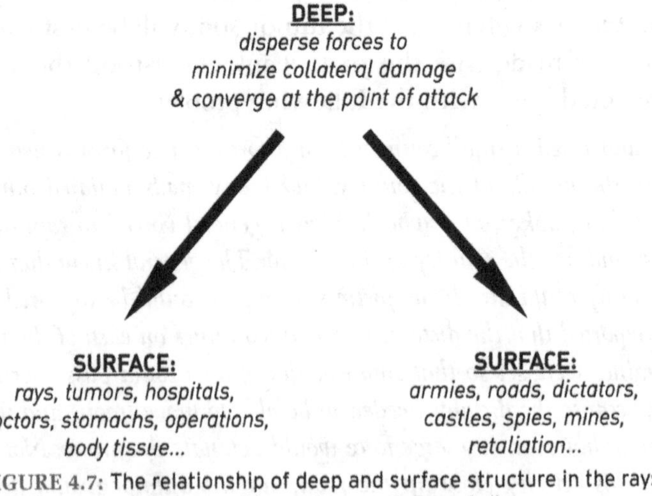

DEEP:
*disperse forces to
minimize collateral damage
& converge at the point of attack*

SURFACE:
*rays, tumors, hospitals,
doctors, stomachs, operations,
body tissue...*

SURFACE:
*armies, roads, dictators,
castles, spies, mines,
retaliation...*

FIGURE 4.7: The relationship of deep and surface structure in the rays-tumor and the armies-fortress problems. Source: © Greg Culley.

hours." In Chapter 2 I emphasized that prior knowledge is necessary to comprehend this sort of text. If you don't know what sort of storms are named and where Belize is, you don't fully understand these sentences. In addition, your background knowledge will also shape how you interpret *what comes next.* The interpretation of these sentences drastically narrows how you will interpret new text. For example, when you see the word *eye* you won't think of the organ that sees, nor of the loop at the top of a needle, nor of a bud on a potato, nor of a round spot on a peacock's feather. You'll think of the center of a hurricane. And if you see the word *pressure* you'll immediately think of atmospheric pressure, not peer-group pressure or economic pressure.

So our minds assume that new things we read (or hear) will be related to what we've just read (or heard). This fact makes understanding faster and smoother. Unfortunately, it also makes it harder to see the deep structure of problems. That's because our cognitive system is always struggling to make sense of what we're reading or hearing, to find relevant background knowledge that will help us interpret the words, phrases, and sentences. But the background knowledge that seems applicable almost always concerns the surface structure. When people read the tumor-and-rays problem, their cognitive system narrows the interpretation of it (just as it does for the hurricane sentences) according to what sort of background knowledge the reader has, and that's likely to be some knowledge of tumors, rays, doctors, and so forth. When the person later reads the other version of the problem, the background knowledge that seems relevant concerns dictators, armies, and fortresses. That's why transfer is so poor. The first problem is taken to be one about tumors, and the second problem is interpreted as being about armies.

The solution to this problem seems self-evident. Why not tell people to think about the deep structure as they read? The problem with this advice is that the deep structure of a problem is not obvious. Even worse, an almost limitless number of deep structures *might* be applicable. As you're reading about the dictator and the castle, it's hard to simultaneously think, Is the deep structure the logical form *modus tollens*? Is the deep structure one of finding the least common multiple? Is the deep structure Newton's third law of motion? To see the deep structure, you must understand how all parts of the problem relate to one another, and you must know which parts are important and which are not. The surface structure, on the other hand, is perfectly obvious: this problem is about armies and fortresses.

The researchers who did the tumor-and-rays experiment also tried telling people, "Hey, that problem about the tumor and the rays might help you in solving this problem about armies and a fortress." When they told them that, almost everyone could solve the problem. The analogy was easy to see. The fortress is like the tumor, the armies are like the rays, and so on. So the difficulty was that people simply didn't realize that the two problems were analogous.

Other times we get poor transfer even when students know that a new problem shares deep structure with another problem they've solved. Picture a student who knows that the algebra word problem he's working on is an illustration of solving simultaneous equations with two unknowns, and there are examples in his textbook outlining the process. The surface structures of the solved textbook problem and the new problem are different – one is about a hardware store's inventory and the other is about mobile phone plans – but the student knows he should disregard the surface structure and focus on the deep structure. To use the textbook example to help himself, however, he must figure out how the surface structure of each problem maps onto the deep structure. It's as though he understands the tumor problem and its solution, but when presented with the fortress problem he can't figure out whether the armies are playing the role of the rays, the tumor, or the healthy tissue. As you might guess, when a problem has lots of components and lots of steps in its solution, it more often happens that transfer is hampered by difficulty in mapping from a solved problem to the new one. Occasionally, the results can be comic (Figure 4.8).

This discussion makes it sound as though it's virtually impossible for knowledge to transfer, as though we are powerless to look beyond the surface structure of what we read or hear. Obviously that's not true. *Some* of the participants in the experiments I described did think of using the problem they had seen before, although the percentage who did so is surprisingly small. In addition, when faced with a novel situation, an adult will usually approach it in a more fruitful way than a child will. Somehow the adult is making use of his or her experience so that knowledge is transferring. In other words, it's a mistake to think of our old knowledge transferring to a

FIGURE 4.8: Comedies sometimes make use of failures to transfer known solutions to new problems. In *Office Space*, the lead characters plan revenge on their company using a plan that worked well in the movie *Superman III*, but their version fails to transfer to their context because they didn't account for relevant differences in the companies. Source: © Getty Images/Handout.

new problem only when the source of that background knowledge is obvious to us. When we see the tumor-and-rays problem for the first time, we don't simply say, "I've never seen that problem or one like it before, so I give up." We have strategies for coming up with solutions, even though they may ultimately not work. Those strategies must be based on our experience – on other problems we've solved, things we know about tumors and rays, and so on. In that sense, we're *always* transferring knowledge of facts and knowledge of problem solutions, even when we feel like we've never seen this sort of problem before. Not very much is known about this type of transfer, however, precisely because it's so hard to trace where it comes from.

In the next chapter I discuss, among other things, how to maximize the chances that knowledge will transfer.

Summary

Understanding happens when we assemble ideas from memory in new ways, for example, when we compare finishers in a horse race to readings on a thermometer as a way of understanding scales of measurement. Abstract ideas are difficult because we rely on what's already in memory to understand new ideas, and most of what's in memory is concrete. Our understanding of new ideas is initially shallow because deep understanding requires more connections among the components of the idea; it simply takes more experience and therefore more time to develop deep understanding. Once we've worked with the same idea in a number of guises, we can appreciate its deep structure – the functional relationships among the components of the idea. But until then, our understanding will cling to the examples we've seen, and transfer will be uncertain.

Implications for the Classroom

The message of this chapter seems rather depressing: it's hard to understand stuff, and when at last we do, it won't transfer to new situations. It's not quite that grim, but the difficulty of deep understanding shouldn't be underestimated. After all, if understanding were easy for students, teaching would be easy for you! Here are a few ideas on how to meet this challenge in the classroom.

Be Wary of Promises of Broad Transfer

The history of education is littered with abandoned attempts to teach students a skill that will "train the mind" and help students think more critically about, well, everything.

In the nineteenth century students studied Latin in the hopes that the logical structure of the grammar would make logical thinking habitual. In one of the early (and notable) successes of educational psychology, Edward Thorndike showed that students who took Latin did no better in their other classes than students who didn't. The logic of Latin didn't rub off.[3]

The hope of very broad transfer was reignited in the 1960s, when some educational theorists reasoned that computer programming called for logical thinking, as well as the use of some broadly applicable concepts (e.g., recursion). Maybe if kids learned to code, those thinking skills would apply broadly. It works a little better than teaching them Latin, but only a little.

Some people think learning chess will make kids logical thinkers, others advocate for teaching them to play a musical instrument. What you've seen in this chapter is the persistent specificity of learning. I think that playing chess is wonderful and so is playing an instrument, but if you want children to think logically about science, teach them how science works. If you want them to learn to evaluate an argument in expository prose, teach that. Don't teach a different skill in the vain hope that it will burnish some other skill.

To Help Student Comprehension, Provide Examples and Ask Students to Compare Them

As noted earlier, experience helps students to see deep structure, so provide that experience via lots of examples. Another strategy that might help is to ask students to compare different examples. Thus an English teacher trying to help her students understand the concept of *irony* might provide the following examples:

- In *Oedipus Rex,* the Delphic Oracle predicts that Oedipus will kill his father and marry his mother. Oedipus leaves his home in an effort to protect those he believes to be his parents, but in so doing sets in motion events that eventually make the prediction come true.
- In *Romeo and Juliet,* Romeo kills himself because he believes that Juliet is dead. When Juliet awakens, she is so distraught over Romeo's death that she commits suicide.
- In *Othello,* the noble Othello implicitly trusts his advisor Iago when he tells Othello that his wife is unfaithful, whereas it is Iago who plots against him.

The students (with some prompting) might come to see what each example has in common with the others. A character does something expecting one result, but the opposite happens because the character is missing a crucial piece of information: Oedipus is adopted, Juliet is alive, Iago is a deceiver. The audience knows that missing piece of information and therefore recognizes what the outcome will be. The play is even more tragic because as the audience watches the events unfold, they know that the unhappy ending could be avoided if the character knew what they know.

Dramatic irony is an abstract idea that is difficult to understand, but comparing diverse examples of it may help students by forcing them to think about deep structure. Students know that the point of the exercise is not shallow comparisons such as, "Each play has men and women in it." As discussed in Chapter 2, we remember what we think about. This method of getting students to think about deep structure may help.

Make Deep Knowledge the Spoken and Unspoken Emphasis

You very likely let your students know that you expect them to learn what things mean – that is, to learn the deep structure. You should also ask yourself whether you send unspoken messages that match that emphasis. What kind of questions do you pose in class? Some teachers pose mostly factual questions, often in a rapid-fire manner: "What does b stand for in this formula?" or "What happens when Huck and Jim get back on the raft?" The low-level facts are important, as I've discussed, but if that's all you ask about, it sends a message to students that that's all there is.

Assignments and assessments are another source of implicit messages about what is important. When a project is assigned, does it demand deep understanding or is it possible to complete it with just a surface knowledge of the material? If your students are old enough that they take quizzes and tests, be sure these test deep knowledge. Students draw a strong implicit message from the content of tests: if it's on the test, it's important.

Make Your Expectations for Deep Knowledge Realistic

Although deep knowledge is your goal, you should be clear-eyed about what students can achieve and about how quickly they can achieve it. Deep knowledge is hard won and is the product of much practice. Don't despair if your students don't yet have a deep understanding of a complex topic. Shallow knowledge is much better than no knowledge at all, and shallow knowledge is a natural step on the way to deeper knowledge. It may be years before your students develop a truly deep understanding, and the best that any teacher can do is to start them down that road or continue their progress at a good pace.

In this chapter I've described why abstract ideas are so difficult to understand and why they are so difficult to apply in unfamiliar situations. I said that practice in thinking about and using an abstract idea is critical to being able to apply it. In the next chapter I talk at greater length about the importance of practice.

Notes

*You may have noticed a problem. If we understand things by relating them to what we already know, how do we understand the *first* thing we ever learn? To put it another way, how do we know what *beginning* means? If we look that word up we see that it means "a start." And if we look up the word *start* we see it defined as "a beginning." It seems, then, that defining words with other words won't really work, because we quickly run into circular definitions. This is a fascinating issue, but it's not central to the discussion in this chapter. A short answer is that some meanings are directly understandable from our senses. For example, you know what *red* means without resorting to a dictionary. These meanings can serve as anchors for other meanings and help us avoid the circularity problem that we saw in the *ab ovo* example.

†Not everyone is persuaded by Searle's argument. Different objections have been raised, but the most common is that the example of the person alone in a room doesn't capture what computers might be capable of.

Further Reading

Less Technical

De Bruyckere, P., Kirschner, P.A., & Hulshof, C. D. (2020). If you learn A, will you be better able to learn B? *American Educator, 44* (1), 30–34 . Given what's known about transfer, considers the question "should all students learn to play a musical instrument? Or learn to play chess?"

Hofstadter, D., & Sander, E. (2013). *Surfaces and Essences: Analogy as the Fuel and Fire of Thinking*. New York: Basic Books. This book is "less technical," but it's far from breezy; a 500-page consideration of the centrality of analogy to human thought. It's dense, but Pulitzer Prize–winner Hofstadter writes beautifully.

More Technical

Carey, S. (2011). The origin of concepts: a précis. *Behavioral and Brain Sciences, 34,* 113–167. A summary of a much longer book, this article describes Carey's theory of how children (and adults) come to understand new concepts, with particular emphasis on the idea that there is an innate starting point for human conceptual development.

Goldstone, R., & Day, S. B. (2012). New conceptualizations of transfer of learning. *Educational Psychologist, 47*(3). The entire issue of this prominent journal was devoted to transfer, including articles on what makes it difficult and the best ways to promote it.

Holyoak, K. J. (2012). Analogy and relational reasoning. In: *The Oxford Handbook of Thinking and Reasoning* (eds K. Holyoak & R. Morrison). 234–259. New York: Oxford University Press. Very useful overview of the psychology underlying analogy.

Hoyos, C., & Gentner, D. (2017). Generating explanations via analogical comparison. *Psychonomic Bulletin & Review, 24*(5), 1364–1374. An example of the power of comparison in helping to understand new ideas, here applied in six-year-olds.

Mayer, R. E. (2004). Teaching of subject matter. *Annual Review of Psychology, 55,* 715–744. A comprehensive overview of specific subject matter domains, with special attention to transfer.

Sala, G., & Gobet, F. (2017). Does far transfer exist? Negative evidence from chess, music, and working memory training. *Current Directions in Psychological Science, 26*(6), 515–520. This article summarizes a good deal of research, concluding that studying chess or learning to play a musical instrument makes you proficient in those activities, but doesn't transfer to overall mental acuity.

Scherer, R., Siddiq, F., & Viveros, B. S. (2018). The cognitive benefits of learning computer programming: a meta-analysis of transfer effects. *Journal of Educational Psychology* 111(5): 764–792. Article showing that teaching students to program a computer leads to some positive transfer to measures of creative thinking, mathematics, metacognition, spatial skills, and reasoning. There's not transfer to verbal tests, consistent with the idea that the transfer may not be a matter of generalized logical thinking but of overlap of the training and the transfer tests.

Discussion Questions

1. Deep knowledge is hard won and therefore takes time to develop. Not all knowledge will be deep. How important is it for adults – teachers, parents – to decide what knowledge ought to be deep, versus for students themselves to decide? What are the trade-offs?

2. What is the student's perspective on "rote knowledge"? Why might acquiring "rote knowledge" actually seem appealing? I mentioned the role of testing as one example of what a teacher might (unwittingly) do to encourage students to learn by rote. What other factors might play a role?

3. It would seem that the transfer problem might be very troublesome in teacher education; future teachers often study in university classrooms about how to be a teacher and then are expected to implement that knowledge as teachers in their own classrooms.

How well did this knowledge transfer in your own experience? Reflect on what features of your teacher education led to good or poor transfer.

4. What are some of the more profound and useful "deep structures" of the classroom that you've learned? What have you learned about students or about classroom situations or dynamics that might look different on the surface in different classrooms but reflects a deeper truth across situations?

5. I've said that deep knowledge is hard won; it requires working with ideas in many contexts, and that often takes significant time. This makes it likely that, in your classroom, there are some ideas that students will have some familiarity with from the previous year but still need to work with more, and other ideas that you will introduce, understanding that student knowledge will be probably shallow at the end of the year, but you know will be revisited next year. How confident are you about the communication in your school about what this knowledge is and communication about the competence of individual students around this knowledge? If you're not confident, what might be done to improve communication?

6. Shallow knowledge seems like it might go hand in hand with responding on autopilot, as described in Chapter 1. You perceive situation X and know that response Y generally leads to a good outcome, so you don't think any more deeply about X, for example, whether other situations that appear different on the surface have the same deep structure as X. Two results might follow. You don't see that Y might be useful in other situations, and because you never think much about X, you never come to a deeper understanding of it. Everyone has Xs and Ys in their practice. What are yours? What are the situations that you solve on autopilot and might benefit from deeper reflection?

5

Is Drilling Worth It?

Question: Drilling has been given a bad name. The very use of the military term drill in place of the more neutral term practice implies something mindless and unpleasant that is performed in the name of discipline rather than for the student's profit. Then too, the phrase "drill and kill" has been used as a criticism of some types of instruction; the teacher drills the students, which is said to kill their innate motivation to learn. On the other side of this debate are educational traditionalists who argue that students must practice in order to learn some facts and skills they need at their fingertips – for example, math facts such as $5 + 7 = 12$. Few teachers would argue that drilling boosts students' motivation and sense of fun. Does the cognitive benefit make it worth the potential cost to motivation?

Answer: The bottleneck in our cognitive system is the ability to juggle several ideas in our mind simultaneously. For example, it's easy to multiply 19×6 in your head, but nearly impossible to multiply $184\,930 \times 34\,004$. The processes are the same, but in the latter case you "run out of room" in your head to keep track of the numbers. The mind has a few tricks for working around this problem. One of the most effective is practice, because it reduces the amount of "room" that mental work requires. The cognitive principle that guides this chapter is:

> It is virtually impossible to become proficient at a mental task without extended practice.

You cannot become a good soccer player if, as you're trying to control the ball while running, you focus on how hard to hit the ball, which surface of your foot to use, and so on. Low-level processes like this must become automatic, leaving room for more high-level concerns, such as game strategy. Similarly, you cannot become good at algebra without knowing math facts by heart. Students must practice some things. But not everything needs to be practiced. In this chapter I elaborate on why practice is so important, and I discuss which material is important enough to merit practice and how to implement practice in a way that students find maximally useful and interesting.

Why practice? One reason is to gain a minimum level of competence. A child practices tying her shoelaces with a parent's or teacher's help until she can reliably tie them without supervision. We also practice tasks that we can perform but that we'd like to improve. A professional tennis player can hit a serve into his opponent's court almost every time, but he nevertheless practices serving in an effort to improve the speed and placement of the ball. In an educational setting, both reasons – mastery and skill development – seem sensible. Students might practice long division until they master the process, that is, until they can reliably work long-division problems. Other skills, such as writing a persuasive essay, might be performed adequately, but even after students have the rudiments down, they should continue to practice in an effort to refine and improve their abilities.

These two reasons to practice – to gain competence and to improve – are self-evident and probably are not very controversial. Less obvious are the reasons to practice skills when it appears you have mastered something and it's not obvious that practice is making you any better. Odd as it may seem, that sort of practice is essential to schooling. It yields three important benefits: it reinforces the basic skills that are required for the learning of more advanced skills, it protects against forgetting, and it improves transfer.

Practice Enables Further Learning

To understand why practice is so important to students' progress, let me remind you of two facts about how thinking works.

Figure 5.1 (which you also saw in Chapter 1) shows that working memory is the site of thinking. Thinking occurs when you combine information in new ways. That information might be drawn from the environment or from your long-term memory or from both. For example, when you're trying to answer a question like "How are a butterfly and a dragonfly alike?" your thoughts about the characteristics of each insect reside in working memory as you try to find points of comparison that seem important to the question.

A critical feature of working memory, however, is that it has limited space. If you try to juggle too many facts or to compare them in too many ways, you lose track of what you're doing. Suppose I said, "What do a butterfly, a dragonfly, a chopstick, a pillbox, and a scarecrow have in common?"* That's simply too many items to compare simultaneously. As you're thinking about how to relate a pillbox to a chopstick, you've already forgotten what the other items are.

This lack of space in working memory is a fundamental bottleneck of human cognition. You could dream up lots of ways that your cognitive system could be improved – more accurate memory, more sharply focused attention, better vision, and so on – but if a genie comes out of a lamp and offers you one way to improve your mind, ask for more working memory capacity. People with more capacity are better

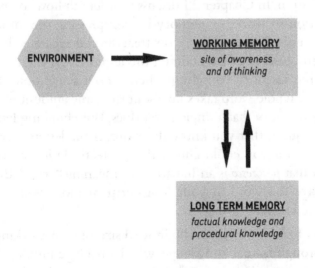

 FIGURE 5.1: Our simple model of the mind. Source: © Greg Culley.

thinkers, at least for the type of thinking that's done in school. There is a great deal of evidence that this conclusion is true, and most of it follows a very simple logic: Take 100 people, measure their working memory capacity, then measure their reasoning ability,[†] and see whether their scores on each test tend to be the same. To a surprising degree, scoring well on a working-memory test predicts scoring well on a reasoning test, and a poor working-memory score predicts a poor reasoning score. (Working memory is not everything, however – recall that in Chapter 2 I emphasized the importance of background knowledge.)

Well, you're not going to get more working-memory capacity from a genie. And because this chapter is about practice, you might think I'm going to suggest that students do exercises that will improve their working memory. Sadly, such exercises don't exist. As far as anyone knows, working memory is more or less fixed – you get what you get, and practice does not change it. The last 10 years have seen many attempts to develop a training regimen to improve working memory, and there's been plenty of hype surrounding these programs, but research shows that an effective one has not yet been developed.

Though you can't increase working memory capacity, you can cheat this limitation. In Chapter 2 I discussed at length how to keep more information in working memory by compressing the information. In a process called *chunking*, you treat several separate things as a single unit. Instead of maintaining the letters *c, o, g, n, i, t, i, o,* and *n* in working memory, you chunk them into a single unit, the word *cognition.* A whole word takes up about the same amount of room in working memory that a single letter does. But chunking letters into a word requires that you know the word. If the letters were *p, a, z, z, e, s, c,* and *o,* you could chunk them effectively if you happened to know that *pazzesco* is an Italian word meaning "crazy." But if you didn't have the word in your long-term memory, you could not chunk the letters.

Thus, the first way to cheat the limited size of your working memory is through factual knowledge, which enables chunking. There is a second way: you can make the processes that manipulate information in working memory more efficient. In fact, you can make them so efficient that they are virtually cost free. Think about learning to tie your shoes. Initially it requires your full attention and thus absorbs all of working memory, but with practice you can tie your shoes *automatically* (Figure 5.2).

What used to take all of the room in working memory now takes almost no room. As an adult you can tie your shoes while holding a conversation or even while working math problems in your head (in the unlikely event that the need arises).

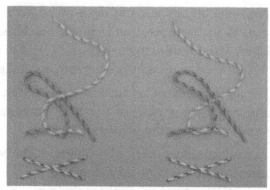

FIGURE 5.2: There is a right and a wrong way to tie your shoes. It's all about the relationship of the bottom and top ties, similar to the difference between a square knot (which is secure) and a false knot (which isn't). Researchers actually showed, through simulated walking, that the right knot stays tied much longer. If a process is going to become automatic, make sure you do it right! Source: From "The roles of impact and inertia in the failure of a shoelace knot" by Christopher A. Daily-Diamond, Christine E. Gregg, & Oliver M. O'Reilly in *Proceedings of the Royal Society A: Mathematical, Physical and Engineering Sciences* 473(2200): 20160770, figure 14b. © Creative Commons CC BY 4.0.

Another standard example, as I've already mentioned, is driving a car. When you first learn to drive, doing so takes all of your working-memory capacity. As with tying your shoes, it's the stuff you're *doing* that takes up the mental space – processes like checking the mirrors, monitoring how hard you're pressing the accelerator or brake to adjust your speed, looking at the speedometer, judging how close other cars are. Note that you're not trying to keep a lot of things (like letters) in mind simultaneously; when you do that, you can gain mental space by chunking. In this example, you're trying to do a lot of things in rapid succession. Of course, an experienced driver seems to have no problem in doing all of these things and can even do other things, such as talk to a passenger.

Mental processes can become automatized. Automatic processes require very little working memory capacity. They also tend to be quite rapid in that you seem to know just what to do without even making a conscious decision to do it. An experienced driver glances in the mirror and checks her blind spot before switching lanes, without thinking to herself, "OK, I'm about to switch lanes, so what I need to do is check my mirrors and glance at the blind spot."

For an example of an automatic process, take a look at Figure 5.3 and name what each of the line drawings represents. Ignore the words and name the pictures.[1]

As you doubtless noticed, sometimes the words matched the pictures and sometimes they didn't. It probably felt more difficult to name the pictures when there was a mismatch. That's because when an experienced reader sees a printed word, it's quite difficult not to read it. Reading is automatic. Thus the printed word *pants* conflicts with the word you are trying to retrieve, *shirt*. The conflict slows your response. A child just learning to read wouldn't show this interference, because reading is not automatic for him. When faced with the letters *p, a, n, t,* and *s,* the child would need to painstakingly (and thus slowly) retrieve the sounds associated with each letter, knit them together, and recognize that the resulting combination of sounds forms the word *pants.*

Automaticity can not only happen by mental processes increasing in efficiency, but also through the development of mental representations. Instead of sounding out *p, a, n, t,* and *s,* you locate a visual representation in memory that matches that letter string. As we noted in Chapter 1, relying on memory is much faster than relying on mental processing – this is a crucial aspect of learning to read.

Math facts that become automatic operate the same way. When students are first introduced to arithmetic, they often solve problems by using counting strategies. For example, they solve 5 + 4 by beginning with 5 and counting up four more numbers to yield the answer 9. This strategy suffices to solve simple

FIGURE 5.3: Name each picture, ignoring the text. It's hard to ignore when the text doesn't match the picture, because reading is an automatic process. Source: © Anne Carlyle Lindsay.

problems, but you can see what happens as problems become more complex. For example, in a multidigit problem like 97 + 89, the student who has not memorized math facts might add 7 and 9 by counting and get 16 as the result. Now the student must remember to write down the 6, then solve 9 + 8 by counting, while remembering to add the carried 1 to the result.

The problem is much simpler if the student has memorized the fact that 7 + 9 = 16, because she arrives at the correct answer for that subcomponent of the problem at a much lower cost to working memory. Finding a well-practiced fact in long-term memory and putting it into working memory places almost no demands on working memory. It is no wonder that students who have memorized math facts do better in all sorts of math tasks than students whose knowledge of math facts is absent or uncertain. And it's been shown that practicing math facts helps low-achieving students do better on more advanced mathematics.

Both reading and math offer good examples of the properties of automatic processes: (i) They happen very quickly. (ii) They are prompted by a stimulus in the environment, and if that stimulus is present, the process may occur (or the relevant memory may be retrieved) even if you wish it wouldn't. Thus you know it would be easier not to read the words in Figure 5.3, but you can't seem to avoid doing so. If you're an experienced driver and you're a passenger in a car that gets in a dangerous situation, your foot reaches out to push on a phantom brake pedal – the response is automatic. (iii) You are not aware of the components of the automatic process. For example, the component processes of reading (such as identifying letters) are never conscious. The word *pants* ends up in consciousness, but the mental processes necessary to arrive at the conclusion that the word is *pants* do not. The process is very different for a beginning reader, who is aware of each constituent step.

The example in Figure 5.3 gives a feel for how an automatic process operates, but it's an unusual example because the automatic process interferes with what you're trying to do. Most of the time automatic processes help rather than hinder. They help because they make room in working memory. Processes that formerly occupied working memory now take up very little space, so there is space for *other* processes. In the case of reading, those "other" processes would include thinking about what the words actually mean. Beginning readers slowly and painstakingly sound out each letter and then combine the sounds into words, so there is no room left in working memory to think about meaning (Figure 5.4).

The same thing can happen even to experienced readers. When I was in high school a teacher asked a friend to read a poem out loud. When he had finished reading, she asked for his reaction to it. He looked blank for a moment and then admitted he had been so focused on reading without mistakes that he hadn't really noticed what the poem was about. Like a first grader, his mind had focused on word pronunciation, not on meaning. Predictably, the class laughed, but what happened was understandable, if unfortunate.

To review, I've said that working memory is the place in the mind where thinking happens – where we bring together ideas and transform them into something new. The difficulty is that there is only so much room in working memory, and if we try to put too much stuff in there, or to do too much with it, we get mixed up and lose the thread of the problem we were trying to solve, or the story we were trying to follow, or the factors we were trying to weigh in making a complex decision. People with larger working-memory capacities are better at these thinking tasks. Although we can't make our working memory larger, we *can* make the contents of working memory smaller in two ways: by making facts take up less room through

16 9 3 20 21 18 5
20 8 9 19
3 15 13 13 15 14 16 12 1 3 5
19 3 5 14 5

FIGURE 5.4: This sentence is written in a simple code: 1 = A, 2 = B, 3 = C, and so on, with a new line denoting a new word. The efforts of a beginning reader are a bit like your efforts to decode this sentence, because the value of each letter must be figured out. If you make the effort to decode the sentence, try doing it without writing down the solution; like the beginning reader, you will likely forget the beginning of the sentence by the time you are decoding the end of the sentence.[2]
Source: © Greg Culley.

chunking, which requires knowledge in long-term memory as is discussed in Chapter 2; and by making the processes we use to bring information into working memory more efficient *or* to remove the need for those processes in the first place by creating a memory representation.

The next obvious question is: What is required to make these processes efficient or to create these memory representations? You know the answer: practice. There may be a workaround, a cheat, whereby you can reap the benefits of automaticity without paying the price of practicing. There may be one, but if there is, neither science nor the collected wisdom of the world's cultures has revealed it. As far as anyone knows, the only way to develop mental facility is to repeat the target process again and again and again.

You can see why I said that practice enables further learning. You may have "mastered" reading in the sense that you know which sounds go with which letters, and you can reliably string together sounds into words. So why keep practicing if you know the letters? You practice not just to get faster. What's important is getting so good at recognizing letters that retrieving word meaning becomes automatic. If it's automatic, you have freed working-memory space that used to be devoted to retrieving the sounds from long-term memory – space that can now be devoted to thinking about the meaning of sentences and paragraphs.

What's true of reading is true of most or all school subjects and of the skills we want our students to have. They are hierarchical. There are basic processes (like retrieving math facts or using deductive logic in science) that initially are demanding of working memory but with practice become automatic. Those processes must become automatic in order for students to advance their thinking to the next level. The great philosopher Alfred North Whitehead captured this phenomenon in this comment: "It is a profoundly erroneous truism, repeated by all copybooks and by eminent people when they are making speeches, that we should cultivate the habit of thinking of what we are doing. The precise opposite is the case. Civilization advances by extending the number of important operations which we can perform without thinking about them."[3]

Practice Makes Memory Long Lasting

Several years ago I had an experience that I'll bet you've had. I happened on some papers from my high school geometry class. I don't think I could tell you three things about geometry today, yet here were problem sets, quizzes, and tests, all in my handwriting, and all showing detailed problem solutions and evidence of factual knowledge.

This sort of experience can make a teacher despair. The knowledge and skills that my high school geometry teacher painstakingly helped me gain have vanished, which lends credence to the occasional student complaint, "We're never gonna *use* this stuff." So if what we teach students is simply going to vanish, what in the heck are we teachers doing?

Well, the truth is that I remember a *little* geometry. Certainly, I know much less now than I did right after I finished the class – but I do know more than I did before I took it. Researchers have examined student memory more formally and have drawn the same conclusion: we rapidly forget much (but not all) of what we have learned.

In one study, researchers tracked down students who had taken a one-semester, college-level course in developmental psychology between 3 and 16 years earlier.[4] The students took a test on the course material. Figure 5.5 shows the results, graphed separately for students who initially got an A in the course and students who got a B or lower. Overall, retention was not terrific. Just three years after the course, students remembered half or less of what they learned, and that percentage dropped until year seven, when it leveled off. The A students remembered more overall, which is not that surprising – they knew more to start with. But they forgot just like the other students did, and at the same rate.

So, apparently, studying hard doesn't protect against forgetting. If we assume that A students studied hard, we have to acknowledge that they forget at the same rate as everyone else. But something else does protect against forgetting: *continued* practice. In another study, researchers located people of varying ages and administered a test of basic algebra.[5] More than one thousand subjects participated

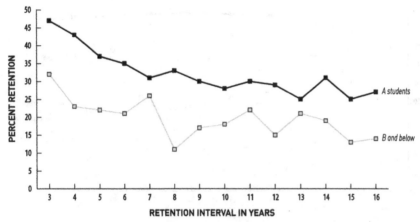

FIGURE 5.5: A graph showing how much students remembered of the material from a one-semester course in developmental psychology taken between 3 and 16 years earlier. Separate lines show the results for students who got an A in the course and those who got a B or lower. Source: "Very long-term memory for information taught in school" by J. A. Ellis, G. B. Semb, and B. Cole in *Contemporary Educational Psychology* 23: 419–433, figure 1, p. 428. Copyright © 1998. Reprinted with permission from Elsevier.

in the experiment, so there were lots of people with varied backgrounds. Most important was that they varied in how much math they had taken.

Have a look at Figure 5.6, which shows scores on an algebra test.[§] Everyone took the test at the same time, for the purpose of the experiment. The scores are separated into four groups on the basis of how many math courses people took in high school and college. Focus first on the bottommost curve. It shows the scores of people who took one algebra course. As you move from left to right, the time since they took the course increases, so the leftmost dot (around 60% correct) comes from people who *just* finished taking an algebra course, and the rightmost dot represents people who took algebra 55 years ago! The bottommost curve looks as you would expect it to; the longer it was since they took an algebra course, the worse they did on the algebra test.

The next curve up shows the scores of people who took more than one algebra course. As you might hope, they did better on the test but showed evidence of forgetting, just like the other group. Now look at the topmost line. These are the scores of people who took math courses beyond calculus. What's interesting about this line is

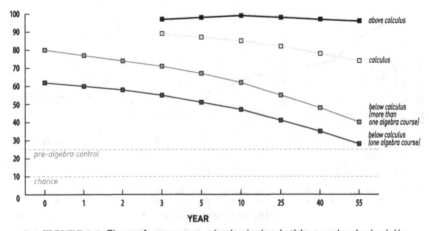

FIGURE 5.6: The performance on a basic algebra test by people who took the course between 1 month and 55 years earlier. The four lines of data correspond to four groups, separated by how much math they took after basic algebra. Source: From "Lifetime maintenance of high school mathematics content" by H. P. Bahrick and L. K. Hall in *Journal of Experimental Psychology: General* 120: 20–33, figure 1, p. 25. Copyright © 1991 by the American Psychological Association.

that it's flat! People who took their last math course more than 50 years ago still know their algebra as well as people who took it 5 years ago!

What's going on here? This effect is *not* due to people who go on to take more math courses being smarter or better at math. It's not shown in the graph, but just as in the previous study of developmental psychology, separating out students who got As, Bs, or Cs in their first algebra course makes no difference – they all forget at the same rate. To put it another way, a student who gets a C in his first algebra course but goes on to take several more math courses will remember his algebra, whereas a student who gets an A in his algebra course but doesn't take more math will forget it. That's because taking more math courses guarantees that you will continue to think about and *practice* basic algebra. If you practice algebra enough, you will effectively never forget it. Other studies have shown exactly the same results with different subject matter, such as Spanish studied as a foreign language, and street names from ones childhood neighborhood.

One thing these studies don't make clear is whether you get longer-lasting memory because you practice *more* or because your practice is stretched out over time. It's very likely that both matter.

It's also likely that you get benefits of practice to memory in the short run as well. Now, it's pretty obvious that reviewing helps memory: if I want to know that the French word for "umbrella" is "parapluie," I'm better off reviewing that fact five times than once. But suppose that I already seem to know that fact. I've got a long list of English–French vocabulary you're helping me learn, and I'm struggling with some, but the last two times we've run through the list when you said "umbrella" I was able to respond "parapluie." I feel I've got it. Is there any reason to keep studying it, or should it be discarded from my practice list?

The answer seems to be "keep studying it." This type of review is called *overlearning* – continued study after you seem to know something. It's exactly the type of practice we've been discussing in that it feels like it's not doing any good. You keep saying "umbrella" and I keep saying "parapluie," and I'm thinking "what's the point of this?"

But think of it this way. Suppose I knew each of the vocabulary items as well as I know umbrella/parapluie; I've gotten each of the items on the list correct two times in a row. If I'm tested three days from now, how will I do? Will I get 100% correct?

Probably not. Over the course of three days I'll forget some. And that's the benefit of overlearning. It offers protection against forgetting. It's hard to make ourselves do it, however, because the practice feels pointless; we're reviewing content it feels like we *know*. But we're ensuring that we will know it later. Now one obvious thing we could do to make overlearning feel less boring and pointless would be spread the studying out over time. I might be more inclined to study umbrella/parapluie if, a couple of days from now, I struggle to remember the right translation.

Researchers have also investigated the importance of *when* you study. The *when* refers not to time of day but to how you space your studying. Let me put it this way: The previous section emphasizes that studying for two hours is better than studying for one. OK. Suppose you decide to study something for two hours. How should you distribute those 120 minutes? Should you study for 120 minutes in a row? Or for 60 minutes one day, then 60 minutes the next? How about 30 minutes each week for four weeks?

Doing a lot of studying right before a test is commonly known as *cramming*. When I was in school students would brag about having done well on a test but that they couldn't remember any of the material a week later, because they had crammed. (An odd thing to brag about, I know.) Research bears out their boasts. If you pack lots of studying into a short period, you'll do okay on an immediate test, but you will forget quickly. If, on the other hand, you study in several sessions with delays between them, you may not do quite as well on the immediate test but, unlike the crammer, you'll remember the material longer after the test (Figure 5.7).

SUNDAY	MONDAY	TUESDAY	WEDNESDAY	THURSDAY	FRIDAY	SATURDAY
		1	2	3	4	5
6	7 Study	8 Study	9 Study	10 Study **STUDY** **STUDY** **STUDY** **STUDY**	11 Test **TEST**	12
13	14	15	16	17	18 Test **TEST**	19
20	21	22	23	24	25	26
27	28	29	30	31		

FIGURE 5.7: This simple figure illustrates what cognitive scientists call the spacing effect in memory. Student 1 (all capitals) studied four hours the day before the first test, whereas Student 2 (lowercase) studied for one hour on each of four days prior to the test. Student 1 will probably do a bit better on this test than Student 2, but Student 2 will do much better on the second test, administered a week later. Source: © Greg Culley.

The spacing effect probably does not surprise teachers; certainly we all know that cramming doesn't lead to long-lasting memory. In contrast, then, it makes sense that spreading out your studying would be better for memory. It's important, however, to make explicit two important implications of the spacing effect. We've been talking about the importance of practice, and we've just said that practice works better if it's spaced out. Distributing practice in the way we've described allows you to get away with *less practice* compared to bunching practice together. Spacing practice has another benefit. The type of practice we're discussing in this chapter means continuing to work at something that you've already mastered. By definition, that sounds kind of boring, even though it brings cognitive benefits. It will be somewhat easier for a teacher to make such tasks interesting for students if they are spaced out in time.

Practice Improves Transfer

In Chapter 4 I discussed at length the challenges of transferring what you already know to new situations. Remember the problem of attacking a castle with small groups of soldiers? Even when subjects had just heard an analogous story that contained the problem solution (attacking a tumor with the rays), they didn't transfer the knowledge to the castle-soldiers problem. As I mentioned then, transfer *does* occur, even when there is no obvious surface similarity between the situations. It occurs, but it's rare. What can we do to increase the odds? What factors make a student more likely to say, "Hey, I've seen problems like this before and I remember how to solve them!"?

It turns out that many factors contribute to successful transfer, but a few of them are especially important. As I've said, transfer is more likely when the surface structure of the new problem is similar to the surface structure of problems seen before. That is, the coin collector will more likely recognize that she can work a problem involving fractions if the problem is framed in terms of exchanging money rather than if a mathematically equivalent problem is framed as one of calculating the efficiency of an engine.

Practice is another significant contributor to good transfer. Working lots of problems of a particular type makes it more likely that you will recognize the underlying structure of the problem, even if you haven't seen this particular version of the problem before. Thus, reading the tumor-and-rays story makes it just a little more likely that you'll know what to do when you encounter the soldiers-and-castle problem; but if you've read *several* stories in which a force is dispersed and converges at a target point, it is much more likely that you'll recognize the deep structure of the problem.

To put it another way, suppose you read the following problem:

> You live in Canada and you're planning a trip to Mexico. You learn that you will save a significant charge if you bring Canadian dollars, exchange them for Mexican pesos once there, and pay for your hotel in cash. You're staying four nights and the hotel costs 100 Mexican pesos per night. What other information do you need in order to calculate how many dollars to bring, and what calculations will you make?

Why does an adult immediately see the deep structure of this problem but a fourth grader does not?

Researchers think there are a couple of reasons that this is so. The first reason is that practice makes it more likely that you will have understood the problem *before* this reading, and that you will remember the solution you used. If you didn't understand it at the time or you don't remember what you did to solve it, there's not much hope of it transferring to a new situation. That's pretty obvious. But suppose a fourth grader does understand the basic math underlying the problem. Why doesn't he see that it would be useful in solving the dollars/pesos problem? And how come you do?

Remember that in Chapter 4 I said that as you read, the possible interpretations of what comes next are drastically narrowed. I used the example of a brief description of a hurricane and said that if you later saw the word *eye*, it wouldn't make you think of the eye with which you see, nor of the bud on a potato, and so on. The point is that as you're reading (or listening to someone talk), you are interpreting what is written, based on your associations with similar topics. You know about a lot of things that are associated with the word *eye*, and your mind picks out the right associates on the basis of the context of what you're reading. You don't have to make that selection consciously, thinking to yourself, "Hmm . . . now, I wonder which meaning of *eye* is appropriate here?" The right meaning just pops into mind.

Contextual information can be used not only for understanding individual words with several possible meanings but also for understanding the *relationships* of different things in what you read. For example, suppose I start to tell you a story: "My wife and I vacationed on a small island, and there is a peculiar law there. If two or more people are walking together after dark, they must each have a pen with them. The hotel had a reminder on the door and pens everywhere, but when we went out to dinner the first night, I forgot to bring mine."

As you read this story, you effortlessly understand the point: I violated a rule. Note that you don't have relevant background knowledge about the surface structure – you've never heard a rule like this before and it doesn't make much sense. But you have lots of experience with the functional relationship of the story elements; the story centers on a *permission*. In a permission relationship, you must fulfill a precondition before you are permitted to take an action. For example, in order to drink alcohol, you must be at least 21 years old. In order to be out at night on a small island with another person, you must have a pen. You also know that permissions not only have rules, they also usually have a consequence for breaking the rule. Thus, when I start telling you my odd story, you can likely predict where the story will go next: it's going to center on whether I got caught without my pen, and if I did get caught, what the consequences were. A sympathetic listener would humor me by saying, "Oh no! Did you get caught without your pen?" If instead a listener said, "Really? What kind of pens did the hotel give you?" I would think he didn't understand the point of the story.

When I tell you the story about the pen, the idea of a "permission rule" pops into your mind as automatically as the meaning of "center of a hurricane" does when you read the word *eye* in the hurricane story. You understand *eye* in context because you have seen the word *eye* used to refer to the center of a hurricane many times before. In the same way, the deep structure of a permission rule pops into mind when you hear the story about the pens, and for the same reason – you have lots of practice thinking about permission rules (Figure 5.8). The only difference between a permission rule and an eye is that the latter is a single word and the former is an idea shaped by the relationship of a few concepts. Your mind stores functional relationships between concepts (such as the idea of a permission) just as it stores the meaning of individual words.

The first time someone tells you that *eye* can refer to the center of a hurricane, you don't have any trouble understanding it; but that doesn't mean that the next time you encounter *eye* the correct meaning will pop into mind. It's more likely that you'll be a little puzzled and need to work out from the context what it means. For *eye* to be interpreted automatically the right way, you will need to see it a few times – in short, you will need to practice it. The same is true of deep structures. You might understand a deep structure the first time you see it, but that doesn't mean you're going to recognize

 FIGURE 5.8: When you think about it, deep understanding of permissions are complicated. It's not that you're forbidden from playing at the water table, and it's not that you must where a smock. It's that if you choose to play at the water table, then you must wear a smock. Yet children as young as three show fairly good understanding of these rules, likely because they encounter them so frequently. Source: © Shutterstock/DGLimages.

it automatically when you encounter it again. In sum, practice helps transfer because practice makes deep structure more obvious.

In the next chapter I talk about what happens when we have had a great deal of practice with something. I compare experts and beginners and describe the radical differences between them.

Summary

I began this chapter by pointing out that there are two obvious reasons to practice: to gain minimum competence (as when a teenager practices driving with a manual shift until he can reliably use it) and to gain proficiency (as when a golfer practices putts to improve her accuracy). I then suggested there are reasons to continue practicing mental skills, even when there are not obvious improvements in our abilities. Such practice yields three benefits: (i) it can help the mental process become automatic and thereby enable further learning; (ii) it makes memory long lasting; and (iii) it increases the likelihood that learning will transfer to new situations.

Implications for the Classroom

We've seen three benefits of this sort of practice, but the downside is probably obvious: It is boring to practice something if we're not improving. In fact, it's more than boring, it's dispiriting! Here are some ideas about how we can reap some of the benefits of practice while minimizing the costs.

What Should Be Practiced?

Not everything can be practiced extensively. There simply isn't time, but fortunately not everything needs to be practiced. The benefits that I've said will accrue from practice provide some direction as to what sorts of things should be practiced. If practice makes mental processes automatic, we can then ask, *Which processes need to become automatic?* Retrieving number facts from memory seems to be a good candidate, as does retrieving letter sounds from memory. A science teacher may decide that his students need to have at their fingertips basic facts about evolution. In general, the processes that need to become automatic are probably the building blocks of skills that will provide the most benefit if they are automatized. Building blocks are the things one does again and again in a subject area, and they are the prerequisites for more advanced work. Given the other benefits of practice we might also ask ourselves, *Which problems come up again and again in this discipline, making it important that students recognize their deep structure?* And we can ask, *What factual information is so central to the field that it ought to be overlearned, so that students will be sure to remember it?*

Space Out the Practice

There is no reason that all of the practice with a particular concept needs to occur within a short span of time or even within a particular unit. In fact, there is good reason to space out practice. As noted earlier, memory is more enduring when practice is spaced out, and practicing the same skills again and again is apt to be boring. It is better to offer some change. An additional benefit of spacing may be that students will get more practice in thinking through how to apply what they know. If all of the practice of a skill is bunched together, students will know that every problem they encounter must be a variant of the skill they are practicing. But if material from a week or a month or three months ago is sometimes included, students must think more carefully about how to tackle the problem, and about what knowledge and skills they have that might apply. Then too, remember that you are not the only teacher your students will encounter. An English teacher might think it's very important for her students to understand the use of imagery in poetry, but the knowledge and skills necessary to appreciate imagery will be acquired over years of instruction.

Fold Practice into More Advanced Skills

You may target a basic skill as one that needs to be practiced to the point of mastery, but that doesn't mean that students can't also practice it in the context of more advanced skills. For example, students may need to practice retrieving sounds in response to printed letters, but once students are ready for it, why not put that practice into the context of interesting reading? A competent bridge player needs to be able to count the points in a hand as a guide to bidding, but if

I were a bridge instructor I wouldn't have my students do nothing but count points until they could do so automatically. Automaticity takes *lots of practice*. The smart way to go is to distribute practice not only across time but also across activities. Think of as many creative ways as you can to practice the really crucial skills, but remember that students can still get practice in the basics while they are working on more advanced skills.

Make Sure There's Variety

I've said that practice helps you see deep structure, but I should be a bit more precise. There's increasing evidence that practice *with variation in surface structure* helps you see deep structure. A recent experiment tested people who spend a lot of time thinking about the likely winners of professional basketball games: coaches, commentators, and others.[6] These people are very good at a particular type of probability calculation: if you think team A will beat team B, say, 60% of the time, what are the chances that team A will win a seven-game series in exactly four games? Or that team B will win in exactly five games? Researchers found that experienced observers of professional basketball games were terrific at this type of calculation but could not perform the same calculation with a different surface structure, for example, that old favorite of probability experts, drawing different colored marbles from an urn. The lesson for us is that students don't just need practice in problems with a particular deep structure in order to recognize that deep structure in different guises; they need to practice the problem *in different guises in the first place*. We might say that the student learns, with practice, which aspects of the problem are irrelevant and so better appreciates what matters.

Notes

*These items may have other features in common, but I selected them because they are all compound words.

†Working memory capacity is usually tested by having people do some simple mental work while they simultaneously try to maintain some information in working memory. For example, one measure requires the subject to listen to a mixture of letters and digits (for example, 3T41P8) and then recite back the digits followed by the letters, in order (that is, 1348PT). This task requires that the subject remember which digits and letters were said while simultaneously comparing them to get the order right. The experimenter

administers multiple trials, varying the number of digits and letters to get an estimate of the maximum number the subject can get right. There are lots of ways to measure reasoning; standard IQ tests are sometimes used or tests more specifically focused on reasoning, with problems like "If P is true, then Q is true. Q is not true. What, if anything, follows?" There is also a reliable relationship between working memory and reading comprehension.

‡This exercise could be taken as another example of how background knowledge can help you to learn. The sentence translates to "Picture this commonplace scene," which is the first sentence from another book I wrote, *The Reading Mind*. Think how much easier the decoding would have been, and how much easier the translation would be to remember, if the coded sentence were something in your long-term memory, such as, "In the beginning, God created the heavens and the earth."

§You'll notice that the curves in this graph seem remarkably smooth and consistent. There are actually many factors that contribute to students' retention of algebra. This graph shows performance after these other factors have been statistically removed, so the graph is an idealization that makes it easier to visualize the effect of the number of math courses taken. You're not seeing the raw scores on this graph, but it is a statistically accurate representation of the data.

Further Reading

Less Technical

Pashler, H., Bain, P. M., Bottge, B. A., Graesser, A., Koedinger, K., McDaniel, M., & Metcalfe, J. (2007). *Organizing Instruction and Study to Improve Student Learning. IES Practice Guide. NCER 2007-2004*. Washington, DC: National Center for Education Research. https://ies.ed.gov/ncee/wwc/PracticeGuide/1 (accessed 13 July 2020). Although it's over 10 years old, this brief booklet offers solid advice about how to organize student practice to make learning as easy as it can be.

Willingham, D. T. (2015). Do students remember what they learn in school? *American Educator*, 39(3), 33–38. A lengthier consideration of why educators should not be discouraged about students forgetting.

More Technical

Kim, A. S. N., Wong-Kee-You, A. M. B., Wiseheart, M., & Rosenbaum, R. S. (2019). The spacing effect stands up to big data. *Behavior Research Methods*, 51(4), 1485–1497. Many laboratory studies show an advantage to learning if practice is spaced. This study took advantage of natural variation in the timing of workplace training sessions and observed a spacing advantage in this setting.

Nelson, P. M., Parker, D. C., & Zaslofsky, A. F. (2016). The relative value of growth in math fact skills across late elementary and middle school. *Assessment for Effective Intervention*, 41(3), 184–192. One of many studies showing that knowing math facts is associated with success in math generally, at least into the middle school years

Soveri, A., Antfolk, J., Karlsson, L., Salo, B., & Laine, M. (2017). Working memory training revisited: a multi-level meta-analysis of n-back training studies. *Psychonomic Bulletin & Review*, 24(4), 1077–1096. One of many review articles published in the last decade that summarizes research on working memory training. Like most others, this one concludes that such training makes you better at the task you've practiced, but not to other working memory tasks. In short, working memory training doesn't work.

Swanson, H. L., & Alloway, T. P. (2012). Working memory, learning, and academic achievement. In: *APA Educational Psychology Handbook, Vol 1: Theories, Constructs, and Critical Issues* (ed. K. Harris): Washington, DC: American Psychological Association Press, 327–366. A broad review of the crucial role working memory plays in academic achievement.

Discussion Questions

1. What do you do if your students *should* have something automatized, but many don't? It's hard not to be frustrated that their former teachers didn't ensure they have this knowledge . . . but now what do you do?

2. One problem with spacing is that students feel "we did this already!" How could you fight that?

3. A key feature of the sort of permanent storage discussed for algebra is that it requires repeated practice across years and thus is not the province of a single teacher. Teachers must coordinate to ensure this practice. How should such consensus be reached? If, in your context, teachers have no say in this sort of curricular decision, who's making it, and how might teachers have a stronger voice?

4. In this chapter I discussed practice of a particular sort – that which feels like it's not helping learning. I took for granted that if students are practicing a skill that they haven't yet mastered (like long division) or one that can be developed further (like writing a persuasive essay) and so need for practice is self-evident. It surely is to you, but is it to your students? Can you characterize students who don't see the value of practice? What beliefs or experiences might lie behind that attitude? What might change it?

5. In this chapter we've used the term automaticity, which is apt, but it seems closely related to what are commonly called habits. We can think of other instances where a stimulus in the environment automatically leads to a response. For example, your phone pings (stimulus) and you redirect your attention away from what you're doing to your phone (response). Or perhaps a student has a particular trigger – when teased about, say, his weight (stimulus), he automatically feels anger (response). Does framing what could inappropriate classroom behaviors (inattention, anger) as automatic make you feel differently about them? Does it change how you think about trying to help the student overcome them?

6. The cruel fact of memory and forgetting is that much of what we teach students *will* be forgotten. In an ideal world students will get repeated exposure to certain core ideas, and those will stick with them. But not everything can be repeated, and so much will, like my knowledge of geometry, be forgotten. I've always consoled myself by thinking "at least students were exposed to this content, and for some, perhaps that ignited a flame of interest, and they will pursue the subject on their own, even if it's not repeated at school." What's your take on this problem? Should we be more bothered by student forgetting? And if so, what should we do about it?

7. Get specific about content. By the time students get to you, what knowledge and/or skills do you hope are automatic? And what new knowledge or skills do you hope will be automatic by the time they leave you?

6

What's the Secret to Getting Students to Think Like Real Scientists, Mathematicians, and Historians?

Q*uestion:* Educators and policy makers sometimes express frustration that curricula seem so far removed from the subjects they purport to cover. For example, history curricula emphasize facts and dates. The good curricula try to give students some sense of the debates within history. (I once heard an educator rail at the idea of a textbook summing up "the causes of the US Civil War" as though they were a settled matter.) But very few curricula encourage students to think as historians do — that is, to analyze documents and evidence and build a case for an interpretation of history. Similarly, science curricula have students memorize facts and conduct lab experiments in which predictable phenomena are observed, but students do not practice actual scientific thinking, the exploration and problem solving that are science. What can be done to get students to think like scientists, historians, and mathematicians?

A*nswer:* This protest against school curricula has a surface plausibility: How can we expect to train the next generation of scientists if we are not training them to do what scientists actually do? But a flawed assumption underlies the logic, namely that students are cognitively capable of doing what scientists or historians do. The cognitive principle that guides this chapter is:

> Cognition early in training is fundamentally differ-
> ent from cognition late in training.

It's not just that students know less than experts; it's also that what they know is organized differently in their memory. Expert scientists did not think like experts-in-training when they started out. They thought like novices. In truth, no one thinks like a scientist or a historian without a great deal of training. This conclusion doesn't mean that students should never try to write a poem or conduct a scientific experiment; but teachers and administrators should have a clear idea of what such assignments will do for students.

Think back to your science classes in middle and high school. If you're like me, they were structured as follows: (i) at home you read a textbook that explained some principle of biology, chemistry, or physics; (ii) the next day the teacher explained the principle; (iii) with a partner you conducted a laboratory exercise meant to illustrate the principle; and (iv) that night you completed a problem set in order to practice the application of the principle.

These activities don't seem to give students any practice in what scientists actually *do*. For example, scientists don't know the outcome of an experiment before they do it – they do the experiment to find out what will happen, and they must interpret the results, which are often surprising or even self-contradictory. In fact, high schoolers know that laboratory exercises have predictable outcomes, so their focus is usually not on what the lab is meant to illustrate but more on whether they "did it right." Likewise, historians don't read and memorize textbooks – they work with original sources (birth certificates, diaries, contemporary newspaper accounts, and the like) to construct sensible narrative interpretations of historical events. If we're not giving students practice in doing the things that historians and scientists actually do, in what sense are we teaching them history and science?

Real scientists are experts. They have worked at science for 40 hours (likely many more) each week for years. It turns out that those years of practice make a qualitative, not quantitative, difference in the way they think compared to how a well-informed amateur thinks. Thinking like a historian, a scientist, or a mathematician turns out to be a very tall order indeed. I'll start this discussion by giving you a sense of what expert thinkers do and how they do it.

What Do Scientists, Mathematicians, and Other Experts Do?

Obviously, what experts do depends on their field of expertise. Still, there are important similarities among experts, not only in scholarly fields such as history, math, literature, and science, but also in applied fields such as medicine and banking and in recreational pursuits such as chess, bridge, and dancing.

The abilities of experts are often well illustrated in the television show *House,* in which the grumpy, brilliant Dr. House (Figure 6.1) solves mysterious medical cases that leave other physicians stumped.

Following is a synopsis of one of House's cases that will help us understand how experts think.[1]

1. House sees a 16-year-old boy who complains of double vision and night terrors. House notes that if there's been no trauma to the brain, night terrors in teens are most commonly associated with terrible stress such as witnessing a murder or being sexually abused. *Tentative diagnosis: sexual abuse.*

2. House finds out that the boy's brain *was* subject to trauma; he was hit in the head during a lacrosse game. Irritated to learn this fact so late in the interview, House concludes that the boy has a concussion and snappishly

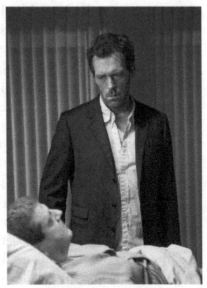

FIGURE 6.1: Hugh Laurie as the expert diagnostician Gregory House. Source: © Getty Images/NBC.

says that the emergency room doctor who examined him after the game obviously "screwed up." *Tentative diagnosis: concussion.*

3. The boy is sitting on a counter swinging his leg as House leaves. House notices the boy's leg jerk and identifies it as the sort of movement our bodies makes when we're falling asleep – but the boy isn't falling asleep. This observation changes everything. House suspects a degenerative disease. He orders the boy admitted to the hospital.

4. House orders a sleep test (which appears to confirm the night terrors), blood work, and a brain scan, on which other doctors see nothing but on which House sees that one brain structure is slightly misshapen, which he guesses is due to fluid pressure. *Tentative diagnosis: a blockage in the system that bathes the brain in protective fluid. The blockage causes pressure on the brain, which causes the observed symptoms.*

5. House orders a procedure to test whether the fluid around the brain is moving normally. The test reveals blockages, so surgery is ordered.

6. During surgery, chemical markers associated with multiple sclerosis are discovered in the fluid around the brain – but the damage to the brain that is associated with the disease is not observed. *Tentative diagnosis: multiple sclerosis.*

7. The patient has a hallucination. House realizes that the boy has been having hallucinations, not night terrors. That makes it unlikely that he has multiple sclerosis, but likely that he has an infection in his brain. Tests showed no evidence of an infection, but House comments that false negatives for neurosyphilis occur about 30% of the time. *Tentative diagnosis: neurosyphilis.*

8. The patient has another hallucination, which leads House to believe that the boy doesn't have neurosyphilis; if he did, he would be getting better from the treatment. House learns that the patient was adopted – the parents hid this fact, even from the boy. House speculates that the boy's biological mother was not vaccinated for measles and that the boy contracted measles sometime before age six months. Although he recovered, the virus mutated, traveled to the brain, and went dormant for 16 years. *Final diagnosis: subacute sclerosing panencephalitis.*

Naturally, I've skipped a great deal of the information in this episode – which is a lot more entertaining than this recap – but even this summary shows some of the behaviors that are typical of experts.

House, like any other physician, is bombarded with information: data from his own examination, results from multiple laboratory tests, the facts of the medical history, and so forth. We normally think that having more information is good, but that's not really true – just think of your reaction when you use Google and get five million results. Medical students have a hard time separating the wheat from the chaff, but experienced doctors seem to have a sixth sense about what is important and what should be ignored. For example, House shows little concern for the patient's double vision. (He initially says, "get glasses.") He focuses his attention on the night terrors. Experience also makes House more sensitive to subtle cues that others miss; he alone notices the odd jerk in the boy's leg, and later, the slight deformation of one structure on the brain scan.

As you would expect from the discussion in Chapter 2, experts have a lot of background knowledge about their fields. But it takes more than knowledge to be an expert. Experts-in-training often know as much (or nearly as much) as experts. The doctors who train under House seldom look blank when he makes a diagnosis or calls their attention to a symptom. But House can access the *right* information from memory with great speed and accuracy. It's information that the more junior doctors have in their memories but just don't think of.

Expertise extends even to the types of mistakes that are made. When experts fail, they do so gracefully. That is, when an expert doesn't get the right answer, the wrong answer is usually a pretty good guess. House is frequently wrong on his way to the correct diagnosis (the show would last just five minutes if he never made mistakes), but his guesses are portrayed as making sense, whereas the tentative assessments of his junior associates often do not. House will point out (usually with withering sarcasm) that one of the patient's symptoms (or absence of symptom) makes the proposed diagnosis impossible.

A final feature of expert performance is not illustrated in the preceding example, but it is quite important. Experts show better transfer to similar domains than novices do. For example, a historian can analyze documents outside her area of expertise and still come up with a reasonable analysis. The analysis will take longer and will not be as detailed or likely as accurate as it would be for material in her own area, but it will be more like an expert's analysis than a novice's. You can imagine what might happen if someone who had reviewed movies for *Time* for the last 10 years were asked to write a financial advice column for the *Wall Street Journal*. Much of his expertise would be bound to writing about movies, but many of his writing skills (like the ability to write clear sentences and well-organized paragraphs) *would* transfer, and the resulting columns would certainly be more professional than those undertaken by a random amateur.

Compared to novices, experts are better able to single out important details, produce sensible solutions, and transfer their knowledge to similar domains. These abilities are seen not only in doctors but also in writers, economists, landscapers – and teachers. For example, novice teachers often fail to notice misbehaviors whereas experts rarely miss them. (No wonder students often wonder at an experienced teacher seeming to have "eyes in the back of her head"!) Like House, expert teachers can also access information rapidly. Compared to novices, they can think of more ways to explain a concept, and they can think of these alternatives more quickly.

What Is in an Expert's Mental Toolbox?

I've described what experts are able to do. So how are they able to do it? What problem-solving abilities or specialized knowledge is required? And how can we make sure that students have whatever it takes?

The mechanisms that experts rely on are a bit like the ones I've talked about before. In Chapter 1 I identified working memory as a significant bottleneck to effective thinking. Working memory is the workspace in which thought occurs, but the space is limited, and if it gets crowded, we lose track of what we're doing and thinking fails. I identified two ways of getting around the limitation of working memory: background knowledge (Chapter 2) and practice (Chapter 5). Novices can get an edge on thinking through either mechanism. Experts use both too, but their extensive experience makes these strategies even more effective.

Remember, background knowledge helps us overcome the working-memory limitation because it allows us to group, or "chunk," pieces of information – such as treating the letters *B, B,* and *C* as the single unit *BBC.* It will surely not surprise you to learn that experts have lots of background knowledge in their area of expertise. But the expert mind has another edge over the minds of the rest of us. It's not just that there is a lot of information in an expert's long-term memory; it's also that the information in that memory is organized differently from the information in a novice's long-term memory.

Experts don't think in terms of surface features, as novices do; they think in terms of *functions,* or deep structure. For example, one experiment compared chess experts and novices.[2] Subjects were briefly shown a chess board with the pieces in a midgame position. They were then given an empty chess board and told to try to recreate the position they had just seen. The experimenters paid particular attention to the order in which subjects placed the pieces. People put the pieces back in clusters, meaning they put back four or five pieces rapidly, then paused, then put down another three or four pieces, then paused, and so forth. They paused as they took a moment to remember the next cluster of pieces. The experimenters found that novices' clusters were based on position; for example, a novice might first place all of the pieces that were in one corner of the board, then the pieces that were in another corner of the board, and so on. The experts, in contrast, used clusters based on *functional* units; that is, pieces were in the same cluster not because they were next to each other but because one piece threatened the other or because one piece supported the other in defense (Figure 6.2).

We can generalize by saying that experts think abstractly. Remember that in Chapter 4 I said that people find abstract ideas hard to understand because they focus on the surface structure, not on the deep structure. Experts don't have trouble understanding abstract ideas because they see the deep structure of problems. In a classic demonstration of this idea, physics novices (undergraduates who had

 FIGURE 6.2: In this experiment, people get a brief look at a chess board and then must replicate the configuration of pieces on a blank board. Experts and novices both do so in chunks – they put a few pieces on the board, then pause as they recall the next cluster from memory, then place the next few pieces, and so on. Novices tend to group pieces based on proximity – nearby pieces go in the same chunk, as shown on the left board whereas experts group pieces by function – pieces that are strategically related in the game go in the same chunk, as shown on the right board. Source: © Daniel Willingham.

taken one course) and physics experts (advanced graduate students and professors) were given 24 physics problems and asked to put them into categories.[3] The novices created categories based on the objects in the problems; problems using springs went into one category, problems using inclined planes went into another, and so on. The experts, in contrast, sorted the problems on the basis of the physical principles that were important to their solution; for example, all of the problems that relied on conservation of energy were put into the same group whether they used springs or planes (Figure 6.3).

This generalization – that experts have abstract knowledge of problem types but novices do not – seems to be true of teachers too. When confronted with a classroom management problem, novice teachers typically jump right into trying to solve the problem, but experts first seek to define the problem, gathering more information if necessary. Thus expert teachers have knowledge of different *types* of classroom management problems. Not surprisingly, expert teachers more often solve these problems in ways that address root causes and not just the behavioral incident. For example, an expert is more likely than a novice to make a permanent change in seating assignments.

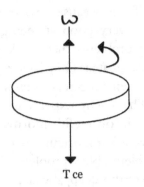

Novice 2: "*Angular velocity, monentum, circular things*"

Novice 3: "*Rotational* kinematics, *angular* speeds, *angular* velocities"

Novice 6: "Problems that have something *rotating: angular* speed"

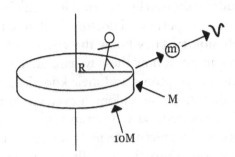

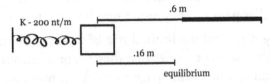

Expert 2: "*Conservation of Energy*"

Expert 3: "*Work-Energy Theorem.* They are all straightforward problems"

Expert 4: "These can be done from energy considerations. Either you should know the *Principle of Conservation of Energy*, or work is lost somewhere."

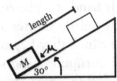

FIGURE 6.3: Novices tended to put the top two figures in the same category because both figures involve a rotating disk. Experts tended to put the two figures on the bottom in the same category because both figures use the conservation-of-energy principle in their solution. Source: From "Categorization and representation of physics problems by experts and novices" by M. T. H. Chi, P. J. Feltovich, and R. Glaser in *Cognitive Science* 5: 121-152, figure 1, p. 126. Copyright © 1981 Lawrence Erlbaum Associates. Reprinted by permission of John Wiley and Sons, via Copyright Clearance Center.

In Chapter 4 I said that transfer is so difficult because novices tend to focus on surface features and are not very good at seeing the abstract, functional relationships among problems that are key to solving them. Well, *that* is what experts are great at. They have representations of problems and situations in their long-term memories, and those representations are abstract. That's why experts are able to ignore unimportant details and home in on useful information; thinking functionally makes it obvious what's important. That's also why they show good transfer to new problems. New problems differ in surface structure, but experts recognize the deep, abstract structure. That's also why their judgments usually are sensible, even if they are not quite right. For example, experienced doctors think in terms of the body's underlying physiology. They know the systems of the body well enough that they can intuit how these systems are behaving on the basis of the outward symptoms, and their knowledge of the systems is rich enough that they will seldom, if ever, say something about them that is self-contradictory or absurd. In contrast, beginning medical students can recognize patterns of symptoms that they've memorized, but they don't think functionally, so when they encounter an unfamiliar pattern, they aren't sure how to interpret it.

The second way to get around the limited size of working memory is to practice procedures so many times that they become automatic. That way the procedures don't take space in working memory. Tie your shoes a few hundred times and you no longer need to think about it; your fingers just fly through the routine without any direction from thought processes that would crowd working memory. Experts have automatized many of the routine, frequently used procedures that early in their training required careful thought. Expert bridge players know the strength of their hand at a glance, without consciously sizing it up. Expert surgeons can tie sutures automatically. Expert teachers have routines with which they begin and end class, call for attention, deal with typical disruptions, and so on. It's interesting to note that novice teachers often script their lessons, planning exactly what they will say. Expert teachers typically do not. They plan different ways that they will discuss or demonstrate a concept, but they don't write out scripts, which suggests that the process of translating abstract ideas into words that their students can understand has become automatic.

So, experts save room in working memory by acquiring extensive, functional background knowledge, and by making mental procedures automatic. What do they do with that extra space in working memory? One thing they do is talk to themselves. What sort of conversation does an expert have with herself? Often she talks about a problem she is working on and does so at that abstract level I just described. The physics expert says things like "This is probably going to be a conservation of energy problem, and we're going to convert potential energy into kinetic energy."[4]

What's interesting about this self-talk is that the expert can draw implications from it. The physics expert just mentioned has already drawn a hypothesis about the nature of the problem, and as she continues reading, she will evaluate whether her hypothesis is right. Indeed, this expert next said, "Now I'm really sure, because we're going to squash the spring and that is going to be more potential energy." Thus experts do not just narrate what they are doing. They also generate hypotheses and so test their own understanding and think through the implications of possible solutions in progress. Talking to yourself demands working memory, however, so novices are much less likely to do it. If they do talk to themselves, what they say is predictably more shallow than what experts say. They restate the problem, or they try to map the problem to a familiar formula. When novices talk to themselves they narrate what they are doing, and what they say does not have the beneficial self-testing properties that expert talk has.

How Can We Get Students to Think Like Experts?

I've discussed the capabilities of scientists, historians, mathematicians, and experts in general. They see problems and situations in their chosen field functionally rather than at the surface level. Seeing things that way enables them to home in on important details among a flood of information, to produce solutions that are always sensible and consistent (even if they are not always right), and to show some transfer of their knowledge to related fields. In addition, many of the routine tasks that experts perform have become automatic through practice.

FIGURE 6.4: New York City's Carnegie Hall is a renowned concert venue. An old joke has a young man stopping an older woman on the street in Manhattan and asking, "Pardon me, ma'am. How do I get to Carnegie Hall?" The woman soberly replies, "Practice, practice, practice." The FAQ page of the Carnegie Hall website refers to this joke, and psychological research indicates that it's true.[5] Expertise does require extensive practice. Source: © Getty Images/Roy Rochlin.

Sounds great. How can we teach students to do that? Unfortunately, the answer to this question is not exactly cheering. It should be obvious that offering novices advice such as "talk to yourself" or "think functionally" won't work. Experts do those things, but only because their mental toolbox enables them to do so. The only path to expertise, as far as anyone knows, is practice (Figure 6.4).

A number of researchers have tried to understand expertise by examining the lives of experts and comparing them to what we might call near-experts. For example, one group of researchers asked violin players to estimate the number of hours they had practiced the violin at different ages.[6] Some of the subjects (professionals) were already associated with internationally known symphony orchestras. The others were music students in their early twenties. Some of the students (the best violinists) had been nominated by their professors as having the potential for careers as international soloists; others (the "good" violinists) were studying with the same goal, but their professors thought they had less potential. Subjects in the fourth group were studying to be music teachers, not professional performers. Figure 6.5 shows the average cumulative number of hours that each of the four groups of violinists practiced between the ages of 5 and 20. Even though the good violinists and the best violinists were all studying at the same music academy, there was a significant difference in the amount of practice since childhood reported by the two groups. Other research shows the importance of practice to a wide range of skills, from sports to games like chess and Scrabble.

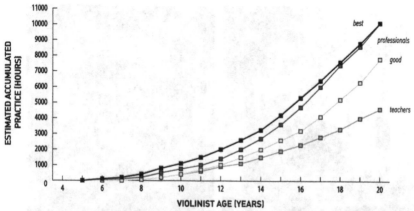

FIGURE 6.5: Experimenters asked violinists how many hours per week (on average) they practiced at different ages. This graph shows the total number of hours accumulated over the years, making it easier to see trends. The best students reported practicing about as much as the middle-aged professionals (up to the age of 20), which is more than the good violinists say they practiced; indeed, by age 20 the best violinists had accumulated almost 50% more time than the good violinists. Not surprisingly, the future music teachers had practiced much less (although they are of course quite competent violinists by most standards). Source: K. A. Ericsson, R. T. Krampe, and C. Tesch-Romer in *Psychological Review* 100: 363-400, figure 9, p. 379. Copyright © 1993 by the American Psychological Association.

Other studies have taken a more detailed biographical approach. Over the last 50 years there have been a few instances in which a researcher has gained access to a good number (10 or more) of prominent scientists, who have agreed to be interviewed at length, take personality and intelligence tests, and so forth. The researcher has then looked for similarities in the backgrounds, interests, and abilities of these great men and women of science. The results of these studies are fairly consistent in one surprising finding. The great minds of science were not distinguished as being exceptionally brilliant, as measured by standard IQ tests; they were very smart, to be sure, but not the standouts that their stature in their fields might suggest. What *was* singular was their capacity for sustained work. Great scientists are almost always workaholics. Each of us knows his or her limit; at some point we need to stop working and watch a stupid television program, hop on Facebook, or something similar. Great scientists have incredible persistence, and their threshold for mental exhaustion is very high (Figure 6.6).

FIGURE 6.6: Thomas Alva Edison, famous for inventing or greatly improving the light bulb, the fluoroscope, the phonograph, and motion pictures. Edison is also famous for his work habits; 100-hour work weeks were not uncommon. Edison often took cat naps on this cot kept next to his desk in his laboratory, rather than sleeping at home. Source: © Getty Images/Bettmann.

Angela Duckworth examined this quality not just in scientists, but in musicians, West Point cadets, spelling bee competitors, and others. Just as the most successful scientists are not necessarily those with the highest IQ, so too researchers had a hard time identifying characteristics of very successful people in other fields, other than "they've put more work into it than others." Duckworth identified two essential personality components – persistence and passion for a long-term goal – and called the combination "grit."

The concept caught the popular imagination in many countries and has been mischaracterized and abused in many ways. I think it's useful as a scientific construct – that is, it helps scientists understand why some people would work very diligently for *years* at a single goal. I think it's gravely mistaken to suppose we can make students gritty, much less gritty about a topic of *our* choosing (schoolwork). Half of grit is passion – it's about what the student loves.

Gritty or not, you won't become an expert until you've put in your hours – that's another implication of the importance of practice. A number of researchers have endorsed what has become known as the "10-year rule": one can't become an expert in any field in less than 10 years, be it physics, chess, golf, or mathematics.[7] This rule has been applied to fields as diverse as musical composition, mathematics, poetry, competitive swimming, and car sales. It has been argued that prodigies such as Mozart, who began composing at age five, are not exceptions to the 10-year rule, because their early output is usually imitative and is not recognized by their peers as exceptional. Even if we were to allow for a few prodigies every century, the 10-year rule holds up pretty well.

There's nothing magical about a decade; it just seems to take that long to learn the background knowledge and to develop the automaticity that I've been talking about in this chapter.* Indeed, it's been shown that those who have less time to practice take longer than a decade, and in fields where there is less to learn – short-distance sprinting or weightlifting, for example – one can achieve greatness with only a few years of practice. In most fields, however, 10 years is a good rule of thumb. And study and practice do not end once one achieves expert status. The work must continue if the status is to be maintained (Figure 6.7).

FIGURE 6.7: Experts still practice. (a) Brilliant jazz pianist Hank Jones, shown here on the day he won his Lifetime Achievement Grammy award. At age 87 Jones was asked whether he still practiced. His response: "Oh, of course, of course, yes. I don't see how anybody can do without practicing, you know. I do scales, exercises . . ."[8] (b) The legendary martial arts expert Pan Qingfu, shown here in the movie *Iron and Silk*, put his views on practice more bluntly: "Masters eat bitter every day of their lives, and that's that."[9] In this context "eating bitter" means enduring the suffering that comes from tireless practice. Source: Jones © Getty Images/Rick Diamond; Qingfu © Getty Images/ Michael Ochs Archives.

Summary

We started by reviewing four characteristics of experts. First, they seem to have a sixth sense about which information they can safely ignore and which information is important. Second, they notice subtle aspects of that information that novices miss, because the expert pays close to attention to particularly important features, so the subtleties are more obvious to them. Third, they fail gracefully, meaning that even when they make a mistake, their course of action was, in retrospect, sensible. Fourth, their knowledge transfers to new situations better than that of novices. Experts are able to do these four things because their experience allows them to see deep structure. Finally, we reviewed research showing that the key ingredient to becoming an expert is extended practice.

Implications for the Classroom

Experts are not simply better at thinking in their chosen field than novices are; experts actually think in ways that are qualitatively different. Your students are not experts, they are novices. How should that affect your teaching?

Students Are Ready to Comprehend but Not to Create Knowledge

After reading this chapter you should have a good idea of how mathematicians, scientists, and historians differ from novices. They have worked in their field for years, and the knowledge and experience they have accumulated enable them to think in ways that are not open to the rest of us. Thus, trying to get your students to think like them is not a realistic goal. Your reaction may well be, "Well, sure. I never really expected that my students are going to win the Nobel Prize! I just want them to understand some science." That's a worthy goal, *and it is very different from the goal of students thinking like scientists.*

Drawing a distinction between *knowledge understanding* and *knowledge creation* may help. Experts create. For example, scientists create and test theories of natural phenomena, historians create narrative interpretations of historical events, and mathematicians create proofs and descriptions of complex patterns. Experts not only understand their field, they also add new knowledge to it.

A more modest and realistic goal for students is *knowledge comprehension*. A student may not be able to develop his own scientific theory, but he can develop a deep understanding of existing theory. A student may not be able to write a new narrative of historical fact, but she can follow and understand a narrative that someone else has written.

Student learning need not stop there. Students can also understand how science works and progresses, *even if they are not yet capable of using that process very well or at all.* For example, students could learn about landmark findings in science as a way of understanding science as a method of continual refinement of theory rather than as the "discovery" of immutable laws. Students might read different accounts of the Yalta Conference as a way of learning how historians develop narratives.

You may find it useful to think of the development of expertise in stages. First, understand and appreciate what experts achieve and why it's special. Second, understand the methods of experts by analyzing how they achieve what they do. Third, work toward using the methods themselves, even if they don't have the requisite knowledge and experience, as a way of deepening their understanding.

Just Because Students Can't Create Like Experts Doesn't Mean They Shouldn't Create

I've said that a key difference between the expert and the well-informed amateur lies in the expert's ability to create new knowledge versus the amateur's ability to understand concepts that others have created. Well, what happens if you ask students to create new knowledge? What will be the result if you ask them to design a scientific experiment or analyze a historical document? Nothing terrible is going to happen, obviously. The mostly likely outcome will be that they won't do it very well; for reasons I've described in this chapter and in Chapter 2, a lot of background knowledge and experience are required.

But a teacher might have other reasons for asking students to do these things. For example, a teacher might ask her students to interpret the results of a laboratory experiment not with the expectation that she is teaching them to think like scientists but instead to highlight a particular phenomenon or to draw their attention to the need for close observation of an experiment's outcome.

Assignments that demand creativity may also be motivating. A music class may well emphasize practice and proper technique, but it may also encourage students to compose their own works simply because the students would find it fun and interesting. Is such practice necessary or useful in order for students to think like musicians? Probably not. Beginning students do not yet have the cognitive equipment in place to compose, but that doesn't mean they won't have a great time doing so, and that may well be reason enough.

The same is true of science fairs. I've judged a lot of science fairs, and the projects are mostly – not to put too fine a point on it – terrible. The questions that students try to answer are usually lousy, because they aren't really fundamental to the field; and students don't appear to have learned much about the scientific method, because their experiments are poorly designed and they haven't analyzed their data sensibly. But some of the students are really proud of what they have done, and their interest in science or engineering has gotten a big boost. So although the *creative* aspect of the project is usually a flop, science fairs seem to be good bets for motivation. (And it's not always a flop. On occasion students do something really creative and substantive!)

The bottom line is that posing to students challenges that demand the creation of something new is a task beyond their reach – but that doesn't mean you should never pose such tasks. Just keep in mind what the student is or is not getting out of it.

Encourage, and Remember "Practice Makes Progress"

The research on practice may prompt a rethinking of how we talk with students about their hopes and dreams. On the one hand, the research offers a truly hopeful message: biology is not destiny, if by "biology" we mean inherited talent. We'll look further at this issue in Chapter 8, but we've already seen that what really sets apart the extremely successful from the ordinary is sustained hard work. Thus, we can and should encourage the student who wants to be a great scientist or novelist, even if she doesn't show exceptional talent now. The research we've reviewed indicates that the student should be told that she can succeed if she works really hard.

But on the other hand, that sort of encouragement comes with its own set of problems. Wouldn't encouragement amount to saying "Yes, you absolutely can be a great scientist! Just be a workaholic for a minimum of 10 years!" You're obviously not going to offer that dispiriting advice, but is there a more sensible way to think about practice and students' futures?

Remember that the 10-year rule applies to *exceptional* achievement. Not just being darn good at something, but being an innovator, in some way a pioneer in the discipline. Your student may turn out not to be a workaholic and may not achieve that status, but she may still make a contribution to her field and be quite happy in doing so.

Even that more modest goal still requires a great deal of hard work over a long period of time. But happily, the learner can see evidence of improvement along the way, and I think that's the key to maintaining motivation over a long period of time. Don't focus so much on the ambitious goal itself, but on way stations, the intermediate stages of success. Replace the mantra "practice makes perfect" with "practice makes progress."

Don't Expect Novices to Learn by Doing What Experts Do

When considering how to help students gain a skill, it seems only natural to encourage them to emulate someone who already knows how to do what you want them to do. Thus, if you want students to know how to program Python, find someone who is a good Python programmer and start training them in the methods this person uses. As logical as this technique sounds, it can be a mistake because, as I've emphasized, there are significant differences between how experts and novices think.

Consider this example: How should we teach reading? Well, if you watch expert readers read, they make fewer eye movements than unskilled readers do. So it could be said that the better way to read is

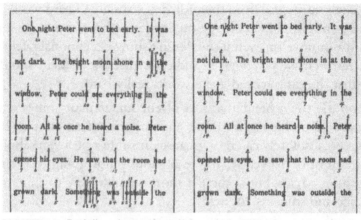

FIGURE 6.8: Each line shows where the reader's eyes paused when reading a paragraph. At left are typical results for a beginning reader, and at right are results for an expert reader. It's true that experts' eyes stop less often compared to the eyes of beginners (if you've never done so before, watch someone's eyes as they read - it's interesting), but that doesn't mean an expert's strategy is one that beginners can use. Source: *Fundamental Reading Habits: A Study of Their Development* by Guy T. Buswell, Supplemental Educational Monographs, published in conjunction with *The School Review* and *The Elementary School Journal*, No. 21, June 1922. Copyright © 1922 by The University of Chicago.

by recognizing entire words and that students should be taught that method from the start, because that's how good readers read. Indeed, an older educational psychology textbook on my shelf cites the eye movement data shown in Figure 6.8 and makes exactly this argument.[10]

Such arguments should be viewed with suspicion. In this case we know from other data that expert readers can take in whole words at a time, but they didn't start off reading that way. In the same way expert tennis players spend most of their time during a match thinking about strategy and trying to anticipate what their opponent will do. But we shouldn't tell novices to think about strategy; novices need to think about footwork and about the basics of their strokes.

Whenever you see an expert doing something differently from the way a nonexpert does it, it may well be that the expert used to do it the way the novice does it, and that doing so was a necessary step on the way to expertise. Ralph Waldo Emerson put it more artfully: "Every artist was first an amateur."[11]

Notes

*You may have heard the figure 10 000 hours, rather than a decade, as the time it takes to acquire expertise. That figure came from Malcolm Gladwell's book *Outliers*, and Anders Ericsson, in his own book *Peak* goes into a number of ways that the calculation is inaccurate. The main thing to keep in mind is that, when you're aiming at expertise, you're looking at a process that takes years.

Further Reading

Less Technical

Bloom, B. S. (1985). *Developing Talent in Young People*. New York: Ballantine Books. A classic, this book is the product of a survey of 100 world-class experts in their fields: athletes, scientists, musicians, and so on. The book's message is that experts are not born but made, and it describes the methods by which experts train.

Duckworth, A. (2016). *Grit: The Power of Passion and Perseverance*. New York: Scribner. Nice overview of grit as a scientific construct, with wonderful storytelling.

Ericsson, A., & Pool, R. (2016). *Peak: Secrets from the New Science of Expertise*. Houghton Mifflin Harcourt. Highly readable book about how experts become experts. Ericsson is widely considered a pioneer in this field.

Simon, H. A., & Chase, W. G. (1973). Skill in chess. *American Scientist, 61*, 394–403. A classic article on expertise that includes the proposal of the 10-year rule and the estimate that 50 000 game positions are stored in the minds of chess masters.

More Technical

Ericsson, K. A., Hoffman, R. R., & Kozbelt, A. (Eds.). (2018). *The Cambridge Handbook of Expertise and Expert Performance, 2*. Cambridge, UK: Cambridge University Press. Comprehensive handbook of psychological research on how experts become experts.

Hogan, T., Rabinowitz, M., & Craven, J. A. (2003). Representation in teaching: inferences from research of expert and novice teachers. *Educational Psychologist, 38*, 235–247. This article reviews research on the differences between novice and expert teachers from a cognitive perspective of expertise.

König, J., Blömeke, S., Klein, P., Suhl, U., Busse, A., & Kaiser, G. (2014). Is teachers' general pedagogical knowledge a premise for noticing and interpreting classroom situations? A video-based assessment approach. *Teaching and Teacher Education, 38*, 76–88. This study shows that the interpretation of classroom situation is influenced by teachers' pedagogical knowledge.

Mo, Y., & Troia, G. A. (2017). Predicting students' writing performance on the NAEP from student- and state-level variables. *Reading and Writing, 30*(4), 739–770. This study showed that students who did more writing at school tended to score better on the writing portion of the National Assessment of Educational Progress (the "nation's report card"). This is one of those studies where it's natural to react "well, of course." But it's still important to do this research, even if you think you know how it will come out. As you've seen by this time in the book, sometimes we're surprised!

Wolff, C. E., Jarodzka, H., van den Bogert, N., & Boshuizen, H. P. (2016). Teacher vision: expert and novice teachers' perception of problematic classroom management scenes. *Instructional Science*, 44(3), 243–265. Study of eye movements in novice and expert teachers. Just as chess experts focus on parts of the game board that carry the most information, expert teachers mostly gaze at parts of the classroom that carry much information.

Discussion Questions

1. Research shows that preschool teachers tend to describe science as an identity ("today we'll act like scientists"). In one study, researchers had them describe it as an activity ("today we'll do science") and they found that children persisted longer on science tasks days later. That was just one study so it's far from definitive, but it's worth thinking about the question more broadly; how can we make expertise – that of a scientist, a historian, a writer – seem more available to students, more close at hand, more possible?

2. We reviewed several differences in the cognition of novices and experts: experts have automatized routine parts of common tasks, they have widespread knowledge that enables chunking, and their knowledge is organized functionally. Think about your teaching, perhaps considering classroom management and instruction separately. (Or break it down any way you see fit.) Do you feel you have these three cognitive capabilities in your teaching? (Or if you're relatively new to teaching, do you see them developing?) Which of the three could use more work? Can you imagine a way for you to get increased practice or better feedback as you work to develop it?

3. Students obviously will not come to be experts in everything – we've examined how difficult it is to become a true expert in just one thing. Have we been assuming, however, that schools should take it as a goal that each student should be an expert in *some*thing? Another plausible goal is that students need not be an expert in anything but should be competent at a number of things. Simply because of time and resources, there's a tension between hoping students will be capable in many subjects versus capable in fewer, but on the road to expertise in one thing. What is your school doing now? How would it change if the goal changed?

4. Grit refers to passion for and persistence in pursuing a long-term goal. Not every student is going to be especially gritty, and of those who are, it may be no more than a handful who are gritty about things that relate to schoolwork: one may be gritty about beekeeping, another about fishing, and a third about mountain climbing. What, if any, responsibility does a school have to encourage and enable the passions of students that fall outside of typical school subjects?

5. One of the reasons grit has been so controversial is that it can be read as dumping on the child all the responsibility to learn. That is, if the child doesn't learn, it's not because her family struggles with poverty, nor because her teacher is unskilled, nor because the curriculum is disorganized, nor because her school is underfunded . . . she's just not gritty enough. Ludicrous as that position would be, one can move too far in the other direction. There are challenges beyond a student's control that we should acknowledge affect his success (and that we should try to remediate) but as students grow, we *do* start to expect that they will take more responsibility for their own learning. They are asked to read at home, to prepare for tests on their own, and so on. Is there a sensible way to

think about this tension? Can we get beyond the bland conclusion that the answer lies somewhere in the middle?

6. I've taken what might be considered an extreme view on the question of student creativity, claiming that very, very few have the skills and knowledge to actually think like a scientist, a historian, or other expert. But you might argue in turn that very little effort goes into identifying those kids who could excel to that level. "Gifted" or "honors" is usually just another name for a tracked class, geared to a relatively large number of generally academically successful students. What about the 1 in 100 or 1 in 1000 who are still kind of bored in this class because they could really soar in their one domain? Does the school owe them a tutor? An opportunity to attend a local college? Or is it enough to figure that will happen in time?

7

How Should I Adjust My Teaching for Different Types of Learners?

Question: All children are different. Is it true that some students learn best visually (they have to see it to learn it) and some auditorily (they have to hear it to learn it)? How about linear thinkers versus holistic thinkers? It seems that tailoring instruction to each student's cognitive style is potentially of enormous significance; perhaps struggling students would do much better with other teaching methods. At the same time, analyzing and catering to multiple learning styles in the same classroom seems like an enormous burden on the teacher. Which differences are the important ones?

Answer: It's important to keep in mind what the hypothesis behind learning styles actually is. The prediction of any learning styles theory is that teaching method A might be good for Javier but bad for Donna, whereas teaching method B might be good for Donna but bad for Javier. Further, this difference between Javier and Donna persists; that is, Javier consistently prefers one type of teaching and Donna prefers another. An enormous amount of research exploring this idea has been conducted in the last 50 years, and finding the difference between Javier and Donna that would fit this pattern has been the holy grail of educational research, but no one has found consistent evidence supporting a theory describing such a difference. The cognitive principle guiding this chapter is:

> Children are more alike than different in terms of how they think and learn.

Note that the claim is not that all children are alike, nor that teachers should treat children as interchangeable. Naturally, some kids like math whereas others are better at English. Some children are shy and some are outgoing. Teachers interact with each student differently, just as they interact with friends differently; but teachers should be aware that, as far as scientists have been able to determine, there are not categorically different types of learners.

Styles and Abilities

Let's start with a couple of questions. Suppose you're an 11th-grade biology teacher. You have a student, Kathy, who is really struggling. She seems to be trying her best, and you've spent extra time with her, but she's still falling further behind. You discuss the problem with some fellow teachers and learn, among other things, that Kathy is regarded as a gifted poet. Would you consider asking Kathy's English teacher to work with you to relate poetry to her biology lessons in the hope that she will better grasp the concepts?

Here's another case. Like Kathy, Lee is struggling in your biology class. He likes science, but he had a great deal of trouble understanding the unit on the Krebs citric acid cycle. His low score on a quiz prompts his parents to come in for a conference. They believe the problem lies in the way the material was presented; the Krebs cycle was presented in a linear fashion and Lee tends to think holistically. They politely ask whether there is a way to expose Lee to new material in a holistic manner rather than a sequential one, and they offer to support such teaching at home. What would you say to them?

It's obvious that students are different. The stories just presented exemplify the great hope inherent in this fact: that teachers can use these differences to reach students. For example, a teacher might take a student's strength and use it to remedy a weakness, such as using Kathy's knowledge of poetry to help her grasp science. A second possibility is that teachers might take advantage of students' different ways of learning; for example, if Lee doesn't understand a concept very well, it may be because of a poor match between how he learns best and how the content was taught. Relatively minor changes in the presentation may make difficult concepts easier to understand.

Now, it must be admitted that these exciting possibilities imply more work for the teacher. Playing to a student's strengths (as in Kathy's case) or changing how you present material (as in Lee's case) means changing your instruction and potentially doing something different for each student in the class. That sounds like a lot of extra work. Would it be worth it?

Research by cognitive scientists into the differences among students can shed light on this question, but before I get into that research, it is important to clarify whether I'm talking about differences in cognitive *abilities* or differences in cognitive *styles*.* The definition of *cognitive ability* is straightforward: it means capacity for or success in certain types of thought. If I say that Sarah has a lot of ability in math, you know I mean she tends to learn new mathematical concepts quickly. In contrast to abilities, *cognitive styles* are biases or tendencies to think in a particular way, for example, to think sequentially (of one thing at a time) or holistically (of all of the parts simultaneously).

Abilities and styles differ in a few important ways. Abilities are how we deal with content (for example, math or language arts) and they reflect the level (that is, the quantity) of what we know and can do. Styles are how we prefer to think and learn. We consider having more ability as being better than having less ability, but we do not consider one style as better than another. One style might be more effective for a particular problem, but all styles are equally useful overall, by definition. (If they weren't, we would be talking about abilities, not styles.) To use a sports analogy, we might say that two soccer players have equal ability even if they have different styles on the field (Figure 7.1).

In the chapter's introductory paragraphs I said that students' ways of learning are more alike than different. How can that be true given that the differences among students seem so obvious and often so large? In the remainder of this chapter I consider styles and abilities in turn and try to reconcile the differences among students with the conclusion that these differences don't mean much for teachers.

FIGURE 7.1: Marta Vieira da Silva and Abby Wambach are considered among the best soccer players of the last 20 years. In terms of ability, most fans would say they are comparable; but in terms of style, they differ, with Marta known for her flair and quick feet and Wambach for playing a more physical, direct game. Source: Marta © Getty Images/Brad Quality Sports Images; Wambach © Getty Images/Jeffery Kane Gammons.

Cognitive Styles

Some people are impulsive, whereas others take a long time to make decisions. Some people enjoy diving into complexity, others relish simplicity. Some people like to think about things concretely, others prefer abstractions. We all have intuitions about how people think, and beginning in the 1940s, experimental psychologists took a strong interest in testing these intuitions. The distinctions they tested were usually framed as opposites (for example, broad/narrow or sequential/holistic), with the understanding that the styles were really a continuum and that most people fall somewhere in the middle of the two extremes. Table 7.1 shows a few of the distinctions that psychologists evaluated.

As you read through the table, which shows just a fraction of the dozens of classification schemes that have been proposed, you'll probably think that many of the schemes sound at least plausible. How can we know which one is right or if several of them are right?

Note that these are not theories of instruction, they are theories of how the mind works. As such, they are relatively easy to test in laboratory situations, and psychologists use a few techniques. First, they try to show that cognitive style is stable within an individual. In other words, if I say you have a particular cognitive style, that style

TABLE 7.1: Some of the many distinctions among cognitive styles that have been proposed and tested by psychologists.

Cognitive styles	Description
Broad/narrow	Preference for thinking in terms of a few categories with many items versus thinking in many categories with few items
Analytic/nonanalytic	Tendency to differentiate among many attributes of objects versus seeking themes and similarities among objects
Leveling/sharpening	Tendency to lose details versus tendency to attend to details and focus on differences
Field dependent/field independent	Interpreting something in light of the surrounding environment versus interpreting it independently of the influence of the environment
Impulsivity/reflectiveness	Tendency to respond quickly versus tendency to respond deliberately
Automatization/restructuring	Preference for simple repetitive tasks versus preference for tasks that require restructuring and new thinking
Converging/diverging	Logical, deductive thinking versus broad, associational thinking
Serialist/holist	Preference for working incrementally versus preference for thinking globally
Adaptor/innovator	Preference for established procedures versus preference for new perspectives
Reasoning/intuitive	Preference for learning by reasoning versus preference for learning by insight
Visualizer/verbalizer	Preference for visual imagery versus preference for talking to oneself when solving problems
Visual/auditory/kinesthetic	Preferred modality for perceiving and understanding information

ought to be apparent in different situations and on different days; it should be a consistent part of your cognitive makeup. Cognitive styles should also be consequential; that is, using one cognitive style or another ought to have implications for the important things we do. If I claim that some people think serially and other people think holistically, then these two types of people ought to differ in how they learn mathematics, for example, or history, or in how they understand literature. Finally, we have to be sure that a cognitive style is not really an ability measure. Remember, styles are supposed to represent biases in how we prefer to think; they are not supposed to be measures of how *well* we think.

This last point seems kind of obvious, but it has been an issue for some of the distinctions made in Table 7.1. For example, people who are more likely to evaluate something they see independently of the object's relationship to other objects are called *field independent*, whereas *field dependent* people tend to see an object in terms of its relationship to other things (Figure 7.2).

Here is a simple form which we have labeled "x"

This simple form, named "x," is hidden within the more complex figure below:

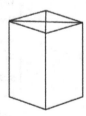

FIGURE 7.2: Two methods of determining field dependence or independence. At left is the rod-and-frame test. The rod and frame are luminous and are viewed in a darkened room. The subject adjusts the rod so that it is vertical. If the subject's adjustment is strongly influenced by the surrounding frame, she is field dependent – if not, she is field independent. At right is one item from an embedded-figures test, in which the subject tries to find the simple figure hidden in the more complex one. Success on tasks like this indicates field independence. Like the rod-and-frame task, it seems to indicate an ability to separate a part of one's visual experience from everything else one is seeing. Source: © Anne Carlyle Lindsay.

People are classified as field dependent or independent only on the basis of visual tests, which don't seem to be very cognitive. But it seems plausible that what's true of vision – that field-dependent people see relationships whereas field-independent people see individual details – may also be true for all sorts of cognitive tasks. That's a neat idea, but the problem is that field-independent people tend to outperform field-dependent people on most cognitive measures. Now, remember that field dependence is supposed to be a cognitive style, and that, on average, people with different styles are not supposed to differ in ability. The fact that they do implies that the tests shown in Figure 7.2 actually measure ability in some way rather than style, although we may not be sure what the mechanism is.

I've said that a cognitive styles theory must have the following three features: it should consistently attribute to a person the same style, it should show that people with different styles think and learn differently, and it should show that people with different styles do not, on average, differ in ability. At this point there is not a theory that has these characteristics. That doesn't mean that cognitive styles don't exist – they certainly might; but after decades of trying, psychologists have not been able to find them. To get a better sense of how this research has gone, let's examine one theory more closely: the theory of visual, auditory, and kinesthetic learners.

Visual, Auditory, and Kinesthetic Learners

The concept of visual, auditory, and kinesthetic learners is probably familiar to you. It states that each person has a preferred way of receiving new information, through one of three senses. Vision (seeing) and audition (hearing) are clear enough, but kinesthesia might require an explanation. Kinesthesia is the sensation that tells you where your body parts are. If you were to close your eyes and I moved your arm as though you were, say, waving, you would know where your arm was even though you couldn't see it. That information comes from special receptors in your joints, muscles, and skin. That's kinesthesia.

The visual-auditory-kinesthesia theory holds that everyone can take in new information through any of the three senses, but most of us have a preferred sense. When learning something new, visual types like to see diagrams, or even just to see in print the words that the teacher is saying. Auditory types prefer descriptions, usually verbal, to which they can listen. Kinesthetic learners like to manipulate objects physically; they move their bodies in order to learn (Figure 7.3).

To give you a backdrop against which to evaluate this theory, I'll start with a few facts about memory that cognitive scientists have worked out. People do differ in their visual and auditory memory abilities.[†] That is, our memory system can store both what things look like and what they sound like. We use visual memory representations when we create a visual image in our mind's eye. For example, suppose I ask you, "What is the shape of a German shepherd's ears?" or "How many windows are there in your classroom?" Most people say they answer these questions by creating a visual image and inspecting it. A great deal of work by experimental psychologists during the 1970s showed that such images do have a lot of properties in common with vision – that is, there's a lot of overlap between your

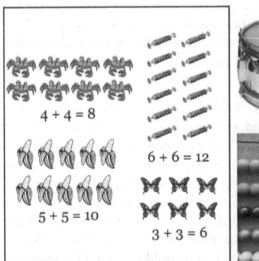

FIGURE 7.3: Learners with different styles might benefit from different ways of presenting the same material. When learning addition, for example, a visual learner might view groupings of objects, an auditory learner might listen to sets of rhythms, and a kinesthetic learner might arrange objects into groups. Source: Sets © Anne Carlyle Lindsay; drum ©Shutterstock/Ronald Summers; abacus ©Shutterstock/Iperion.

"mind's eye" and the parts of your brain that allow you to see. We also store some memories as sound, such as Emma Stone's voice, the roar of the MGM lion, or our mobile phone's ringtone. If I ask you, for example, "Who has a deeper voice: your principal or your superintendent?" you will likely try to imagine each person's voice and compare them. We can store both visual and auditory memories, and as with any other cognitive function, each of us varies in how effectively we do so. Some of us have very detailed and vivid visual memories or vivid and detailed auditory memories; others of us do not.

Cognitive scientists have also shown, however, that we don't store all of our memories as sights or sounds. We also store memories in terms of what they mean to us. For example, if a friend tells you a bit of gossip about a coworker (who was seen at a gas station buying hundreds of lottery scratch-off tickets), you *might* retain the visual and auditory details of the story (for example, how the person telling the story looked and sounded), but you might remember only the content of the story (lottery tickets) without remembering any of the auditory or visual aspects of being told. *Meaning* has a life of its own, independent of sensory details (Figure 7.4).

FIGURE 7.4: What does the word footbath mean? You know it means to soak one's feet, usually when they are sore but also, perhaps, as a way of pampering yourself. Your knowledge of the word footbath is stored as a meaning, independent of whether you first learned the word by seeing someone take a footbath, by hearing a description of it, or by actually soaking your own feet. Most of what teachers want students to know is stored as meaning. Source: ©Shutterstock/musicphone.

Now we're getting to the heart of the visual-auditory-kinesthetic theory. It is true that some people have especially good visual or auditory memories. In that sense there are visual learners and auditory learners. But that's not the key prediction of the theory. The key prediction is that students will learn better when instruction matches their cognitive style. That is, suppose Anne is an auditory learner and Victor is a visual learner. Suppose further that I give Anne and Victor two lists of new vocabulary words to learn. To learn the first list, they listen to a tape of the words and definitions several times; to learn the second list, they view a slideshow of pictures depicting the words. The theory predicts that Anne should learn more words on the first list than on the second whereas Victor should learn more words on the second list than on the first. Dozens of studies have been conducted along these general lines, including studies using materials more like those used in classrooms, and overall the theory is not supported. Matching the "preferred" modality of a student doesn't give that student any edge in learning.

How can that be? Why doesn't Anne learn better when the presentation is auditory, given that she's an auditory learner? *Because auditory information is not what's being tested!* Auditory information would be the particular sound of the voice on the tape. What's being tested is the meaning of the words. Anne's edge in auditory memory doesn't help her in situations where meaning is important. Similarly, Victor might be better at recognizing the visual details of the pictures used to depict the words on the slides, but again, that ability is not being tested.

There are actually experiments showing that some people reinterpret things in an effort to honor what they think of as their learning styles.[1] So people who believe they are verbal learners who are shown a red, striped triangle and told to remember it will make the stimulus verbal by saying to themselves "red, striped triangle." And people who believe they are visual learners who are shown the words "red, striped triangle" will create a visual mental image of the figure. But these efforts don't improve their memory, as the theory predicts it should.

Most of the time students need to remember what things mean, not what they sound like or look like. Sure, sometimes that information counts; someone with a good visual memory will have an edge in memorizing the particular shapes of countries on a map, for example, and someone with a good auditory memory will be better at getting the accent right when learning a new language. But the vast majority of schooling is concerned with what things mean, not with what they look like or sound like.

So does that mean that the visual-auditory-kinesthetic theory is correct some small proportion of the time, such as when students are learning foreign language accents or countries on a map? Not really. Because the point of the theory is that the same material can be presented in different ways to match each student's strength. So what the teacher ought to do (according to the theory) is this: when learning countries on a map, the visual learners should view the shapes of the countries but the auditory learners should listen to a description of each country's shape; and when learning a foreign accent, the auditory learners should listen to a native speaker but the visual learners will learn more quickly if they view a written representation of the sounds. It seems obvious that this approach won't work.

If the visual-auditory-kinesthetic theory is wrong, why does it seem so right? Surveys of educators in various countries in Europe, Central America, North America, and South America show around 85% of educators believe the theory is well supported.

There are probably a few factors that contribute to the theory's plausibility. First, it has become commonly accepted wisdom. It's one of those facts that everyone figures must be right because everyone believes it, a phenomenon called *social proof*. I know that makes people sound like suckers, but we all believe a lot of things for that reason. I believe that the atomic theory of matter is accurate, but I really couldn't describe any of the science supporting it. Everyone talks about it as one of those things that scientists have figured out, so I believe that's the case. People may treat learning styles in the same way.

Another important factor is that something similar to the theory *is* true. Kids do differ in the accuracy of their visual and auditory memories. For example, maybe you've watched in wonder as a student painted a vivid picture of an experience from a class field trip and thought, "Wow, Lacy is obviously a visual learner." As I've described, Lacy may well have a really good visual memory, but that doesn't mean she's a "visual learner" in the sense that the theory implies.

A final reason that the visual–auditory–kinesthetic theory seems right is a psychological phenomenon called the *confirmation bias*. Once we believe something, we unconsciously interpret ambiguous situations as being consistent with what we already believe. For example, suppose a student is having difficulty understanding Newton's first law. You try explaining it a few different ways, and then you give the example of a magician yanking a tablecloth off a table without disturbing the plates and cutlery that lie on top of the cloth. Suddenly the idea clicks for the student. You think, "Aha. That visual image helped him understand. He must be a visual learner." But maybe the example was just a good one and it would have helped any student, or maybe the idea would have clicked for this student after hearing just one more example, visual or not. Why the student understood Newton's first law from the example is ambiguous, and it is only your tendency to interpret ambiguous situations in ways that confirm what you already believe that led you to identify the student as a visual learner (Figure 7.5). The great novelist Tolstoy put it this way: "I know that

FIGURE 7.5: When my first daughter was born, one of the nurses told me, "Oh, it'll be crazy here in a few days. Full moon coming up, you know." Many people believe that all sorts of interesting things happen during a full moon: the murder rate goes up, emergency room admissions increase, as do calls to police and fire departments, and more babies are born, among other things. Actually, this hypothesis has been exhaustively examined, and it's wrong. Why do people believe it? One factor is the confirmation bias. When it's a full moon and the delivery room is busy, the nurse notices and remembers it. When the delivery room is busy and it's not a full moon, she doesn't take note of it. Source: ©Shutterstock/http://Photobank .kiev.ua.

most men, including those at ease with problems of the greatest complexity, can seldom accept the simplest and most obvious truth if it be such as would oblige them to admit the falsity of conclusions which they have proudly taught to others, and which they have woven, thread by thread, into the fabrics of their life."[2]

I've gone into a lot of detail about the visual-auditory-kinesthetic theory because it is so widely believed, even though psychologists know that the theory is not right. What I have said about this theory goes for all of the other learning styles theories as well. The best you can say about any of them is that the evidence is mixed.

Earlier I drew an important distinction between styles and abilities. In this section I've addressed styles – biases or tendencies to think or learn in a particular way. In the next section I discuss abilities.

Abilities and Multiple Intelligences

What is mental ability? How would you characterize someone who is mentally able? A moment of reflection tells us that there are lots of tasks for which we use our minds, and most of us are good at some of them and not so good at others. In other words, we have to talk about mental abilities, not mental ability. We've all known people who seemed gifted with words but could barely handle the math necessary to balance a checkbook, or who could pick out a tune on any musical instrument but seemed to fall all over themselves when attempting anything athletic.

The logic underlying the idea of mental ability is as follows: if there is a single ability – call it intelligence, if you like – underlying different mental activities, then someone who is good at one type of mental activity (for example, math) should be good at all mental activities. But if some people are good at one mental activity (math) and poor at another (reading comprehension), then those activities must be supported by different mental processes. For more than one hundred years, psychologists have been using this logic to investigate the structure of thought.

In a typical study, an experimenter takes 100 people and administers to each of them, say, an algebra test, a geometry test, a grammar test, a vocabulary test, and a reading comprehension test. What we would expect is that each person's scores on the language tests (grammar, vocabulary, and reading comprehension) would hang together – that is, if a person scored well on one of the language tests it would mean he was good at English, so he would tend also to score well on the other language tests. Likewise, people who scored well on one math test would probably score well on the other math test, reflecting high math ability. But the scores on the math and language tests wouldn't be so highly related. If you did this experiment, that's more or less what you'd see.‡

This sounds like pretty obvious stuff. When I was in graduate school, one of my professors called commonsense findings "*bubbe* psychology." *Bubbe* is Yiddish for "grandmother," so *bubbe* psychology is giving scientific-sounding labels to stuff that your grandmother could have told you (Figure 7.6). As far as we've gone, it is pretty obvious stuff. It can get a lot more complicated when we try to get more detailed (and the statistical techniques are pretty complex). But roughly speaking, what you noticed in school is true: some kids are talented at math, some are musical, and some are athletic, and they are not necessarily the same kids.

Educators got much more interested in this type of research in the mid-1980s when Howard Gardner, a professor at Harvard, published his theory of multiple intelligences. Gardner proposed that there are seven intelligences, to which he later added an eighth. They are listed in Table 7.2.

FIGURE 7.6: American biologist E. O. Wilson was a good enough scientist to earn a position at Harvard University where he taught for 40 years, and a good enough writer to win the Pulitzer Prize for General Nonfiction. Twice. Yet he struggled in math, avoiding calculus until he was a 32-year-old professor and even then said he was "never more than a C student."[3] But encountering a great writer and scientist who is an indifferent mathematician would not surprise your *bubbe*. Source: © Getty Images/The Washington Post.

TABLE 7.2: Gardner's eight intelligences.

Intelligence	Description	Profession requiring high levels of given intelligence
Linguistic	Facility with words and language	Attorney, novelist
Logical-mathematical	Facility with logic, inductive and deductive reasoning, and numbers	Computer programmer, scientist
Bodily-kinesthetic	Facility with body movement, as in sports and dance	Athlete, dancer, mime
Interpersonal	Facility in understanding others' emotions, needs, and points of view	Salesperson, politician
Intrapersonal	Facility in understanding one's own motivations and emotions	Novelist
Musical	Facility in the creation, production, and appreciation of music	Performer, composer
Naturalist	Facility in identifying and classifying flora or fauna	Naturalist, chef
Spatial	Facility in the use and manipulation of space	Architect, sculptor

As I've mentioned, Gardner was certainly not the first to generate a list of human abilities, and his list does not look radically different from those that others have described. In fact, most psychologists think Gardner didn't really get it right. He discounted some important work that came before his, for reasons that researchers have thought were not justified, and he made some claims that were known at the time to be wrong – for example, that the intelligences were relatively independent of one another, which he later deemphasized.

Educators were (and are) interested not so much in the particulars of the theory but in three claims associated with the theory:

> Claim 1: The list in Table 7.2 is one of intelligences, not abilities or talents.
>
> Claim 2: All eight intelligences should be taught in school.
>
> Claim 3: Many or even all of the intelligences should be used as conduits when presenting new material. That way each student will experience the material via his or her best intelligence, and thus each student's understanding will be maximized.

Gardner made the first of these claims, and it is an interesting, debatable point. The other two points have been made by others on the basis of Gardner's work, and Gardner disagrees with them. I'll describe why each claim is interesting and try to evaluate what it might mean for teachers.

Let's start with Claim 1, that the list shown in Table 7.2 represents intelligences, not abilities or talents. Gardner has written extensively on this point. He argues that some abilities – namely, logical-mathematical and linguistic – have been accorded greater status than they deserve. Why should those abilities get the special designation "intelligence" whereas the others get the apparently less glamorous title "talent"? Indeed, insisting that musical ability should be called musical intelligence, for example, carries a good share of the theory's appeal. Gardner himself has commented more than once that if he had referred to seven talents instead of seven intelligences, the theory would not have received much attention.[4]

So? Are they intelligences or talents? On the one hand, the cognitive scientist in me agrees with Gardner. The mind has many abilities, and there is not an obvious reason to separate two of them and call them "intelligence" while referring to other mental processes by another label. On the other hand, the term *intelligence* has an entrenched meaning and it's unwise to suppose that a sudden switch of the meaning will not have any fallout. I believe that confusion over Gardner's definition versus the old definitions of *intelligence* helps to explain why other people have made the other two claims – the ones with which Gardner disagrees.

Claim 2 is that all eight intelligences should be taught in school. The argument for this claim is that schools should be places where the intelligences of *all* children are celebrated. If a student is high in intrapersonal intelligence, that intelligence should be nourished and developed, and the student should not be made to feel inferior if he is lower in linguistic and logical–mathematical intelligences, the ones that are usually heavily weighted in school curricula. There is a surface plausibility to this claim. It appeals to our sense of fairness; all intelligences should be on the same footing. Gardner disagrees, however, saying that curricular decisions should be made on the basis of the curricular goals. Curricular goals, in turn, should be based on the values of the community. You pick what students will study based on what you think is important for them to know and be able to do. A theory of intelligence shouldn't set curricular goals.

The claim that all intelligences should be taught in school is, I believe, a reflection of relabeling *talents* as *intelligences*. Part of our understanding of intelligence is that intelligent people do well in school.[§] As a result of this assumption, some people's thinking, has gone this way:

> Children go to school to develop their native intelligence.
> A new intelligence has been discovered.
> Therefore, schools should develop the new intelligence.

Some educators do seem to think that Gardner "discovered" that people have musical intelligence, spatial intelligence, and so forth, whereas musical intelligence is of course the same thing your *bubbe* would have recognized as musical talent. I personally believe that music should be part of school curricula, but the idea that cognitive scientists could tell you anything to support that position is wrong.

The third claim states that it is useful to introduce new ideas through multiple intelligence avenues; for example, when students are learning how to use commas, they might write a song about commas (musical intelligence), search the woods for creatures and plants in the shape of a comma (naturalist intelligence), and create sentences with their bodies, assuming different postures for different parts of speech (bodily-kinesthetic intelligence).[5] The expectation is that different children will come to understand the comma by different means, depending on their intelligence. The idea will click for the student who is high in naturalist intelligence during the search-the-woods exercise, and so on.

This sounds a bit like the matching idea in learning styles, and Gardner has written specifically to point out that his theory concerns ability, not style.[6] Gardner also disavows the matching idea, and he's right to do so. The different abilities (or intelligences, if you like) are not interchangeable. Mathematical concepts have to be learned mathematically, and skill in music won't help.** Writing a poem about the arc that a golf club should take will not help your swing. These abilities are not completely insulated from one another, but they are separate enough that you can't take one skill you're good at and leverage it to bolster a weakness.

Some people have suggested that we might at least be able to get students interested in subject matter by appealing to their strengths. To get the science whiz reading for pleasure, don't hand him a book of Emily Dickinson's poetry; give him the memoirs of physicist Richard Feynman. I think that's a sensible idea, if not terribly startling. I also think it will only take you so far. It's a lot like trying to appeal to students' individual interests, a point I took up in Chapter 1.

Summary

Everyone can appreciate that students differ from one another. What can (or should) teachers do about that? One would hope we could capitalize on those differences to improve instruction. Two basic methods have been suggested. One approach is based on differences in cognitive style – that is, if one matches the method of instruction to the preferred cognitive style of the child, learning will be easier.

Unfortunately, no one has described a set of styles for which there is good evidence.

The second way that teachers might take advantage of differences among students is rooted in differences in abilities. If a student is lacking in one cognitive ability, the hope would be that she could use a cognitive strength to make up for, or at least bolster, the cognitive weakness. Unfortunately, there is good evidence that this sort of substitution is not possible. To be clear, it's the substitution idea that is wrong; students definitely do differ in their cognitive abilities (although the description in Gardner's multiple intelligences theory is widely regarded as less accurate than other descriptions).

Implications for the Classroom

I admit I felt like a bit of a Grinch as I wrote this chapter, as though I had a scowl on my face as I typed "wrong, wrong, wrong" about the optimistic ideas others have offered regarding student differences. As I stated at the start of the chapter, I am not saying that teachers should not differentiate instruction. I hope and expect that they will. But when they do so, they should know that scientists cannot offer any help. It would be wonderful if scientists had identified categories of students along with varieties of instruction best suited to each category, but after a great deal of effort, they have not found such types, and I, like many others, suspect they don't exist. I would advise teachers to treat students differently on the basis of the teacher's experience with each student and to remain alert for what works. When differentiating among students, craft knowledge trumps science.

That said, I do have some positive thoughts on what all of this means for your classroom.

Notions of "Ability" Shouldn't Undercut Hard Work and Modest Achievement

Thinking of many types of ability has an obvious appeal – it seems to make it more likely that everyone will be good at something or even smart at something. I've already said I think that puts "being good at something" on a taller pedestal than it perhaps deserves. But there's another aspect of this we want to watch out for. By wondering what kind of intelligence each child has (or encouraging them to do so) we may encourage a view of intelligence (whether musical, mathematical, whatever) as something that a child just *has*. I see negative ways a child might hear this message, ways that would undercut the message that achievement comes from hard work. If I think "I'm high in musical intelligence," I may take that to mean "That's more important than working hard at music." I'll have more to say about this in Chapter 8, but for now I think the point is intuitive: if I believe I'm good at it, I might assume that means it comes easily, and I shouldn't need to work hard at it.

In contrast if I understand that I'm not naturally good at it, I may take that to mean there's not much point in trying in the first place. Or, I may use my supposed lack of intelligence in this domain as a reason to quit trying after any setback.

From my own experience, I have always had a very hard time with music. I had to play an instrument in middle school band (trombone, disaster) and I saw that other band kids really *got* their instrument; they talked about music as a language. To me, it remained gibberish. I dropped trombone as soon as I could, but for whatever reason, I *did* pick up a guitar at 17 and played, on and off, for the next 20 years. That was usually a question of painstaking memorization; I never developed any feel for it, and in that sense, the language of music remained gibberish. But I did get a type of pleasure from playing unavailable elsewhere. During middle school I thought of music as "really difficult for me." I wonder, had I thought of myself as "low in musical intelligence," would I have tried the guitar at 17?

Think in Terms of Content, Not in Terms of Students

Learning-style theories don't help much when applied to students, but I think they are useful when applied to content. Take the visual-auditory-kinesthetic distinction. You might want students to experience material in one or another modality depending on what you want them to get out of the lesson; a diagram of the Petronas Twin Towers should be seen, the national anthem of Turkmenistan should be heard, and the *cheche* turban (used by Saharan tribes for protection against sun and wind) should be worn. The distinctions in

Table 7.1 provide a number of interesting ways to think about lesson plans: Do you want students to think deductively during a lesson, or to free-associate creatively? Should they focus on similarities among concepts they encounter, or should they focus on the details that differentiate those concepts? Table 7.1 may help you to focus on what you hope your students will learn from a lesson and how to help them get there.

Change Promotes Attention

Every teacher knows that change during a lesson invigorates students and refocuses their attention. If the teacher has been doing a lot of talking, something visual (a video or a map) offers a welcome change. Table 7.1 provides a number of ways to think about change during the course of a lesson. If the students' work has demanded a lot of logical, deductive thinking, perhaps an exercise that calls for broad, associative thinking is in order. If their work has required many rapid responses, perhaps they should do something else that calls for thoughtful, measured responses. Rather than individualizing the required mental processes for each student, give all of your students practice in all of these processes, and view the transitions as an opportunity for each student to start fresh and refocus his or her mental energies.

There Is Value in Every Child, Even If He or She Is Not "Smart in Some Way"

I am willing to bet you have heard someone say, "Every student is intelligent in some way," or ask students to identify "What kind of smart are you?" I think teachers say this in an effort to communicate an egalitarian attitude to students: everyone is good at something. But there are a couple of reasons to be leery of this attitude. First, this sort of statement rubs me the wrong way because it implies that intelligence brings value. Every child *is* unique and valuable, whether or not they are intelligent or have much in the way of mental ability. I admit that being the father of a child with profound mental disability makes me sensitive on this issue. My daughter is not intelligent in any sense of the word, but she is a joyful child who brings a lot of happiness to a lot of people.

Second, it's not necessarily the case that every child is smart in some way. The exact percentage of children who are "smart" would depend on how many intelligences you define and whether "smart" means "top 10%" or "top 50%," and so on. It doesn't much matter – there will always be some kids who are in fact not especially gifted in any of the intelligences. In my experience, telling kids that they have a skill they don't possess seldom works. (If a child is briefly fooled, her peers are usually happy to bring reality crashing down on her head.)

Third, for reasons I describe in the next chapter, it is *never* smart to tell a child that she's smart. Believe it or not, doing so makes her less smart. Really.

Don't Worry – and Save Your Money

If you have felt nagging guilt that you have not evaluated each of your students to assess their cognitive style, or if you think you know what their styles are and have not adjusted your teaching to them – don't worry about it. There is no reason to think that doing so will help. And if you were thinking of buying a book or inviting someone in for a professional development session on one of these topics, I advise you to save your money.

If "cognitive styles" and "multiple intelligences" are not helpful ways to characterize how children differ, what's a better way? Why do some children seem to breeze through mathematics while others struggle? Why do some children love history, or geography? The importance of background knowledge has come up again and again in this book. In Chapter 1 I argued that background knowledge is an important determinant of what we find interesting; for example, problems or puzzles that seem difficult but not impossible pique our interest. In Chapter 2 I explained that background knowledge is an important determinant of much of our success in school. Cognitive processes (such as analyzing, synthesizing, and critiquing) cannot operate alone. They need background knowledge to make them work.

Still, background knowledge is not the only difference among students. There is something to the idea that some students are simply really clever. In the next chapter I explore that idea, and I focus on what we can do to maximize the potential of all students, regardless of how clever they are.

Notes

*Some people differentiate between cognitive styles (how we think) and learning styles (how we learn). I don't think this distinction is very important, so I use the term *cognitive styles* throughout this chapter, even when I'm talking about learning.

†We differ in kinesthesia too, but the literature on this is more complicated to describe, so I'm going to stick to visual and auditory examples.

‡Actually, the math and English scores are not completely unrelated. Good scores on one are predictive of good scores on the other, but the relationship is weaker than the relationship of one math score to another math score. We'll get into this topic in Chapter 8.

§In fact, modern intelligence testing began in France in the late nineteenth century as a way of predicting who would excel in school and who would not.

**Although music and rhythm can help us to memorize things, including mathematical formulae, they won't help us gain a deep understanding of what the formulae do. The reasons that music helps us memorize things are fascinating, but a discussion of them would take us too far afield.

Further Reading

Less Technical

De Bruyckere, P., Kirschner, P. A., & Hulshof, C. D. (2015). *Urban Myths about Learning and Education*. London: Academic Press. A fun survey of 35 commonly believed myths (e.g., "young people don't read anymore") with evidence showing they are wrong.

Willingham, D. T. (2004). Reframing the mind. *Education Next*, 4(3) 19–24. This article covers the more technical problems in the multiple intelligences theory, explaining why psychologists prefer other accounts of ability over Gardner's.

Willingham, D. T. (2018). Ask the cognitive scientist: does tailoring instruction to "learning styles" help students learn? *American Educator*, 42(2), 28–32. A review of the scientific evidence regarding learning styles, including the fascinating data showing that people sometimes act in accordance with their purported style, even if it hurts task performance.

More Technical

Coffield, F., Moseley, D., Hall, E., & Ecclestone, K. (2004). *Should We Be Using Learning Styles? What Research Has to Say about Practice*. London: Learning and Skills Research Center. http://hdl.voced.edu.au/10707/64981 (accessed 13 July 2020). A review of the literature on learning styles, especially useful because it reviews the many different theories of styles.

Cuevas, J. (2015). Is learning styles-based instruction effective? A comprehensive analysis of recent research on learning styles. *Theory and Research in Education*, 13(3), 308–333. A review of multiple studies that examined whether there is any benefit to matching instruction with student learning style.

Gardner, H., Kornhaber, M., & Chen, J.-Q. (2018). The theory of multiple intelligences: psychological and educational perspectives. In: *The Nature of Human Intelligence* (ed. R. Sternberg), 116–129. Cambridge, UK: Cambridge University Press. A brief, up-to-date account of Gardner's views on intelligence.

Nickerson, R. S. (1998). Confirmation bias: a ubiquitous phenomenon in many guises. *Review of General Psychology, 2,* 175–220. A somewhat dated but still relevant review of the confirmation bias.

Pearson, J. (2019). The human imagination: the cognitive neuroscience of visual mental imagery. *Nature Reviews Neuroscience, 20*(10), 624–634. Contemporary review of the state of research on visual representations in the brain.

Rotton, J., & Kelly, I. W. (1985). Much ado about the full moon: a meta-analysis of lunar-lunacy research. *Psychological Bulletin, 97,* 296–306. This article reviews 37 studies that sought a link between the lunar cycle and various behaviors (such as psychiatric disturbances, homicides, and crisis calls). No relationship is observed.

Discussion Questions

1. You may now believe that learning styles theories don't have scientific support and therefore should not influence your practice, but some parents will not be so easily convinced. Teachers tell me that sometimes parents will say, "My child is struggling in your class because you're not teaching to their learning style." What can you say to these parents?

2. It seems inarguable that Gardner is right in his claim that most schools prize ability with language and ability with numbers over other abilities. Why do you suppose that is? Does it make sense to you? How does your school value different types of intelligence (or ability, if you prefer)? How is this value expressed? Do you wish it were different?

3. Does it matter whether we use the term "ability," "talent," or "intelligence"? Do these terms mean different things to educators, parents, and students?

4. The most consistent difference among students that we *know* matters to success in school is what students already know and can do before the lesson begins. This fact seems to argue plainly for teaching children with different levels of preparation in different classrooms; it's should be much easier for a teacher to meet children where they are if they are mostly in the same place, academically. But when this strategy is adopted, the *very* consistent problem is that the teacher of the children who are further behind has lower expectations for his kids. What can be done to resolve this dilemma?

5. If your goal is to, as much as possible, have students in your classroom with very similar background knowledge, another strategy would be to use a much more consistent curriculum within a district or even state. That way students who have moved would still have been exposed to the same work in the past. A set curriculum of this sort seems to be the opposite result of the implication drawn from a multiple intelligences perspective. That's usually interpreted as crying out for greater individuation, so students can follow their strengths and interests. What is gained and lost in each approach?

6. Do you agree with me that there's an underlying desire in educators for everyone to be smart, or at least to be good at something? What are the benefits of this underlying desire? What are the costs?

8

How Can I Help Slow Learners?

Question: It's a cruel fact that some children just don't seem to be cut out for schoolwork. That's not to say they don't have valuable skills. For example, we've all heard stories of business titans who struggled in school. But certainly we would like all students to get everything they can out of school. How can school be optimized for students who don't have the raw intelligence that other students have?

Answer: Some people view intelligence as a fixed attribute, like eye color. If you win the genetic lottery, you're smart; but if you lose, you're not. This notion of intelligence as a fixed quality has implications for school and work. One implication is that smart people shouldn't need to work hard in order to get good grades – after all, they are smart. As a corollary, if you work hard, that must mean you're not smart. The destructive cycle is obvious: students want to get good grades so that they look smart, but they can't study to do so because that marks them as dumb. But what if you view intelligence as malleable, changeable? If you fail a test or don't understand a concept, you wouldn't take that as evidence that you're stupid – you just haven't mastered that content yet. This attribution is helpful because it tells you that intelligence is under your control. If you are performing poorly, you can do something about it. So which view is correct? Is intelligence fixed or malleable? There is some truth in both. Our genetic inheritance does affect our intelligence, but less than most people believe – indeed, less than scientists believed 20 years ago. There is no doubt that intelligence can be changed. The cognitive principle that guides this chapter is:

> Children do differ in intelligence, but intelligence can be changed through sustained hard work.

It would be nice if all of our students were equally capable – if the only differences in their performance at school were due to differences in how hard they worked. It would somehow make school seem fairer. Regardless of how desirable that might be, many teachers would say it's a pipe dream. Aside from the fact that students have different opportunities to learn outside of school, some students are simply smarter than others. Knowing what to do for the bright ones is not that tough – offer them more challenging work. But what about those who have difficulty keeping up? How can teachers ensure that they are getting all they can from school?

To start, we need to clarify what's meant by *intelligence*. If given a few minutes to write a definition, we might say that intelligent people can understand complex ideas and use different forms of reasoning. They can also overcome obstacles by engaging thought, and they learn from their experiences. I think this definition is in line with common sense, and it happens to be a paraphrase of the definition created by a task force appointed by the American Psychological Association.* Although many finer distinctions could be made, the overall idea – that some people reason well and catch on to new ideas quickly – captures most of what we mean when we say "intelligence."

There are two things to note about this definition. First, it doesn't include abilities in music, athletics, or other fields that Gardner included in his theory of multiple intelligences. As described in Chapter 7, most researchers consider those abilities just as important as those that are considered aspects of intelligence, but calling them intelligences rather than talents muddies the waters of communication and prompts inaccurate inferences, for example, that a cognitive strength can directly make up for a cognitive weakness. Second, this definition seems to include just one intelligence. An implication is that if someone is intelligent, she should be equally good at both math and language arts. We all know people who are *not* equally gifted in these two fields. So how could this definition be right?

There is in fact overwhelming evidence that there is a general intelligence – that is, "if you're smart, you're smart." But it's not the whole story. Here's one way that psychologists research this topic. Suppose I hypothesize that there is a single type of intelligence. It's usually called g, short for general intelligence. You, on the other hand, argue that there are two types of intelligence – one verbal and one mathematical. Now suppose you and I find 100 students, each of whom is willing to take four tests: two math tests (say, a calculation test and a word problem test) and two verbal tests (for example, a vocabulary test and a reading comprehension test). I think "if you're smart, you're smart," so anyone who does well on one of the tests ought to do well on the other three (and anyone who does poorly on one test will do poorly on the others). You, in contrast, think that verbal and mathematical intelligence are separate, so someone who does well on the reading comprehension test is likely to do well on the vocabulary test, but that success should predict nothing about how she will do on the math tests (Figure 8.1).

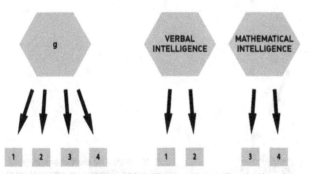

FIGURE 8.1: Two views of intelligence. According to the view on the left, a single type of intelligence underlies all intellectual tasks. So doing well on the vocabulary test implies that you have a lot of g, which implies that you should also do well on the other three tests. In the model on the right, doing well on the vocabulary test implies that you have high verbal intelligence but that tells us nothing about how much mathematical intelligence you have, because the two are separate. Data from hundreds of studies show that neither of these models is correct. The model in Figure 8.2 is commonly accepted. Source: © Greg Culley.

So which of these two models is right? Neither. Data from tens of thousands of people have been evaluated, and they show a pattern that has something in common with each model. The model on the left of Figure 8.1 predicts that verbal and math test scores will be related to one another, whereas the model on the right predicts that they will be unrelated. The data show that the verbal test scores are in fact related to the math test scores – but the verbal test scores are more related to one another than they are to the math test scores. That pattern fits the model shown in Figure 8.2. Separate cognitive processes contribute to verbal and mathematical intelligences, but *g* contributes something to each of them too.

What exactly is *g*? It's really a description of how the data hang together. It's natural to assume that there's a cognitive process underlying *g*, but the data certainly don't tell us what that is. People suggest it might be related to the speed or the capacity of working memory, or even that it's a reflection of how quickly the neurons in our brains can fire. Most recently, some researchers have suggested that a single mental process does *not* underlie *g*; it's not one thing, but several high-level cognitive processes that are themselves closely related and hence appear to be one thing.[1]

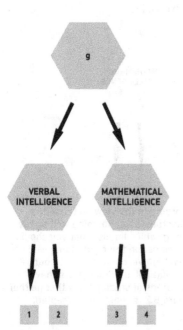

FIGURE 8.2: The dominant view of intelligence. There is a general intelligence that contributes to many different types of mental tasks, but there are also particular types of intelligence that are supported by the general intelligence processes. Almost everyone agrees that there are verbal and mathematical intelligences, although some people think these should be broken down further. Source: © Greg Culley.

g is general intelligence and has an influence on a very broad array of mental abilities. There are also more specific mental abilities, for example those that help you understand language and those that help you deal with numbers. Those vary among people as well, and that accounts for why we observe some people who get As in English, but struggle to get Cs in math, and vice versa.

Even though *g* is not the whole story when it comes to intelligence, researchers often refer to *g* when considering why some people are quite intelligent and others less so, at least in part because having a lot of *g* predicts that one will do well in school and well in the workplace. Now that we better understand what intelligence is, we can turn our attention to the next question: What makes people more or less intelligent?

What Makes People Intelligent?

In Chapters 5 and 6 I emphasized the importance of practice and hard work to expertise in cognitive tasks. Perhaps people who are intelligent are those who have had a lot of practice doing the sorts of tasks that are used to define intelligence; for whatever reason, they have been exposed to lots of complex ideas (and explanations of these ideas), have had many opportunities to reason in a supportive environment, and so on.

The other view is that intelligence is a matter not of work and practice but rather of carefully selecting one's parents. In other words, intelligence is mostly genetic. Some people are born smart and although they might further develop this ability through practice, they will be pretty smart even if they do very little to develop their intelligence (Figure 8.3).

I've proposed two answers to the question *Where does intelligence come from?* and both answers are rather extreme: all nature (that is, genetics) or all nurture (that is, experience). Whenever the question *Is it nature or is it nurture?* is asked, the answer is almost always *both*, and it's almost always difficult to specify how genes and experiences interact. The same answer applies to the question about intelligence, but there has been a significant shift in researchers' points of view in the last 30 years, from thinking that the answer is "both, but probably

FIGURE 8.3: Two views of intelligence. On the left is Charles Darwin, commonly credited as the chief architect and promulgator of the theory of evolution. In a letter to Francis Galton, his half cousin and a brilliant polymath, Darwin said, "I have always maintained that, excepting fools, men [do] not differ much in intellect, only in zeal and hard work." Not everyone agrees. On the right is actor Keanu Reeves. "I'm a meathead. I can't help it, man. You've got smart people and you've got dumb people. I just happen to be dumb."[2] Source: Darwin © Getty Images/Bettmann; Reeves © Getty Images/ Ron Galella.

more genetic" to thinking it's "both, but probably more environmental." Let me describe the evidence on both sides. Once we better understand why people are intelligent, we'll better understand how to help students who seem to lack intelligence.

I've just said that intelligence is very likely a product of genetic *and* environmental factors combining in complex ways. So how can we untangle them?

For decades, the key strategy was to compare the intelligence of pairs of people who vary in their genetic similarity. For example, identical twins share 100% of their genes and fraternal twins (like all siblings) share 50% of their genes. So, testing whether identical twins are close to each other in intelligence more often than fraternal twins are will help us determine the importance of genes (Figure 8.4).

In addition, we can examine whether the intelligence of siblings raised in the same household is more similar than the intelligence of siblings who were raised in different households – that is, siblings who were separated at birth and adopted by different families. Siblings who were raised in the same household didn't have identical environments but they had the same parents, likely went to the same school, had similar exposure to literature, television, the Internet and other sources of culture, and so forth.

 FIGURE 8.4: Identical twins (and American Democratic politicians) Julián and Joaquin Castro were raised in the same household and share 100% of their genes. Fraternal twins Scarlett and Hunter Johansson were raised in the same household but, like all non-twin siblings, share just 50% of their genes. Comparing how similar the intelligence of identical twins is to how similar the intelligence of fraternal twins is helps researchers evaluate the importance of genetics to intelligence. Source: Castro © Getty Images/Joe Raedle; Johansson © Getty Images/Steve Zak Photography.

Table 8.1 compares several types of relationships and tells us a lot about the relative importance of genetics and how we are raised.

Hundreds of sibling pairs in each category were tested and researchers evaluated how similar twins were in intelligence and other attributes The results of these studies were startling. Genetics seemed to play a huge role in general intelligence; that is, our genes seem to be responsible for something like 50% of our smarts.

TABLE 8.1: This table shows different sibling relationships and the genetic and environmental similarities within each pair.

Relationship	Percentage of genes shared	Environment
Identical twins, raised together	100	Similar
Fraternal twins, raised together	50	Similar
Identical twins, raised apart	100	Different
Fraternal twins, raised apart	50	Different
Adoptive siblings	0	Similar

Some research laboratories (notably one at the University of Minnesota) are in contact with hundreds of pairs of twins who were raised apart, many of whom met for the first time as part of the study.[1]

But data using other research methods call that conclusion into question.

The human genome project was completed in 2003, and people were hopeful it would lead to more specific information about which genes contribute to intelligence. Sure, intelligence is complicated and we know it's not going to be a matter of locating just one or two genes, but if it's half the story of intelligence, we should be able to find *something*. But research targeting the role of specific genes largely came up empty.

During the mid 2000s another research technique was developed. In genome-wide association studies (GWAS), the researcher doesn't need to have a hypothesis about which part of the genome to examine. The entire genome of many people (hundreds of thousands) was analyzed, and powerful statistical techniques connected variations in the genomes with variations in intelligence. This method yielded somewhat more encouraging results, but still nothing close to what studies of twins suggested. The genetic variants associated with intelligence number in the thousands, but each variant offers just a *tiny* increase in predictive power. Together these genetic variations account for, at maximum, 20% of intelligence, not the 50% indicated by twin studies.[3] What's going on? There are a couple of contributing factors.

For one thing, most researchers now think that a good bit of the predictive power of a person's genome for intelligence is actually indirect. Here's what that means. Suppose I conduct my GWAS study on 300000 people and use that to develop a profile of the genetic makeup associated with more or less intelligence. I call that the polygenic score, and I can calculate a polygenic score for each person and use that to predict their intelligence. The fascinating finding is that if I try to use this score to figure out which of two *siblings* is smarter, the predictive power is cut in half.[4] Why?

When we look at a person's genetic makeup and their intelligence, we naturally think of a direct link, (your genes)→(your intelligence). But you get your genes from your parents, of course. So when I look at your genetic makeup I'm also looking (indirectly) at something about your parents. And if genes influence how people parent their kids, then part of the linkage is actually (parents, genes)→(parents, behavior)→(your intelligence). Polygenic scores aren't as effective in predicting which of two siblings is the smarter (compared to predicting which of two strangers is the smarter) because part of the predictive power of a polygenic score is a prediction, based on your genetic makeup and of your parents, genetic makeup; their genetic makeup influences how they raised you.

Genetic makeup may also have an indirect influence because it makes people likely to *seek out* particular environments. Researcher Bill Dickens offers the following analogy.[5] Suppose identical twins are separated at birth and adopted into different families. Their genes make them unusually tall at a young age, and they continue to grow. Because each twin is tall, he tends to do well in informal basketball games around the neighborhood (Figure 8.5). For that reason, each twin asks his parents to put up a net at home. The skills of each twin improve with practice, and each is recruited for his junior high school basketball team. More practice leads to still better skill, and by the end of high school each twin plays quite well – not a future professional, perhaps, but still better than 98% of the population, let's say.

Now, notice what has happened. These are identical twins, raised apart. So if a researcher tracked down each twin and administered a test of basketball skills, she would find that both are quite good, and because they were raised apart, the researcher would conclude that this was a genetic effect, that skill in basketball is largely determined

FIGURE 8.5: Who would you select for your team? Source: ©Shutterstock/XiXinXing.

by one's genes. But the researcher would be mistaken. What actually happened was that their genes made them tall, and being tall nudged them toward environments that included a lot of basketball practice. Practice – an environmental effect – made them good at basketball, not their genes. *Genetic effects can make you seek out or select different environments.*

Now think of how that perspective might apply to intelligence. Maybe genetics has had some small effect on your intelligence. Maybe it has made you a little quicker to understand things, or made your memory a little bit better, or made you more persistent on cognitive tasks, or simply made you more curious. Your parents and teachers noticed this and encouraged your interest. They may not even have been aware that they were encouraging you. They might have talked to you about more sophisticated subjects and used a broader vocabulary than they otherwise would have. As you got older, you saw yourself more and more as one of the "smart kids." You made friends with other smart kids and entered into friendly but quite real competition for the highest grades. Then too, maybe genetics subtly pushed you away from other endeavors. You may be quicker cognitively, but you're a little slower and clumsier physically than others. That made you avoid situations that might develop your athletic skills (such as pickup basketball games) and instead stay inside and read.

If this account is right and genes have less influence on intelligence than we may have thought, then it should be easy to observe some instances where the environment directly changes intelligence. A few varieties of that evidence exist. For example, if a child lives in a relatively deprived home and is then adopted into a family with greater means, the child's intelligence increases.[6] Other studies show that schooling has a substantial impact on intelligence. Children who miss a year of school show a drop in IQ. When Norway added two years to the minimum time children must attend school, the population saw a substantial increase in IQ (measured when people entered the military at age 19). Children who switch from an undemanding school to one with higher expectations and more resources show an increase in intelligence.[7]

Perhaps most persua-
sive is the Flynn effect.
Over the last half-
century IQ scores have
shown quite substan-
tial gains in a num-
ber of nations.[8] For
example, in Holland,
scores went up 21
points in just 30 years
(1952–1982), accord-
ing to scores from
tests of Dutch military
draftees. The effect has
been observed in more
than a dozen countries
throughout the world,
including the United
States (Figure 8.6). Not
all countries have data
available – very large
numbers of people are
needed to be sure that
we're not looking at

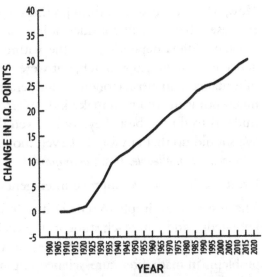

FIGURE 8.6: This graph shows IQ score gains
in all available data, worldwide, between 1909
and 2013. The "Flynn effect" is strong
evidence that the environment has a powerful
impact on intelligence because geneticists
agree that the gene pool could not change
rapidly enough to account for this change in
IQ. Source: From "One Century of Global IQ
Gains: A Formal Meta-Analysis of the Flynn
Effect (1909-2013)" by Jakob Pietschnig &
Martin Voracek in *Perspectives on Psychological Science* 10 (3): 282-306, figure 1, p. 285.

a quirky subset – but where the data are available, the effect has
been found.

If intelligence is largely genetic, we would not expect IQ scores for
a whole country to go up or down much over time, because the
overall gene pool changes very slowly. But that's not what has happened. There have been huge increases in IQ scores – increases that
are much too large to have been caused by changes in genes. Some
of the increase may have come from better nutrition and health
care. Some of it may have come from the fact that our environment
has gotten more complex and people are more often called on to
think abstractly and solve unfamiliar problems – the exact sorts of
things they're asked to do on IQ tests. Whatever the cause, it must
be environmental.[†]

Now, why did I take you through this long story about intelligence? Because what we will consider doing for students who seem unintelligent differs depending on the nature of intelligence. If intelligence just can't change much, if it were determined by your genetic inheritance and wasn't open to influence, then there wouldn't be much point in trying to make kids smarter. Instead, we'd try to get students to do the best they could given the intelligence they have. We should do that anyway, but even more, we should be aware that *intelligence is malleable. It can be improved.*

Great! So how do we improve intelligence?

The answer is as simple to state as it is difficult to execute. You build knowledge and you teach students the analytic skills associated with a broad variety of different disciplines: how to formulate and address problems in math, literature, science, engineering, and so on.

A second thing you'd want to do is more subtle. You want to convince students that intelligence can be improved.

How Beliefs About Intelligence Matter

Consider two hypothetical students. Felix is very concerned that he appears intelligent. When given a choice of tasks, he picks the easy one to be sure that he succeeds. When confronted with a challenging task, he quits after the first setback, usually protesting loudly that he is tired or offering some other excuse. Mel, in contrast, doesn't seem bothered by failure. Given a choice, he picks tasks that are new to him and seems to enjoy learning from them, even if they are frustrating. When a task is difficult and not going well, Mel doesn't withdraw, he persists, trying a new strategy.

You have doubtless had Mels and Felixes in your classroom. What accounts for the differences between them? Psychologist Carol Dweck proposed that what they believe about intelligence is an important factor.[9] Students like Felix are more likely to believe that intelligence is *fixed*, determined at birth; and because it's unchangeable, he's very concerned that he get the "right label," so he picks easy tasks. Felix's beliefs about intelligence really paint him into a corner. He thinks that smart people don't need to work hard to succeed – they succeed through their superior intelligence.

Therefore, working hard is a sign of being dumb. Thus, although it's important to Felix to appear smart, he won't allow himself to work hard to be sure he succeeds because he thinks hard work makes him look dumb!

Mel, conversely, views intelligence as malleable. He thinks he gets smarter by learning new things. Thus failure is not nearly so threatening to Mel as it is to Felix, because he doesn't believe it says anything permanent about his abilities. When Mel fails, he figures he didn't work hard enough or hasn't learned about this particular topic yet. Thus Mel feels that he's in control of his success or failure because he can always work harder if he fails. Mel sees nothing embarrassing in admitting ignorance or in getting a wrong answer. Therefore, he's not motivated to pick easy tasks; instead, he's more likely to pick challenging tasks, because he might learn from them. Mel also doesn't think that working hard is a sign of stupidity – on the contrary, he thinks hard work is a sign that one is trying to get smarter (Figure 8.7). The core belief that intelligence is malleable and can be improved via hard work is called having a growth mindset.

 FIGURE 8.7: You could imagine going to a bar Trivia Night with Felix; he'd offer answers only to the easy questions but would do so loudly to increase the chances he'd appear smart. Mel, in contrast, would guess at everything, not caring much if he was wrong, but eager to learn something new. How would you play? Source: © Getty Images/Jim Donahue.

As you probably know, there has been enormous interest in growth mindset in the last 10 years. Schools have declared themselves "growth mindset schools," courses have been developed to nurture growth mindset in students, and teachers have been urged (and in some cases harangued) to exhibit growth mindset in their classrooms. Has it paid off?

There are two parts to this question. First, is the theory right – does belief in the malleability of intelligence prompt one to set more ambitious goals, fear failure less, and ultimately achieve more? Second, if the theory is right, can we get students to adopt a growth mindset?

There's good data that the theory is right. The most telling evidence comes from an enormous study conducted by the Organisation for Economic Cooperation and Development (OECD). Every three years, the OECD oversees the administration of tests of reading, math, and science to 15-year-olds. In 2018, they asked students in 74 countries a range of questions related to their attitudes toward school, including whether they agreed or disagreed with this statement: "Your intelligence is something about you that you cannot change very much." Those who disagreed or disagreed strongly were categorized as having a growth mindset.

As the theory predicted, a growth mindset was associated with students' self-reported tendency to stick with tasks, to set more ambitious learning goals, and to attribute greater value to school. Growth mindset was *negatively* associated with fear of failing at academic tasks. Of course it might be that all these expectations and attitudes are affected by income, so the researchers statistically removed the effect of socioeconomic status as part of the analysis.[10]

Now that's a start, but these are correlations, and we know correlation does not allow us to draw a causal conclusion. For example, maybe it's not that belief in the malleability of intelligence leads to doing better in school. Maybe if you do well in school, growth mindset is appealing; you like to think "I'm doing so well because I work hard and make myself smarter" whereas if you do poorly you'd rather think "It's not really my fault – it's just that I was born not very smart."

To see whether growth mindset *causes* kids to do better in school, we need an experiment – we need to take a large group of people, select some at random, give them a growth mindset, then see if they then persist at difficult tasks, get better grades, and so on.

There are several very carefully conducted experiments showing this effect. One tested 6320 low-achieving ninth-graders drawn from a nationally representative sample of high schools in the United States.[11] Each group completed two 25-minute instructional sessions online. The growth mindset intervention focused on three ideas: (i) trying hard or asking for help doesn't mean that you're dumb; (ii) failure doesn't stem from low ability, but from inexperience; and (iii) there's no need to worry about "looking stupid" by failing or revealing that you don't know something. A control group completed two online instructional sessions about brain anatomy.

Compared to control group students, those in the growth-mindset group earned higher grade point averages at the end of ninth grade, and they were more likely to enroll in a challenging math course at the start of 10th grade. The effects were small, but it's remarkable that they were observed at all, given that they were prompted by a mere hour-long online experience. It may even strike you as too good to believe, but the experiment was repeated with a similar number of students in Norway, with similar results.[12]

What has *not* worked consistently are growth-mindset programs meant for schools or classrooms. As I write in 2020, none of these programs are proven and ready for prime time. It's much more challenging to create a classroom program because it must be flexible enough to adapt to classroom realities, like the different ways that teachers might teach it, the possibility that lessons will be interrupted by a fire drill or eliminated if something more important comes up, and so on. The online version is much easier to control, but even that underwent multiple rounds of pilot-testing and revision over several years. So we may be waiting a while for reliable, in-class growth mindset lessons.

A final thought. Growth mindset offers an object lesson in the use of science to improve education. If you knew the science, you'd know from the start that growth mindset was not going to be a

TABLE 8.2: Percentage of 15-year-olds who took the OECD test who showed a growth mindset (that is, who disagreed with the statement "Your intelligence is something about you that you cannot change very much.").

Greater than 60%	Between 40% and 60%	Less than 40%
United Kingdom	Russia	Poland
United States	Singapore	Lebanon
Canada	Italy	Philippines
Japan	Slovak Republic	Indonesia
Finland	Chile	Kosovo
Germany	Turkey	Panama

This is a sampling of countries, not a complete listing.
Source: Data from OECD (2019), *PISA 2018 Results (Volume III): What School Life Means for Students' Lives*, PISA. Paris: OECD Publishing, figure III.14.1, p. 202.

game-changer. The effect couldn't be huge, because it's supposed to improve motivation, and clearly, many factors contribute to motivation, not just your beliefs about intelligence. Then too, it can only help kids who don't already have a growth mindset, and the OECD data cited previously shows that, in many countries, 15-year-olds already do! (See Table 8.2.) What was most promising about this research was that it was very low cost – you didn't need new equipment or to hire more teachers, you just talked to kids about intelligence differently. But the hype got past the researchers (who, to their credit, tried to scale back expectations) and teachers got thoroughly sick of growth mindset.[13] Still, educators can glean more from this research than an example of application gone wrong.

Summary

You sometimes hear "Intelligence tests tell you nothing more than whether a person is good at taking intelligence tests." This is not true. IQ predicts success in school and in the workplace. For many years, researchers thought that about half of intelligence came from your genes and half from the environment. More recent research indicates that the environment is much more important than people had estimated. We also have good evidence that intelligence can be increased and that schooling makes you smarter. That does take hard work, however, and children will be more willing to do this hard work if they know it will pay off, that is, if they believe that they can get smarter.

Implications for the Classroom

What can we do for slow learners? The point of this chapter is to emphasize that slow learners are not dumb.‡ They probably differ little from other students in terms of their potential. Intelligence can be changed.

This conclusion should not be taken to mean that these students can easily catch up. Slow students may have similar potential as bright students, but they probably differ in what they know, in their motivation, in their persistence in the face of academic setbacks, and in their self-image as students. They may also differ in the resources available to them outside of school. I fully believe that these students can excel, but it must be acknowledged that things have not gone well to this point. To help slow learners improve, we must first be sure they believe that they can do it, and next we must try to persuade them that it will be worth it.

Talk About Intelligence as Growth Mindset Theory Suggests, but Don't Expect Big Changes from That Alone

This recommendation is odd because I'm suggesting you do exactly what I said at the end of the chapter is unsupported by evidence. Let me explain what I recommend you do, then why it's odd, and then why I think you should try it anyway.

The idea is that the teacher talks about intelligence in a way that fosters a growth mindset. You want students to think of their intelligence as under their control, and especially that they can develop their intelligence through hard work. There are three elements to this sort of talk.

First, you praise *processes* rather than ability. When a student succeeds you don't say, "Wow! You're so smart!" That communicates that intelligence is an entity, something the child *is* (which is not under her control). Instead, praise things the child does. Whether they succeed or not, praise her when she undertakes a challenging task, or persists in the face of difficulty, or takes responsibility for her work.

Second, encourage the students to seek out feedback. Anyone needs honest, informative feedback to improve. So it's not enough for a teacher to say, "Wow, I love how much effort you put into your presentation on how to solve today's Challenge Math Problem." You need to add feedback like "The order in which you presented the steps was very clear, but I think the graphs you drew confused some students. Let me explain why I say that."

Third, students must become accustomed to finding new strategies when things go wrong and resourceful in that search. Okay, her graphs weren't good. Now what? Does she know enough about graphing to brainstorm some other methods? If not, does she know where she could find models, or who to talk to about it?

These are the three things Carol Dweck recommended teachers do to encourage a growth mindset. Now, why is it odd that I suggest you do them? Well, as I mentioned, when schools have tried to institutionalize these strategies, it mostly hasn't worked. Reviews of the research show some successes but many failures.[14]

In addition, Dweck herself is concerned that these practices are often implemented incorrectly. In 2015 she published an opinion piece in an education newspaper, expressing dismay that it was not going well.[15] She noted that the most common misapplication was to praise effort . . . and stop there. Such praise actually sends exactly the wrong message. Suppose a child can't work a math problem and the teacher says, "Well, but you did try really hard, and that's great." That praise suggests that there's no point in continuing. The teacher is offering a consolation prize, a verbal participation sticker because the child tried, but that seems to say, "No need to keep trying, because you probably will never be able to do it. Let's just say you're finished."

I nevertheless favor talking with children about intelligence in the way that the growth mindset literature suggests, especially taking care to include all three elements that Dweck recommends. Intelligence, the reasons for success or failure, what to do when one fails – these are inevitable topics of conversation in classrooms. You may as well describe intelligence in ways that are as close to the truth as we know. Growth mindset doesn't suggest you say anything wacky; you tell kids "you can get smarter, but you must work hard, seek feedback, and try new things."

Growth mindset is worthwhile because it's incredibly low cost. It's a change in the way you talk about topics that come up in classrooms anyway. That's easy, and students may get a little boost from it.

Don't Forget to Challenge Them

What is growth mindset preparing students for? It's meant to give them a positive attitude about challenging work. So don't forget to challenge them!

Intelligence comes from learning new things. You cannot gain raw processing speed in the mind, but you can learn new facts and new ways of solving problems. Practice will make recall of those facts automatic, and it will help you recognize problems you've solved before when they are dressed in different clothing.

The main way your students will get smarter is by doing more of this work. You've heard "set high expectations" a million times. I hope this chapter has offered a deeper understanding of why that's important. If the work is not ambitious, students are merely treading water.

Tell Them Explicitly That Hard Work Pays Off

Praising process rather than ability sends the unspoken message that intelligence is under the student's control. There is no reason not to make that message explicit as well, especially as children approach upper elementary school. Tell your students how hard famous scientists, inventors, authors, and other "geniuses" must work in order to be so smart; but even more important, make that lesson apply to the work your students do. If some students in your school brag about not studying, explode that myth; tell them that most students who do well in school work quite hard.

Persuading students of that truth may not be easy. I once had a student who was on the football team and devoted a great deal of time to practice, with little time left over for academics. He attributed his poor grades to his being "a dumb jock." I had a conversation with him that went something like this:

DTW Is there a player on the team who has a lot of natural ability but who just doesn't work very hard, goofs off during practices, and that sort of thing?

STUDENT Of course. There's a guy like that on every team.

DTW Do the other players respect him?

STUDENT Of course not. They think he's an idiot because he's got talent that he's not developing.

DTW But don't they respect him because he's the best player?

STUDENT He's not the best. He's good, but lots of other guys are better.

DTW Academics is just the same. Most people have to work really hard at it. There are a few who get by without working very hard, but not many. And nobody likes or respects them very much.

Students should expect that some of the work they do will be hard. It will *feel* hard. That isn't necessarily negative; there can be satisfaction in that sort of hard work, but it feels worse if you're not used to it. Again, an analogy to physical exercise is apt. When you're first trying to get in shape, it's hard to interpret the hard work of exercise as anything other than discomfort. But as you grow more used to it, it takes on a different cast. It's hard, but it's a satisfying type of hard. The people who do well in school are not ones who don't need to work because they are smart. They are the ones who can capture that feeling of satisfaction in hard work, and they probably got that way by pushing past that initial feeling of "bleah, I want to quit."

Treat Failure as a Natural Part of Learning

If you want to increase your intelligence, you have to challenge yourself. That means taking on tasks that are a bit beyond your reach, and that means you may very well fail, at least the first time around. Fear of failure can therefore be a significant obstacle to tackling this sort of work. But failure should not be a big deal.

My first job after college was in the office of a member of Congress. I didn't see the Big Boss very often, and I was pretty intimidated by him. I remember well the first time I did something stupid (I've forgotten what) and it was brought to his attention. I mumbled some apology. He looked at me for a long moment and said, "Kid, the only people who don't make mistakes are the ones who never do anything." It was tremendously freeing – not because I avoided judgment for the incident, but it was the first time I really understood that you have to learn to accept failure if you're ever going to get things done. Basketball great Michael Jordan put it this way: "I've missed more than nine thousand shots in my career. I've lost almost three hundred games. Twenty-six times I've been trusted to take the game-winning shot and missed. I've failed over and over and over again in my life. And that is why I succeed."

Try to create a classroom atmosphere in which failure, although not desirable, is neither embarrassing nor wholly negative. I've been in classrooms where teachers, when they needed to tell a student that he made a mistake, would choose their words carefully, and unconsciously stiffen. If you're uncomfortable when a child makes a mistake, he will likely sense it. This discomfort shows the child that he's done something pretty bad, and you're trying to spare him the embarrassment.

Instead, see how it feels to just be matter of fact about a student mistake. Failure is no fun, but it means you're about to learn something. You're going to find out that there's something you didn't understand or didn't know how to do. Most important, *model* this attitude for your students. When you fail – and who doesn't – let them see you take a positive, learning attitude.

Don't Take Study Skills for Granted

Make a list of all of the things you ask students to do at home. Consider which of these things have other tasks embedded in them and ask yourself whether the struggling students really know how to do them. For older students, if you announce that there will be a quiz, you assume they will study for it. Do your slower students really know how to study? Do they know how to assess the importance of different things they've read and heard and seen? Do they know how long they ought to study for a quiz? (At the college level, my low-performing students frequently protest their low grades by telling me, "But I studied for three or four hours for this test!" I know that the high-scoring students study about 20 hours.) Do your slower students know some simple tricks to help with planning and organizing their time?

These concerns are especially important for students who are just starting to receive serious homework assignments – in many school systems around age 12. There is a period of adjustment for most students when homework is no longer "bring in three rocks from your yard or the park" and turns into "read Chapter 4 and answer the even numbered questions at the back." All students must learn new skills as homework becomes more demanding – skills of self-discipline, time management, and resourcefulness (for example, knowing what to do when they're stumped). Students who are already behind will have that much more trouble doing work on their own at home, and they may be slower to learn these skills.

Don't take for granted that your slower students have these skills, even if they *should* have acquired them in previous grades. I will tell you that by the time they get to me, in college, most of them still don't know very effective ways to complete tasks like reading textbooks, studying for tests, and organizing their schedule. They got to college in spite of their study skills, not because of them.

Catching Up Is the Long-Term Goal

It is important to be realistic about what it will take for students to catch up. In Chapter 2 I pointed out that the more we know, the easier it is to learn new things. Thus, if your slower students know less than your brighter students, they can't simply work at the same pace as the bright students; doing only that, they will continue to fall behind! To catch up, the slower students must work *harder* than the brighter students.

I think of this situation as analogous to dieting. It is difficult to maintain one's willpower for the extended period necessary to reach a target weight. The problem with diets is that they require difficult choices to be made again and again, and each time we make the right choice, we don't get rewarded with the instant weight loss we deserve! When a dieter makes a wrong choice or two, there is a tendency to feel like a failure and then to give up the diet altogether. A great deal of research shows that the most successful diets are *not* diets. Rather, they are lifestyle changes that the person believes he could live with every day for years – for example, switching from regular milk to skim milk, or walking the dog instead of just letting her out in the morning, or drinking black coffee instead of lattes.

When thinking about helping slower students catch up, it may be smart to set interim goals that are achievable and concrete. These goals might include such strategies as devoting a fixed time every day to homework, reading a weekly news magazine, or streaming one documentary on science or history each week. Needless to say, enlisting parents in such efforts, if possible, will be an enormous help.

Thus far we have devoted all of our attention to students' minds, but of course students use tools as well as their minds, and we might ask what impact those tools have on their thinking. That question has had special urgency in the last 10 years as digital technologies have become widely accessible. In the next chapter we'll consider how technology affects students' thinking.

Notes

*The task force was created after *The Bell Curve* was published. *The Bell Curve* was a very controversial 1994 book that claimed, among other things, that observed differences between the races in IQ test scores are largely genetic – in short, that some races are inherently smarter than others. The leadership of the American Psychological Association felt that there was a lot of misinformation about intelligence in the book and in articles published in response to the book. The task force was assembled to create a summary statement describing what was actually known about intelligence.

†The Flynn Effect is slowing or even reversing in some highly developed nations. Researchers interpret these effects too as environmental. See Bratsberg, B., & Rogeberg, O. (2018). Flynn effect and its reversal are both environmentally caused. *Proceedings of the National Academy of Sciences* 115 (26): 6674–6678.

‡This is not to say that some students don't have specific learning disabilities and that some disabilities do not have a large genetic component.

Further Reading

Less Technical

Dweck, C. (2017). *Mindset: Changing the Way You Think to Fulfil Your Potential*. New York: Random House. Carol Dweck's research has been hugely important to psychologists' understanding of the role of one's attitude toward intelligence in learning and in schooling. This book provides a readable, recently updated overview of her work, from the source herself.

Nisbett, R. E. (2010). *Intelligence and How to Get It*. New York: Norton. A summary of the literature on intelligence, getting dated, but still useful, that leans toward downplaying the importance of *g* and highlighting the role of the environment.

Ritchie, S. (2016). *Intelligence: All that Matters*. London: John Murray Learning. A good companion to Nisbett's book, this one also sticks closely to the scientific facts, but with a more *g*-friendly interpretation.

Segal, N. L. (2012). *Born Together—Reared Apart: The Landmark Minnesota Twin Study*. Cambridge, MA: Harvard University Press. This book focuses on a long-running study at the University of Minnesota, the centerpiece of which is 137 pairs of twins who were separated at birth. If you're comfortable with a bit of statistics with your narrative, this is a thorough, reliable treatment of a complicated scientific issue.

Stanovich, K. E. (2009). *What Intelligence Tests Miss*. New Haven, CT: Yale University Press. An attempt to separate intelligence from what's usually called common sense. It's a problem few researchers have taken on, and Stanovich has an interesting take.

More Technical

Carr, P. B., & Dweck, C. S. (2020). Intelligence and motivation. In: *The Cambridge Handbook of Intelligence* (ed. R. Sternberg), 1061–1086. New York: Cambridge University Press. A recent summary of Dweck's theory.

Carroll, J. B. (1993). *Human Cognitive Abilities: A Survey of Factor-Analytic Abilities*. New York: Cambridge University Press. This book reports the results of Carroll's massive review of testing data, the conclusion of which was the hierarchical model of intelligence, with *g* at the pinnacle and increasingly specific abilities as one moves downward.

Kuncel, N. R., & Hezlett, S. A. (2010). Fact and fiction in cognitive ability testing for admissions and hiring decisions. *Current Directions in Psychological Science*, 19(6), 339–345. Article reviewing data showing that standardized cognitive ability tests predict performance in school and the workplace.

Lazar, I., Darlington, R., Murray, H., et al. (1982). Lasting effects of early education: a report from the Consortium for Longitudinal Studies. *Monographs of the Society for Research in Child Development*, 47(2–3), 1–151. One of many studies showing that environmental interventions (such as changes in schooling) can have large effects on cognitive ability.

Maher, B. (2008). The case of the missing heritability. *Nature, Personal Genomes*, 456, 18–21. Often considered the classic paper despairing the failure to translate the heritability observed in twin studies to straightforward biological pathways.

Neisser, U., Boodoo, G., Bouchard, T. J., et al. (1996). Intelligence: knowns and unknowns. *American Psychologist*, 51(2), 77–101. The American Psychological Association Task Force's statement on intelligence; among other things, provides a generally accepted definition of the construct.

Plomin, R., & von Stumm, S. (2018). The new genetics of intelligence. *Nature Reviews Genetics*, 19, 148–159. Robert Plomin remains one of the more high-profile advocates of the idea that a substantial portion of intelligence is inherited.

Yeager, D. S., Romero, C., Paunesku, D., et al. (2016). Using design thinking to improve psychological interventions: the case of the growth mindset during the transition to high school. *Journal of Educational Psychology, 108*(3), 374–391. It's common for interventions to work in a few classrooms, then fail when they are scaled up. This paper formalizes a method to address the problem, and showed success in a growth mindset intervention with more than 3000 students.

Yeager, D. S., & Walton, G. M. (2011). Social-psychological interventions in education: they're not magic. *Review of Educational Research, 81*(2), 267–301. Very influential article exploring why certain very brief interventions might be expected to influence long-term outcomes like grade point average and persistence in school.

Discussion Questions

1. Think about your students who struggle the most in school. Some may simply see themselves as not all that smart, whereas others may figure that they are not smart in the way that school values, but they have common sense or something similar. Where are these students successful outside of school? In what way do those activities draw on intelligence? Do you think these students actually do have the kinds of smarts that could allow them to do well in school? If so, how could you convince them of that?

2. It's important to note that this chapter has made an assumption about the values of schooling. The view of intelligence presented is closely tied to IQ. It's no accident that IQ is closely tied to schooling; IQ started as a test to predict how well young children would fare in school. Hence, it's unsurprising that doing more of the sorts of work that typically happen in school would make you smarter . . . by that definition of intelligence. It's a pretty mainstream way to view intelligence, but it may be a *less* mainstream way to view school. Some families think school should prepare children for practical life. Some think school should maximize their potential. Would this change how we think about growing intelligence in their children?

3. It's important to communicate to children that intelligence is malleable, but that may not be what they are hearing at home. How can we get parents on board with this message?

4. If culture can make us all smarter, how can we advocate to make that happen? On the one hand, there are instance of government-funded cultural innovations that research has shown really do make kids smarter – the television program *Sesame Street* is an example. You might imagine similar efforts in video gaming, movies, and smartphone apps. On the other hand, government dollars going to such efforts makes some people uneasy. What's your take?

5. As noted in this chapter, one account for the Flynn effect is that intelligence increases when the culture becomes more cognitively challenging, as when, for example, there are more information-economy jobs that present ever-changing problems to employees. Could you imagine a reversal of this trend as digital tools become more sophisticated? For example, it's already known that when people use a GPS, they don't learn a city's layout. Could more and more digital tools free us from cognitive work, and so perhaps make us a bit dumber?

6. Beliefs about someone's intelligence can certainly prejudice how we view their achievements. For example, a few years into my teaching I started grading examination essays without knowing the author's name, and found that, once I matched names with essay grades, I was frequently surprised by the quality of a particular student's essay. What struck me was that I was *more often* surprised when I graded this way, which led me to think that what I thought I knew about a student was probably influencing how I graded their work. It made me suspect that my beliefs were influencing how I interacted with students in class as well. It's not possible to refrain from having beliefs about students; where might they leak into your teaching? What can you do about it?

9

How Can I Know Whether New Technology Will Improve Student Learning?

Question: If you're a teacher with five or more years of experience, you've probably heard at least one of the following:

- "We're going one-to-one with iPads."

- "All your kids should be microblogging."

- "We're putting an interactive whiteboard in your classroom. Here's the manual."

- "Coding is the new math."

- "We're getting a 3D printer. Everyone think about what you will do with it."

- "Have you considered flipping your classroom?"

Teachers have understandably grown wary of each "next big thing" in ed tech. But the power of technology to improve our lives is undeniable. How do you know which claims are legitimate?

nswer: the principle that guides this chapter is:

> Technology changes everything . . . but not the way you think.

In this chapter we look at cognition in a different way. We've been examining individual mental processes – working memory, learning, or attention, for example – and then we've tried to put that knowledge to work with sensible classroom actions. Considering technology in education works in reverse; you start with the classroom action, like giving your students a laptop, or putting homework on a cloud-based platform, and try to anticipate the cognitive consequences.

Because we're starting with actions rather than mental processes, we *could* simply test the effectiveness of the action; for example, identify 20 classrooms where students will be given a laptop and 20 comparable classrooms where they won't, then in six months compare students' learning (or motivation, or attitudes, or whatever was hypothesized would change). There's no need to understand how it affects students' mental processes, because ultimately, the laptops help or they don't. That's what we want to know.

And for innovations that have already been tried, that approach is fine. But tech innovations pop up continuously, and sometimes we need a sense of whether one is likely to help *before* we adopt it. Can we discern a pattern for which innovations have worked in the past and which haven't?

We tend to *think* we can. We look at the proposed intervention and think to ourselves "students will do *this* with it, and that will affect learning in *that* way . . ." These guesses are sometimes so intuitive they can seem *obviously* right, so much so that they don't even feel like guesses. But of course, they can be wrong, especially because an intervention like "go one-to-one with laptops" changes *lots* of mental processes, and all those changes are hard to anticipate. This problem is the source of much mischief in ed tech.

The principle guiding this chapter –"Technology changes everything . . . but not the way you think" – has two meanings. It means tech changes lots of cognitive processes, but not necessarily the way you'd predict. It also refers to a common exclamation you've probably heard: "Technology has changed everything!" So it has, but it hasn't changed the way you think, that is, the way your mind works. And that's where we begin.

This Changes Everything, 1.0:
Your Brain on Tech

My youngest daughter is 13 and she often plays the role of IT consultant to my wife and me. Recently my iPhone couldn't connect to our home network, and I didn't spend 30 seconds trying to figure out why. I called IT support. (That is, I yelled upstairs.) Most adults with a child over 10 can relate. Kids today seem to have a sixth sense for technology.

Except it turns out they don't.

The idea that today's generation are tech wizards is itself about a generation old. It was popularized in a 2001 article by Marc Prensky, in which he used the terms Digital Native and Digital Immigrant.[1] The former represented children who grew up with digital technologies and therefore "spoke the language" like a native. Adults, in contrast, might use tech tools but would never feel as comfortable doing so as Digital Natives do. Prensky characterized this difference as reflecting deep changes in the way children think:

> *"It is now clear that, as a result of this ubiquitous environment and the sheer volume of their interaction with it, today's students think and process information fundamentally differently from their predecessors. These differences go far further and deeper than most educators suspect or realize."*

It sounds plausible, but experiments don't support the idea. For example, in 2006, researchers asked students entering the University of Melbourne about how they use technology. They found that students were very comfortable with a small set of tools used in a limited number of ways. For example, the students could search for information on Google, but most had never logged into a social network, even though MySpace was at its peak at this time, signing 200 000 new users each day.[2]

Other research has shown parallel findings with teachers. For example, in one study researchers asked Finnish first-year student teachers born between 1984 and 1989 (thus meeting the definition of digital native) to create a lesson that made effective use of information and communication technology.[3] The lessons commonly used tools for information gathering and presentation but not for communicating with peers, sharing, or creating content, exactly the next-generation skills that are supposed to be second nature to digital natives.

Comfort with tech comes from your context, not your generation. Teens are motivated to understand and use platforms and devices used by their friends, and those friends are usually willing tutors. Some kids grow interested in tech tools, but most stop where my daughter has stopped; she is an adept deployer of iPhone tricks and Instagram hacks and a solid user of the tools required by her school.

The Digital Native idea posits a positive (or at least, neutral) change to kids' brains. Others have suggested a negative change, particularly to attention. They point out that digital devices usually call for rapid shifts of attention. Web articles invite scanning rather than reading. People multitask, with several apps open at once. Action video games demand frequent shifts of attention, and television programs offer quicker cuts and accelerated dialogue compared to 25 years ago. According to the argument, this rapid shifting of attention becomes habitual, rendering students unable to focus attention for extended periods.

Again, the idea sounds plausible, especially when you consider the time kids spend on screen-based activities. A 2019 survey put time per-day averages at nearly five hours for tweens and over seven hours for teens.[4]

Yet all this exposure is probably not deep-frying teens' brains. If it were, you'd see consequences far beyond the ability to pay attention. Inability to focus would affect reading, math, problem solving, reasoning . . . most any high-level thinking process you can name. Yes, the brain is plastic, it's open to change. But there must be limits to that change, and it seems improbable that something so central to thinking as attention could change so profoundly.

More important, there are data indicating attention hasn't changed. Some measures of attention have been administered to large groups of participants over decades, and the outcomes today are similar to those observed before the advent of the digital age (Figure 9.1).

There's a third common guess about the way digital technologies have affected children's cognition: the extensive practice in doing several things at once has made them adept at multitasking; in fact, they work best that way. Adults often tell kids not to multitask; do one thing at a time, focus on your work! But we think that's best because *we* are not good at multitasking, and we're not good at it because we didn't grow up doing it. So the argument goes.

There's a grain of truth here. Young people are better at multitasking than old people. But it's not because they have practiced it more. Rather, people with larger working memory capacity are bet-

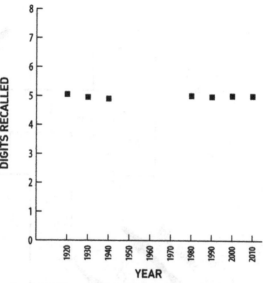

FIGURE 9.1: In the backward digit span task, subjects hear a list of digits, for example, "seven, three, one," and then must repeat them backwards. If they answer correctly, the number of digits increases by one, and the process continues until they make a set number of mistakes. As the graph shows, the average number of digits people can repeat is about five. Importantly, that average hasn't changed over the years. Source: From "The magical numbers 7 and 4 are resistant to the Flynn effect: No evidence for increases in forward or backward recall across 85 years of data" by G. E. Gignac in *Intelligence* 48: 85-95. Copyright © 2015. Reprinted with permission from Elsevier.

ter at multitasking, and working memory capacity peaks in one's early twenties and declines thereafter. But doing a lot of multitasking doesn't make you generally good at multitasking. If anything, students who multitask a lot might be slightly worse at regulating their attention than students who multitask infrequently.

And people (young or old) who say "you'll do better if you concentrate on one thing at a time" are right. The reason may not be intuitive; it's that you can't really share attention between tasks. It may feel like you are, but you're actually switching attention between them.

In a classic experiment (Figure 9.2), subjects viewed a digit-letter pair, for example, "W6." The stimulus appeared in one of four

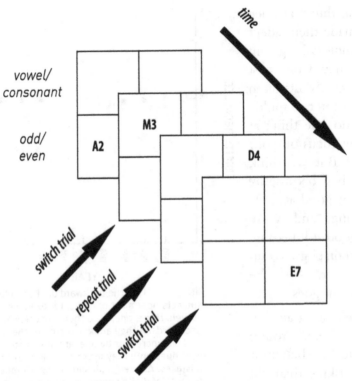

FIGURE 9.2: A typical experiment testing task switching.
Source: © Greg Culley.

quadrants. If it appeared in the top row, the subject was to pay attention to the letter (and classify it as a vowel or consonant). If it appeared in the bottom row, the subject was to pay attention to the digit (and classify it as odd or even).[5] After the participant responded, there'd be a new digit-letter pair that would appear in a new quadrant. When the classification task switched (for example, the participant had just done the odd-even task and now had to do the vowel-consonant task), response times were about 20% slower than if the task was repeated.

Switching tasks requires extra mental steps: resetting your goal ("ignore the digit, attend to the letter") and remembering the rule ("if it's a vowel press the left button, if a consonant press the right"). What's especially interesting about this experiment is that you'd think you'd be able to keep both rules in mind at the same time. That's the heart of multitasking: keeping two things in mind at once and doing both of them. But you can't keep two tasks in mind simultaneously, even when each is very simple.

So when a student texts with her friend while she works on her paper analyzing August Wilson's *Fences*, she is doing a lot of switching. Just as the letter-digit task called for resetting the goal each time there's a switch, so too this multitasking student will switch her train of thought, the formality of what she's writing, and the way she'll type it.

But what if the student is only *sort of* multitasking? Often a student will have the television on as she works, or music playing, and will say, "I'm not even paying attention; it's just background noise."

Experiments consistently show a decrement in reading or other cognitive work when a television is playing, even if students claim they are ignoring it – they are distracted by it, at least every now and then. Music, however, has more complicated effects. Music is distracting, and switching attention between music and work will incur a cost. But music is also energizing and provides an emotional lift. That's why people listen to music when they exercise, and music was once commonly played on factory assembly lines. This trade-off means that the research literature on multitasking with music is mixed: it sometimes seems to improve performance, or degrade it, or have no effect. It all depends on the balance of the energizing benefit and the distracting cost of the music.

This Changes Everything, 2.0: Your Classroom on Tech

When I was about 10, I loved maps, or more exactly, I loved being charged by my parents to monitor a map on family vacations, to ensure that the driver missed no turns. I overestimated the weight of my responsibility, as our long-distance trips usually meant hours on a single interstate highway, but even today, it seems a piloting of a sort. That small pleasure is gone now, of course, as a disembodied lady-in-a-box issues commands to direct us.

It's hard to remember how surprising it was when paper maps were made obsolete in the mid 2000s. Around the same time, digital cameras became the norm, and the little kiosks where you'd drop off your film one day and pick up prints the next began to disappear (Figure 9.3). So too went phone calls to travel agents once you could book your own plane tickets online.

Photography, maps, and travel were three common mid-2000s examples of digital technology upending an industry. Pundits offered an analogy to education that was vague, but ominous: technology will make classrooms unrecognizable, and if you're a teacher you may well be made obsolete. Embracing tech was usually offered as the best preparation for the inevitable.

Until the revolution, students would benefit in small ways from current technology. The advantages new devices would bring to learning seemed so obvious as to require little elaboration. If every classroom had an interactive whiteboard,* for example, the physics teacher could show 3D simulations, the music teacher could show YoYo Ma's bowing technique, and the math teacher could have three children work on the same problem at the board simultaneously, with automated feedback. Britain bet big on

 FIGURE 9.3: A typical Fotomat kiosk. At its peak, there were more than 4000 Fotomats in the United States, and they were, of course, not the only place to get film developed. The rapid demise of film photography was a dramatic, if narrow, change in daily life. Source: Wikimedia author anonymous. http:// wikimedia.org/wiki/File:This_is_a_typical_drive-up_Fotomat_booth.jpg (accessed 24 July 2020) (CC BY-SA 3.0) https://creativecommons.org/licenses/ by-sa/3.0/deed.en

interactive whiteboards and by 2007 close to 100% of schools had at least one.

Around the same time, districts, states, and even countries (Google "Uruguay OLPC") decided to give each student a laptop computer. Again, the benefits seemed self-evident and beyond question. With a laptop, students could access an amazing array of research content. They could collaborate through the cloud. They could read electronic textbooks that would be updated frequently and could integrate video and audio into the reading experience.

But the initiatives to provide interactive whiteboards or laptops didn't improve student learning. Surveys of teachers revealed one reason that probably should have been anticipated. Professional development was far too brief, and teachers varied in their comfort with the new tech. In addition, creating new lessons that really exploit the capabilities of these technologies is not a simple matter. Children may have shown little benefit because teaching didn't change that much.

More recent evaluations offer a brighter picture – greater use of digital technologies in classrooms is associated with a modest increase in student learning – and the ready interpretation is that school systems and jurisdictions figured out that it was a losing strategy to simply drop tech into schools and wait for the magic to happen. Educators today are getting more time and training to learn the tools, and some better off-the-shelf products are available.

Perhaps more important, we may be seeing a shift in expectations. Even in the early 2000s, some researchers were emphasizing that measures of success should be more fine-grained than something like a standardized achievement test in reading or math, because technologies vary in what they make easier or more effective.[6] For example, laptops make it easier for teachers to offer feedback on writing, for teachers to communicate with students and their parents, and for students to collaborate. Interactive whiteboards do none of those things but offer teachers access to better visualization tools and a new set of opportunities for a class to work as a team.

So a more modest claim seems supportable: new technologies don't change everything, and they don't help "learning"; they help some aspect of learning. That perspective squares well with the cognitive analysis in this book. We've been addressing topics like attention and engagement (Chapter 1), learning (Chapter 3), comprehension (Chapter 4), practice (Chapter 5), and critical thinking (Chapter 6). The benefit of considering one mental process at a time is that it's a simpler, more modest goal.

But there's a disadvantage. You may learn something about attention, but when you change a classroom practice to exploit what you've learned, you affect the whole child, not just the single mental process you hope to target. You may affect motivation, for example, in some way you didn't anticipate.

To be sure, sometimes you try to affect just one cognitive process and you succeed. For example, spaced repetition software is designed to capitalize on the spacing effect described in Chapter 5, and a number of products seem to deliver on that promise.[7] Document cameras (also called visualizers) likewise set a limited but useful goal: allow everyone in a class to see. The entire class can watch the instructor as she shows a shading technique as she draws, or the enhanced image of a moth's wing, or watch a peer demonstrate a novel handwriting style (Figure 9.4).

Consider how you'd assess the value of a visualizer. You don't expect test scores to rise because you put one in the classroom. The thinking is more "We have a limited number of microscopes, so kids line up to see a hydra (or whatever), and some aren't sure of what they're looking for, so they don't even know whether they've seen it. With a classroom camera they can all see the same thing at once." Yes, you expect it to help kids learn, but the effect is so distant from a standardized test you don't expect to see the effect there. More simply put, you don't need research to tell whether it's fulfilling your expectations.

So the tentative answer to the question "How can I know whether new technology will improve student learning?" seems to be "Tools that improve one cognitive process will lead to more predictable outcomes than complex tools that influence a lot of cognitive processes." That's a start, but it's not quite that simple.

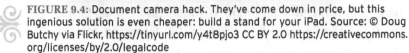

FIGURE 9.4: Document camera hack. They've come down in price, but this ingenious solution is even cheaper: build a stand for your iPad. Source: © Doug Butchy via Flickr, https://tinyurl.com/y4t8pjo3 CC BY 2.0 https://creativecommons.org/licenses/by/2.0/legalcode

This Changes More Than I Expected

Predicting how new technology will interact with the human mind is harder than it sounds. I'll describe three cases from the last 20 years in which predictions were disconfirmed.

First, consider electronic books. E-books are an enormous success, even surpassing print books in sales for a time, although they now lag again.[†] Surprisingly, comprehension when reading on a screen is slightly worse than comprehension when reading paper, especially for nonfiction. The difference is so slight you probably wouldn't notice; you'll still enjoy your Ron Chernow biography if you bring your Kindle on the plane instead of a paperback.

That conclusion changes when we consider textbooks, however. Students find reading e-textbooks harder than reading print, likely because they differ from leisure books. The content is more challenging. We read textbooks for a different purpose (learning, not entertainment) and textbooks are organized by themes, rather than as a narrative. It's not clear how important each difference is, but for whatever reason, the seemingly small change in technology makes a surprisingly large change in cognition.

Here's a second example of a new technology that *seems* to fulfill one narrow cognitive need, and yet doesn't fulfill it quite as we expect. Perhaps the hallmark of the Internet is speedy access to limitless information. That invites the question "why should you memorize anything? You can just look it up" (Figure 9.5).

Indeed you can, but when it comes to providing information for cognitive processing, your brain beats Google in important ways. First, stopping your reading to look something up – the definition of *yegg*, say – is disruptive. It's easy to lose the thread of what you're reading. For that reason, people don't have a lot of patience for this sort of work. It's true that Google is a lot faster than looking things up in books – you're talking about seconds to find an answer, rather than minutes. But your brain is much faster than Google. It takes much less than a second to provide the definition of a word.

The second reason you need the information in your memory is even more important. Your brain is *much* more sensitive to context than Google is. Here's what I mean. Recall this sentence from Chapter 2: "I shouldn't use my new barbecue when the boss comes

 FIGURE 9.5: Why should you commit, say, the quadratic equation, to memory? In 2016, Jonathan Rochelle, director of Google Education Apps at the time, said at an industry conference, "I don't know why [my children] can't ask Google for the answer if the answer is right there."[8] Source: © Getty Images.

to dinner." It made you think of the fact that people aren't always successful in using a new appliance. But suppose the sentence had been "I shouldn't use my new barbecue with this messy brown sugar glaze." Now you'd think of a different characteristic of new appliances: not that people make mistakes when they first use them, but that people like to keep them clean. Or suppose the sentence had read "I shouldn't use my new barbecue until Rob can come over and watch me use his gift." Or "I shouldn't use my new barbecue until I get a different coupling for the gas line." Each sentence draws on different knowledge you have in memory about new appliances: it takes practice to use them properly, people like to keep them nice, people like to show them off, sometimes they require new accessories.

You know a lot about new appliances, but your mind doesn't throw all that information at you when you're reading. Outside of your awareness, the mind selects the right bit of information, given the context, that will help you make sense of what you're reading. Google can't do that. If you were confused by the first sentence and Google "new barbecue," you know quite well what would happen. You'd get millions of hits, and it would be a long, long time before you came on the right information to fill the gap left by the writer.

Our third example of a tech change that seems straightforward but turns out to be complex is the taking of classroom notes with a laptop. This one is slightly different than our previous examples in that the target cognitive process is affected as we'd predict, but the technology affects other cognitive processes as well. Students take notes in classes with laptops because they expect that they can type faster than they write and that they can edit their notes later more easily. They're right about that.[‡]

But students who take notes on a laptop are distracted by the easy availability of the Internet. Snapchat, Pinterest, Zappos – whatever their Internet drug, a hit is just a click away, and that's hard to resist. A few years ago I had a student who admitted to watching YouTube videos during my class "when lecture gets boring." I asked him how he knew when to listen again. Unfazed, he said, "When you

FIGURE 9.6: Even teachers who discourage students from taking note on laptops must remember that for some students, a laptop is assistive technology. To minimize any embarrassment for students, when I go over my policy at the start of the year, I also say that any student who feels this policy is a bad fit for them should come talk to me, and if it makes sense for them to use a laptop, they will. That way peers don't know the reason a peer uses a laptop unless they choose to reveal it. Source: © Getty Images/picture alliance.

get interesting again." So I think having students take notes on a laptop typically isn't worth it (Figure 9.6).

I've heard the counter-argument "Well, sure it's distracting, but that's the world we live in. They need to learn how to resist distraction." This argument is wrong in two ways. First, it aspires to an incredibly difficult standard of resisting distraction; teens are not as good as adults are at controlling impulses, and teens are hypersocial. So social media is a terrible temptation. And come to that, *adults* often don't meet that standard; how often have you been in a meeting and observed others answering e-mail or shopping? (See Figure 9.7.)

Second, psychologists will tell you that the smart way to resist temptation is to change the environment. If you're trying to lose weight, it's stupid to say to yourself, "I must learn to resist the cookies in the cupboard." Just don't buy cookies.

Let me emphasize, my intention is *not* to bash tech tools. I could add many other positive examples to those mentioned, especially assistive tech: closed captioning to allow people with hearing difficulties to watch video, speech-to-text software to enable those with limited motor skills to type, text-to-speech to enable those with limited vision to read, voice recognition, screen enlargers, page turners, background noise masks, talking calculators, and more. These tools render a cognitive process unnecessary or support one that poses a problem and can be a game changer for students and for adults.

My point is that the cognitive outcomes associated with even simple tech tools can surprise you. I think that's been a real problem in the adoption of new technologies. The advantages seem so obvious but then later are not realized, so everyone feels cheated. Be cautious, and believe the benefits when you see them.

FIGURE 9.7: Connie Bernard, a member of the Baton Rouge, Louisiana, school board, made national headlines in 2020 when she was caught shopping during a meeting. That would have been bad enough, but at the time, community members were addressing the board regarding whether to change the name of Robert E. Lee high school to honor someone who better reflected the values of the community. Source: via YouTube, © Gary Chambers Jr.

Tech Changes the Ecosystem

We've considered two ways that technology might "change everything": first, by changing kids' very thought processes (for example, by degrading their attention spans), and second by yielding a product or tool that upends the way we think about learning. Neither has borne out. Instead, tech seems to have produced modest changes to a number of narrower tasks or parts of a task. But if this change supports a cognitive process that's especially troublesome for the student, the benefit to that student may be substantial.

Even if changes brought by tech tools are usually small, there are many such tools, and they affect many areas of children's lives. Tech influences how students socialize, how they eat, how they learn, how they entertain themselves, and more. Perhaps educators should know about and somehow account for the way technology has changed how kids *live*.

Let's consider the nature of that change. In the United States, children's screen time increased steadily until 2015 and then leveled off, probably because access to devices became nearly universal; smartphones became cheap enough that most teens had one. As I've noted, average daily screen time remains high, at just under five hours per day for 8–12 year-olds, and somewhat over seven hours per day for 13–18 year-olds. What are kids doing for those hours each day?

You may remember the optimism of the early 2000s, when high-speed Internet became broadly available in wealthy countries, enabling many kids to access the Internet at home. People who cared about education thought we might be poised for a learning explosion, and given certain assumptions, the prediction made sense. If you believe that children are naturally curious and want to learn, and you believe that schools don't satisfy this curiosity because they regiment what kids must study, then it was natural to suppose that the availability of the Internet meant that kids would finally be able to explore their interests.

That didn't happen because, as described in Chapter 1, humans *are* naturally curious, but curiosity is fragile and evaporates if the conditions aren't right. It's harder to satisfy your curiosity about challenging subjects (for example, European history) because you don't know where to look and because many of the information sources are not artfully designed to maintain your interest. Other content – like social media, vlogs, video games, and infotainment websites like Buzzfeed – are cunningly crafted for quick-fix fun.

As a result, broad Internet access did not lead to a flowering of self-education. Teens spend about 30% of their screen time texting, 25% on video content, 18% on gaming, 5% on video chat, and 18% on various other Internet websites (most of which is likely social media).[9] In other words, kids today are doing with tech more or less what I did at their age without it. Goofing off with their friends.

So has all that screen time with this brew of content had any impact on kids?

Let me be clear that I'm excluding compulsive use of the Internet. Experts disagree on whether there's a classifiable disorder we should call Internet addiction, but some people do show behavior and feelings that are typical of addiction. They use the Internet nearly constantly, they feel guilty about it, their relationships suffer because of their compulsion, they suffer withdrawal if they can't access the Internet, and so on. The study of compulsive Internet use is still in its infancy, but there is good reason to be concerned that it does indeed carry negative consequences for mental health, emotion regulation, and social relationships.

What about someone we wouldn't call an addict, but who, like the typical teen, logs a lot of screen time?

There was a scare in the late 2010s when researchers noticed that the rapid rise in teens' use of social media was accompanied by a rapid rise in depression, anxiety, and suicide. But at the time of this writing, follow-up work indicates that the association was extremely small or possibly absent, once other risk factors were taken into account. Furthermore, although online bullying can certainly be a problem, it is much more common for the character of offline interactions to transfer online. It's usually friends interacting (arranging to meet, discussing common concerns, and so on) and they are usually pleasant to one another.[8]

So although the screen time activities kids pick in their leisure time may not be doing much for them, there's little evidence it is doing much to them. Most of them use tech for the stuff that teens are keenly interested in, which hasn't markedly changed.

But perhaps there's an opportunity cost. That is, if kids weren't online, maybe they'd be doing something beneficial, so online time prevents their gaining that benefit.

One opportunity cost is easy to appreciate: loss of sleep. Kids who take mobile phones or tablets to their bedrooms in the evening sleep less and have lower quality sleep than kids who don't. It's easy to appreciate both because it's logical – we expect kids would rather text with their friends or play a game than go to sleep – but it's also similar to older research showing that kids lose sleep if they play console video games or watch television before bed.

Other observers have worried that screen time has replaced reading as a leisure activity. With so much time soaked up by tech, how much time is left in the day? Indeed, some surveys indicate a reduction in reading in the last 20 years, both among adults[10] and children.[11] Of course, it could be that some factor other than increased use of digital devices contributed to this decline in reading. One indication that's true is that some research shows the reading decline reaches back to the late 1970s, before the onset of the digital age.[12]

Another problem with the "tech is killing reading" hypothesis is that most studies use a less-than-ideal method; people are simply asked about their reading habits. "How much do you read in a typical week?" or "How many books did you read last year?" People may see "I never read" as a socially undesirable answer and so inflate their estimate. The apparent decline in reading over the years may be due to fewer people in the general population worrying about the social acceptability of admitting they don't read.

A better method is employed by the American Time Use Survey, which asks people to keep a diary of all their activities.[13] Because it's a daily diary, memory is less of a problem, and in addition, people would be less reluctant to say, "I didn't read at all today," because, after all, even a regular reader might not happen not to read on any given day.

The American Time Use Survey points to two important conclusions (Figure 9.8).

First, there has been a decline in leisure reading since 2003 (the first year that data were collected) but the decline is not observed among supposedly tech-addled teens. It's older people who are reading less. Second, there hasn't been much of a chance to observe a decline in reading among kids, because kids do so little reading in the first place.

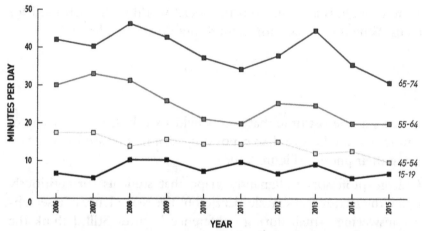

FIGURE 9.8: Data showing how much the average American (of different ages) reads each day and how that figure has changed across years. Source: © Greg Cully, data assembled by Daniel Willingham from American Time Use Survey, https://www.bls.gov/tus#

So to sum up this section, Internet compulsion is bad, and taking mobile devices to bed is bad. But there's not much data revealing a general problem caused by typical teen screen time.

And yet I admit I'm uncomfortable with the amount of screen time the average teen logs. First, as I noted, screen time hasn't cut into reading because when digital devices became commonplace, teens weren't reading, so reading time couldn't decline. If there's any hope of that changing, teens need some breathing room in their out-of-school hours. If every moment is consumed with videos, gaming, texting, and the rest, reading, exercise, volunteer work, or any other activity cannot gain a toehold.

Second, the fact that teens are online so much means that peer influence is ever present. I'll put it this way. I was a typical teen in that I was obsessed with my relationships (and lack of relationships) with my peers, and that led to emotional highs and lows each school day. But when I got home my world mostly narrowed to my parents and siblings. I might stew a bit about that day's social triumphs and defeats, but I would usually engage with my family. When teens are constantly online, there's no break from the social world; I just don't think that's good. Family time matters.

Why, though, is a break from the social world such a hard sell for teens? Why is it so hard for them to put down the phone?

Why Are They So Frantic About Their Phones?

When was the last time that you beheld a work of art or a scene of nature that was beautiful, so captivating, that no one around you was using their phone? (Figure 9.9).

College professors indignantly gripe that students surreptitiously text if the lecture lacks razzle-dazzle, but I've seen plenty of researchers answering e-mail during conference lectures. Still, I think the hunger to stay online may be more extreme in teens than in adults. If you're an educator or a parent, you can't help but notice that teens' passion for connection interrupts other activities. What's behind it?

A few factors contribute. First, humans are seekers of information. As described in Chapter 1, curiosity is aroused when we judge that there is something in the environment to be learned, and a mobile phone notification is an extremely clear signal that there's something to learn. Whether it's a new like, Instagram post, or text message, you can be certain it's novel and relevant to *you*. Now of course that doesn't mean that you're

FIGURE 9.9: This photo of a woman texting in front of the Shwedagon pagoda is staged, but I'm sure you've witnessed similar scenes. I've seen people texting at the top of the CN tower and at the foot of Niagara Falls. Source: © Getty Image/EyesWideOpen.

going to think it's especially interesting or important once viewed. It's testimony to the power of our bias to seek information that, even though we know notifications usually signal something trivial, we still want to investigate them.

This compulsion will be more powerful in teens, because phone notifications often carry social information, and teens are hyper-social. Although adults usually think teens care about their peers' opinion more than they should, psychologists have suggested it's a feature, not a bug.[14] Teens are obsessed with their peers because they are approaching the age when they must separate from their parents. Close study of their peers is the method by which they learn to navigate the world outside their home.

But there's another way that "urgent" takes on special meaning for teens. Follow me through a thought experiment described in Figure 9.10.

Rewards have more value when we contemplate getting them right away. When we anticipate getting something in the future, it has less reward value. That's why it's easier to turn down ice cream that you don't anticipate eating for hours, compared to a bowl you can eat seconds later.

FIGURE 9.10: Imagine you're at the grocery store and you spy chocolate chip ice cream, your favorite, and you think, "What a nice dessert that would make tonight!" But you remember that your doctor told you to avoid fatty foods, so you must resist buying the ice cream. Now imagine that you're at home and you've just finished supper. Your spouse brings a bowl of ice cream to the table and says, "How thoughtless of me. I got myself ice cream and didn't ask if you wanted dessert. Would you like this bowl?" In which situation is it harder to resist the ice cream? Source: Freezer © Getty Images/Jamie Squire; bowl ©Shutterstock/http://Photobank.kiev.ua/Slavica Stajic.

You can imagine, then, a curve with a downward slope, show-ing how the value of a reward declines as it moves into the future (Figure 9.11). This slope is steeper for children than it is for adults; rewards lose value more rapidly for kids. Early elementary teachers learn this lesson the first time they tell their class, "If everyone is well behaved this week, we'll have a pizza party on Friday." A pizza party is great fun for a first-grader if it's happening *now*; if it's happening a few days from now, it's about as exciting as being told some other kid is having a pizza party. In Paris.

When we're frustrated that teens are glued to their phones, we often suggest that they put the phone away and check it every two hours or so. But now you can see why that strategy doesn't appeal to them. It's like showing them a bowl of ice cream and suggesting they set it aside for a couple of hours, instead of eating it now.

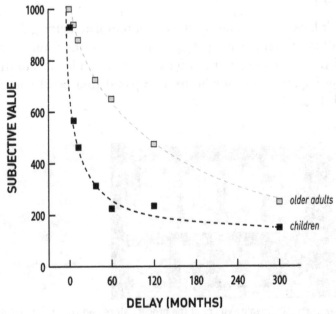

FIGURE 9.11: The experimenter might ask, "Would you rather have $200 a month from now, or $1000 a year from now?" By posing many such questions (using different dollar amounts and times), the researcher can work out how valuable money seems at different points in the future. As you can see, as the prospect of getting money moves further in the future, it loses value. But that loss is much more rapid for children than older adults. Source: From "Discounting of Delayed Rewards Across the Life Span: Age Differences in Individual Discounting Functions," by L. Green, J. Myerson, and P. Ostaszewski, in *Behavioral Processes* 46: 89-96. Copyright © 1999. Reprinted with permission from Elsevier.

But there's still another aspect to the value of new text messages and TikToks. Note that in the ice cream example, the ice cream is objectively just as valuable at noon or in the evening – the psychological value differs, but it's still delicious ice cream at both times. But social information changes value with time. It's perishable. The gossip that I'm dying to tell you now – Gina posted something terrible about Olivia on her feed, here's the link, you won't believe it – will be much less interesting in just a few hours, partly because everyone will know, and partly because it will have been replaced by fresh news.

So to recap, everyone – teens and adults – is primed to check their phones, because they know that it offers new information that is likely to be personally relevant. This tendency is amplified in teens because (i) the information tends to be social, and teens are especially interested in social information; (ii) delaying rewards is difficult for anyone, but it's even harder for teens than for adults; and (iii) social information is often perishable, further exaggerating the difference in value between checking one's phone now and checking it later.

Summary

This chapter reviewed data that indicate that the changes wrought by new technologies are more modest than most predicted they would be. First, your brain is plastic and changes with experience, but the fundamental architecture of the mind is probably not open to change, so tech has not "changed the way today's kids think," for better or for worse. Second, technology has not made over education entirely as some predicted would happen. Third, the smaller ways that tech changes cognition are hard to anticipate; changes that seem like they should affect cognition little, if at all (e.g., reading from a screen instead of paper) sometimes have consequential effects on student learning and emotion. Fourth, the broader idea that being immersed in tech will have noticeable effects on children's lives seems not to have materialized either for good (kids routinely using the Internet for self-education) or ill (increasing rates of anxiety and depression). The most noticeable change seems to be that teens today (and many adults) really love their phones.

Implications for the Classroom

In other chapters we focused on what a cognitive analysis implied for classroom practice. But the prominent role technology plays in students' lives outside of school means that educators will want to think not just of what tech means at school but what it means at home. Most of the educators I know respect parents' autonomy in this matter, of course, but also feel that teachers have a responsibility to let parents know about the in-school consequences of their at-home decisions. Hence, I'll comment on both school-based and home-based recommendations.

Equity

Equity takes on a different cast where technology is concerned. It's more than assessing whether all students have equivalent access to similar digital equipment and opportunities to learn at school; it's a recognition that "home" plays a significant role in tech learning, in two ways.

First, there's a hardware issue. Ten years ago, this concern was described as "the digital divide"; wealthy children had access to computers at home whereas poorer children often did not. Today, schools are sometimes able to provide laptops or tablets for students. That's helpful, of course, but the digital divide remains in the form of Internet access at home; poor families may have slow or unreliable Internet access or none at all, and be forced to seek public Wi-Fi. Ideally, schools issuing hardware will choose devices with enough internal memory to store programs and files and to choose software that is not cloud based. Teachers should also strive to assign homework that does not require Internet access. An alternative is for schools to lease wireless hotspots that students can check out and take home.

Second, there's a curriculum issue. If wealthy children have easy access to digital devices at home, won't they gain a comfort with technology that poor children will lack? Given that so many jobs require comfort with technology as a matter of course, doesn't that represent a terrible disadvantage for poor kids? I think this issue is very important, but we should be also be aware of opportunity costs.

As we've seen, most kids are not learning anything very high level in their leisure screen time. But certainly they learn to navigate one or more operating systems and some common applications, and they learn conventions that apply across platforms like hierarchical file structures. It seems crucial that those who do not get that experience at home get it at school.

But it doesn't make sense to address the digital divide by offering classes in programming or other technical subjects. Wealthy kids are not learning that content at home, and there's a potential opportunity cost; what's being cut to make time for programming? And although an employer would expect that any employee can navigate Windows, they would likely be understanding of an employee who didn't know the difference between an object-oriented and a relational database. It's routine to hire employees who lack narrow technical expertise – or whose technical expertise has grown dated – with the idea that they will take a class to bolster their skills. Hiring employees who lack skills in reading, writing, or math is not routine.

Adoption of Tech Products

About 10 years ago I was chatting with a professor of educational technology when a light suddenly flashed in his eyes. "Oh! I want you to look at this!" It was an early model of a pen that created an audio recording as you wrote. The notebook paper looked ordinary, but it enabled the user to easily coordinate between the written notes and recording – hence, if you were looking over your class lecture notes and didn't understand a graph you had drawn, you could find the spot in the audio recording corresponding to the graph. The professor demonstrated the product and then said, "The manufacturer sent me this hoping I'd suggest how to use it. Any ideas?"

In my experience, that's not an unusual approach in schools; teachers are told, "We've got access to this new tool. What problems can you solve with it?" It seems self-evident that the process should be inverted; start with the problems in your practice that seem most pressing, then look for solutions, tech or otherwise.

Then again, you may miss out on something great if you close your mind to any innovation except those that seem relevant to the problem you've identified. Here's a list of questions I ask myself about new teaching tools.

1. Is there good reason to be an early adopter? By "early" I mean before there are published data or at least fairly detailed impressions from other educators I trust. Does it make sense to wait until someone else has tried it out?

2. How confident am I that I can guess the impact on my students? If I'm looking at published data, were the students and school context similar to mine? Think about the distinction drawn in this chapter: I'll be more successful in guessing how useful a tool will be if it serves a single narrow purpose (e.g., a visualizer) than something broad (e.g., an iPad).

3. When new technology replaces old, *something* is sacrificed. I want to be sure I'm clear on what that is and that I'm comfortable with it. An example of this principle involves old technologies: using an overhead projector instead of a blackboard. An overhead projector allowed teachers to prepare transparencies in advance (and so they could be carefully designed and neatly executed), and they could be used with a photocopy machine so a figure from a book could be reproduced and projected to the class. But there's one easily overlooked feature of a blackboard: a teacher can start at the left side and add content, moving right, so as the lesson advances, it's easy for the teacher to refer back to an earlier part of the lesson; even if the teacher doesn't, students can. That's lost with transparencies. How much does it matter?

4. Make a plan for evaluation. When I visit districts contemplating a major tech initiative (or in the midst of one), I'm often surprised by the vagueness of the objective. The motivation often seems a feeling that using technology makes schools up to date, which is obviously good. I recommend being more specific and having clear answers to these questions: (i) What are we hoping to change? (ii) How will we know whether or not it has changed? (iii) By when is it supposed to change? and

(iv) What are we going to do if it changes, and what are we going to do if it doesn't? (I say much more about this approach in my book *When Can You Trust the Experts?*)

Use Tech to Support Children with Disabilities

Sometimes it might seem that, for students with disabilities, tech tools could be support that backfires; the student is able to avoid practicing important skills by using a tech work-around. For example, the parent of a sixth-grader who struggles with reading asks whether his son might listen to an audio version of the novel that other students are reading. The motivation for the request is clear enough – the father wants his child to understand the novel – but if the child's reading fluency is not what it should be, doesn't the child need to practice reading whenever possible?

Clearly there is a balance to be struck here, but I'd argue in these situations that you'd rather err on the side of providing too much tech support than too little. My concern would be that the student will not only fail to understand this one assignment very well, but will, over time, fall further and further behind as his peers accumulate subject matter knowledge (see Chapter 2). Worse, he may come to see school as a place where he's asked, again and again, to do things that do not come naturally to him and plainly are easy for his peers. A much more fruitful way for him to see the fluency problem is as a small glitch that he'll work on but not something that will prevent him from succeeding in school and enjoying it.

As I said, there's a balance to be struck here, and you do want the student to work on improving whatever gives him trouble. But what's the worst-case scenario if you allow too much tech support? Progress will be slower on the troubled skill, which seems to me much the less of two evils.

Have a Consistent Acceptable Use Policy for Personal Devices

Most aspects of a school or district's acceptable use policy are easy for teachers to agree on: websites that should be off limits, for example, or the forbidding of cyberbullying. More controversial is student use of personal devices during school hours.

There's not a clear research-based answer as to what policy is best – it depends too much on other goals the school strives for and school culture. I've seen successful policies where students have complete access to their devices and successful policies where students have none.

The policy that causes the most problems, in my experience, leaves the choice in the hands of individual teachers. It sounds far-seeing and flexible, but it creates a problem for those teachers who don't want students to access their phones in class. As I've described, students' phones demand attention because they offer timely, relevant social information. If a student knows that others have access to their phone – and so might be posting social media or texting – but they can't see it, that's a terrible distraction.

There's another sense of "consistent" when it comes to acceptable use policies – consistent enforcement. I've been to schools with well-thought-out acceptable use policies, which are duly signed by parents and students in the fall and then forgotten, unless there's an egregious violation of rules. If it's thought out, it ought to be consistently enforced, but the burden should not fall mainly on teachers. Policy is not the same as procedures. The policy may be fine, but if the procedures turn teachers into ever-vigilant cops, the procedure ought to be reviewed.

Offer Practice in Sustained Attention

I've said that students' attention span has not been affected by their use of digital devices. But surveys show teachers who have been in the classroom a while absolutely sense a change. Surveys of teachers show that they feel students *are* more distractible and that they (teachers) must engage in song and dance to hold their attention.

I don't think these teachers are wrong, but I don't think students *can't* pay attention; I think they don't want to. Paying attention is not just a matter of ability, it's a matter of desire.

A common feature of the digital age is incredible ease of accessing entertainment. If you carry a smartphone, there is always something to watch, listen to, or play with. Further, you need to do almost nothing to access it – just press a button. Before such easy access to an endless variety of amusements, kids sometimes got bored. They may have learned a valuable lesson from that: sometimes an activity is boring, but gets more interesting if you hang in there. I remember having that very thought that as a child when home sick from school. I was watching television, but there weren't very many channels, and the only thing on was a "movie for grown-ups," which I reluctantly watched, as the other choices were still worse. And, after a half hour or so, I found I rather liked it. (It was *The Lady Eve* with Barbara Stanwyck and Henry Fonda.)

You could consider a practice similar to one instituted by Jennifer Roberts, a professor of art history at Harvard. Roberts noticed that her students seemed impatient and quickly bored, attributes that might be useful for tasks that call for quick thinking and brisk action. What students were poorly practiced in, she thought, was slow, deliberative thinking and immersive attention. So she gave them practice in that. Each student was asked to select a work of art at a local museum and spend three full hours examining it and taking note of their observations and questions.

As Roberts notes, a few features of this experience are likely crucial. First, the time is striking – it seems excessive, as though it couldn't possibly pay off. Second, it *does* pay off. What makes the experiment work is that students are so sure they won't notice anything new about the artwork after, say, 10 minutes. But they do. Third, the quiet of the museum is almost certainly a factor, providing the distraction-free environment for students to become immersed.

If this hypothesis – that what looks like a decreased span of attention is really a quickening of the conclusion "I'm bored" – then the twenty-first century skill that may be in the greatest demand may be the ability to deploy patient, alert vigilance.

Educate Parents

I've cited data showing that the typical student spends a lot of time in front of screens. The typical parent is not happy about this state of affairs, which is curious, when you think about it. The usual scenario (I'm guessing) is that parents find screen-based entertainment an extremely reliable way to get a little peace and quiet when children are very young. (How many times have you seen a frustrated parent give their phone to their whiny six-year-old in a restaurant?) As psychologist David Daniel put it, "People think smartphones and tablets provide instant gratification for kids. It's really instant gratification for parents."

The next thing the parent knows their child is 11 and spends hours on screens each day, doing stuff her parents don't think is *terrible*, but that they wish added up to more like 30 minutes.

How can a teacher help with this problem, given that it's happening at home? Teachers can play three important roles.

First, some parents simply need reassurance. They don't have the information in this chapter and are unsure whether limiting their child's screen time is in some way robbing them of technical prowess. Sometimes they just need to be reminded that they can say "no."

Second, all parents could use some practical help in thinking through strategies; things like a time to park the phone in the evening, recommendations for software that monitors phone use if that's deemed appropriate, and so on. If someone at your school has the time and interest, it's an ideal topic for a parent workshop. It's not just about giving parents tips on restricting device use; you can also update them regarding research on multitasking and other topics I've covered here.

Third, teachers are ideally situated to serve as communication hubs regarding this issue, and communication can be vital because consistency across households helps, just as I emphasized was the case with acceptable use policy at school. The battle to get my daughter to park her phone at 8 p.m. will be less fierce if she knows that all of her friends are doing the same.

Notes

*If you're unfamiliar with these devices, an interactive whiteboard is like a regular classroom whiteboard, but it also serves as a large computer display and touchscreen.

†It's actually difficult to compare print to e-book sales. You and I would assume such comparisons are made based on the number of books sold, but Amazon does not release that figure for e-books. So the comparison is sales revenue, which is more complicated to interpret.

‡There have been some reports that taking notes on a laptop makes it more likely you'll write without thinking. You're able to type so fast, you try to get every word, and you're really just taking dictation, whereas writing on paper is slower, so you must summarize, which requires thinking about meaning. As I write, the issue is not settled.

Further Reading

Less Technical

Carr, N. (2010). *The Shallows: What the Internet Is Doing to our Brains.* New York: WW Norton & Company; and Wolf, M. (2018). *Reader, Come Home: The Reading Brain in a Digital World.* New York: Harper. Two high-profile books arguing that long-term Internet use makes it difficult to sustain attention.

Odgers, C. (2018). Smartphones are bad for some teens, not all. *Nature,* 554: 432–434. This researcher argues that online life is fine for most teens, but those suffering problems offline may find their problems transferring online and perhaps expanding.

Organisation for Economic Cooperation and Development. (2015). *Students, Computers and Learning: Making the Connection. PISA.* Paris: OECD Publishing. doi: http://dx.doi.org/10.1787/9789264239555-en (accessed 13 July 2020). Comprehensive but readable review of computer use in education, including chapters on equity, association of technology with learning, comparison of standardized test taking online vs. paper, and more.

Pinker, S. J. (2010). Not at all. https://www.edge.org/responses/how-is-the-internet-changing-the-way-you-think (accessed 13 July 2020). Short piece, the title of which answers the question "How is the Internet changing the way you think?"

Roberts, J. L. (2013). The power of patience. *Harvard Magazine* (November-December). https://www.harvardmagazine.com/2013/11/the-power-of-patience. (accessed 19 July 2020). Article describing the author's reasoning for asking her students to practice patient observation by extended viewing of a single painting.

Willingham, D. T. (2017). You still need your brain. *New York Times* (21 May), p. SR5. Why Google is not enough.

Willingham, D. T. (2019). The high price of multitasking. *New York Times* (15 July), p. A21. More on what's happening when we multitask, in a variety of contexts.

More Technical

Bork, A. (2003). Interactive learning: twenty years later. *Contemporary Issues in Technology and Teacher Education,* 2(4): 608–614. Written by an early proponent of the idea that computers would "change everything" in education, this retrospective considers why it didn't. Note the date!

Carter, B., Rees, P., Hale, L., Bhattacharjee, D., & Paradkar, M. S. (2016). Association between portable screen-based media device access or use and sleep outcomes: a systematic review and meta-analysis. *JAMA Pediatrics* 170(12): 1202–1208; and Hale, L., & Guan, S. (2015). Screen time and sleep among school-aged children and adolescents: a systematic literature review. *Sleep Medicine Reviews:* 21, 50–58. Two reviews showing sleep loss when children have access to tech devices in their rooms at bedtime.

Chukharev-Hudilainen, E., & Klepikova, T. A. (2016). The effectiveness of computer-based spaced repetition in foreign language vocabulary instruction: a double-blind study. *Calico Journal* 33(3): 334–354. You would think that an app meant simply to remind you when to study, using experimental data on how to space out practice sessions, ought to be straightforward to implement . . . and it is! A number seem to do what they claim.

Clinton, V. (2019). Reading from paper compared to screens: a systematic review and meta-analysis. *Journal of Research in Reading* 42(2): 288–325. Review showing the small disadvantage to reading from a screen.

Creighton, T. B. (2018). Digital natives, digital immigrants, digital learners: an international empirical integrative review of the literature. *Education Leadership Review* 19(1): 132–140. Review and evaluation of the Digital Natives/Digital Immigrant distinction.

Delgado, P., Vargas, C., Ackerman, R., & Salmerón, L. (2018). Don't throw away your printed books: a meta-analysis on the effects of reading media on reading comprehension. *Educational Research Review* 25: 23–38. Review showing that comprehension is slightly better on paper than on a screen.

Donald, J. N., Ciarrochi, J., & Sahdra, B. K. (2020, June 18). The consequences of compulsion: a 4-year longitudinal study of compulsive internet use and emotion regulation difficulties. *Emotion* doi: http://10.1037/emo0000769. Online ahead of print. Study showing the toll that compulsive use of the Internet takes on one's emotional life.

Gaudreau, P., Miranda, D., & Gareau, A. (2014). Canadian university students in wireless classrooms: what do they do on their laptops and does it really matter? *Computers & Education* 70: 245–255. In this study researchers both asked students what they do with their laptops during class time *and* electronically monitored the laptops of a different set of students (with student consent, of course). The results of both showed that students spend a lot of time on activities unrelated to class, and the more such time they spend, the lower their grades, even after statistically controlling for attitudes toward school, Internet addiction, and other factors.

Jeong, S. H., & Hwang, Y. (2016). Media multitasking effects on cognitive vs. attitudinal outcomes: a meta-analysis. *Human Communication Research* 42(4): 599–618. Summary article reviewing the effects of having television or music playing while trying to complete mental work.

Odgers, C. L., & Jensen, M. R. (2020). Annual research review: adolescent mental health in the digital age: facts, fears, and future directions. *Journal of Child Psychology and Psychiatry* 61(3): 336–348; and Coyne, S. M., Rogers, A. A., Zurcher, J. D., et al. (2020). Does time spent using social media impact mental health?: an eight year longitudinal study. *Computers in Human Behavior* 104: 106–160. Early work noted an association between social media use and mental health issues (especially anxiety and depression, and especially in girls) but more complete analyses indicate that there is not causality in the correlation. Other factors are responsible.

Salthouse, T. A., Hambrick, D. Z., Lukas, K. E., & Dell, T. C. (1996). Determinants of adult age differences on synthetic work performance. *Journal of Experimental Psychology: Applied*, 2(4), 305. This paper shows that young people are, on average, better multitaskers than older people.

Shi, Y., Zhang, J., Yang, H., & Yang, H. H. (2020). Effects of interactive whiteboard-based instruction on students' cognitive learning outcomes: a meta-analysis. *Interactive Learning Environments*, 1–18; and Zheng, B., Warschauer, M., Lin, C. H., & Chang, C. (2016). Learning in one-to-one laptop environments: a meta-analysis and research synthesis. *Review of Educational Research*, 86 (4): 1052–1084. Two recent articles reviewing the impact of introducing technology to classrooms, and reporting a modest boost, on average.

Somerville, L. H. (2013). The teenage brain: sensitivity to social evaluation. *Current Directions in Psychological Science*, 22(2), 121–127. Review of brain changes associated with the hypersociality of teenage years.

Uncapher, M. R., & Wagner, A. D. (2018). Minds and brains of media multitaskers: current findings and future directions. *Proceedings of the National Academy of Sciences of the United States of America*, 115(40), 9889–9896. Brief review of the complicated literature on the long-term effects of media multitasking (that is, multitasking with video or music).

Wiradhany, W., & Nieuwenstein, M. R. (2017). Cognitive control in media multitaskers: two replication studies and a meta-analysis. *Attention, Perception, & Psychophysics*, 79(8), 2620–2641. A review of studies examining the relationship between media multitasking and attentional control. Early studies made it look like there was definitely a negative relationship, but follow up work made it appear somewhat less clear.

Discussion Questions

1. I've suggested caution in adopting new tech tools to your classroom or school, implicitly asking whether you have a good reason to be a guinea pig, so to speak. Why not let someone else take the risk of giving a new tech device a try, and then finding out how they thought it went? That invites the question whose opinion would you trust? What would you ask them? And how long must they remain enthusiastic before you're ready to jump in the water?

2. It's all very well that I've reassured you that students *can* pay attention, they just have a lower threshold of boredom . . . that still leaves you with students who are more impatient, more desirous of classroom entertainment than you would have had 10 or 15 years ago. I've heard very different responses from teachers to this problem. Some say, "The classroom is not a theater, and students need to learn to pay attention, and even to endure some slow moments." Others say, "This is the new reality and it's our duty to meet students where they are." What's your take?

3. Most people would say, "I don't like or dislike tech per se; I evaluate new tech on the basis of whether I think it will help my students." But of course we do have opinions about "tech per se." Some people delight in exploring new software and devices, and some are very reluctant adopters indeed. How would you characterize yourself on this dimension? Although it sounds prejudiced to let your views about tech influence your adoption (or restraint) when it comes to new innovations, one could argue that your enthusiasm or reluctance is a factor in whether it's likely to work in your classroom. But then again, maybe your preconceptions are something to be overcome. So how are we to think about this issue? What role, if any, should your personal feelings about tech play in your use of tech in the classroom?

4. In March 2020, schools throughout Europe and North America moved to distance learning, with many relying heavily on video conferencing. Many teachers were able to see the conditions in which children were trying to learn at home – siblings passing by or interfering, pets wandering about, and so on. Even when they are attending school as usual, many students still have work to complete at home, and the pandemic made obvious something that teachers probably could have guessed: parents don't know how to prepare an environment for learning. Suggesting that parents "reserve a space for homework" is fine, but isn't realistic for many families. What concrete strategies can you suggest for parents, to maximize the success of their children when they work at home?

5. How do you interact with students on social media? Most educators I know shrink from students glimpsing their personal lives on Facebook or Instagram, but others create accounts specifically so that they can interact with students; and, some have told me with candor, they create these accounts so they can see what their students are up to on social media. Do social media play a useful role in your teaching?

6. Reflect on your school's acceptable use policy. Do students really know what it says? Do faculty? Does it work equally well for all students? If it's not taken as seriously as it ought to be, what do you think might be done to enhance its presence?

7. Have you yourself ever taken a digital holiday, staying off all devices for, say, 48 hours? What was your experience? Would you recommend it to your students? If so, why? And how would you convince them to try it?

8. I've said that, despite the fact that you can learn or experience nearly *anything* on the Internet, students explore only a very limited range of activities. Why do you suppose that is? What might you do to make them more adventurous?

10

What About My Mind?

Question: Most of this book has focused on the minds of students. What about the minds of teachers?

Answer: In Chapter 1 I outlined the cognitive requirements for students to think effectively: they need space in working memory, relevant background knowledge, and experience with applicable mental procedures. Throughout the rest of the chapters I detailed principles of the mind that illustrate how those requirements might be met. The cognitive principle that guides this chapter is:

> Teaching, like any complex cognitive skill, must be practiced to be improved.

Thus far, all of our discussion has focused on the minds of students. What about you? Isn't teaching a cognitive skill? So couldn't we apply these findings from cognitive science to *your* mind?

Teaching is indeed a cognitive skill, and everything I have said about students' minds applies to yours. Let's bring back the picture of the mind from Chapter 1 so I can briefly refresh your memory about the cognitive apparatus that must be in place for any type of effective thinking to occur, including effective teaching (Figure 10.1).

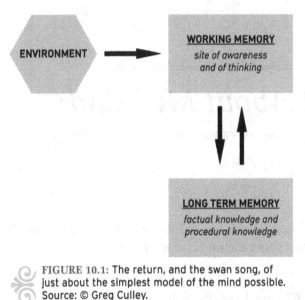

FIGURE 10.1: The return, and the swan song, of just about the simplest model of the mind possible. Source: © Greg Culley.

Thinking is the putting together of information in new ways – for example, comparing the structure of the solar system with the structure of an atom and recognizing that they have some similarities. This sort of manipulation of information happens in working memory, which is often called the staging ground of thought. The information manipulated in working memory might come from the environment (from things we see or hear, for example, such as a teacher describing the structure of an atom) or from long-term memory (from things we already know, for example, the structure of the solar system).

We use mental *procedures* to manipulate information (for example, a procedure that compares features of a solar system and features of an atom). Our long-term memory can store simple procedures as in "compare features of these two objects," as well as complex, multi-stage procedures to support tasks with lots of intermediate steps. For example, you might have stored the procedure to make pancakes or to change the oil in a car or to write a well-organized paragraph.

To think effectively, we need sufficient room in working memory, which has limited space. We also need the right factual and procedural knowledge in long-term memory. Let's think about how teaching fits into this framework.

Teaching as a Cognitive Skill

I have described to teachers how cognitive psychologists talk about working memory: they refer to it as a mental place where we juggle several things at once and where, if we try to juggle too many things, one or more things will be dropped. Teachers always respond in the same way: "Well, of course! You've just described my work day." Research confirms this strong intuition; teaching is very demanding of working memory.

It's just as evident that factual knowledge is important to teaching. Many observers have emphasized that teachers ought to have rich subject-matter knowledge – that is, if you're going to teach history, you should know history – and there do seem to be some data that students of these teachers learn more, especially in middle and high school and especially in math. Somewhat less well known but just as important are other data showing that *pedagogical content knowledge* is also important. That is, for teachers, just knowing algebra really well isn't enough. You need to have knowledge particular to *teaching* algebra. Pedagogical content knowledge might include such things as knowledge of a typical student's conceptual understanding of slope, or the types of errors students often make when factoring, or the types of concepts that require a lot of practice and those that don't. When you think about it, if pedagogical content knowledge were *not* important, then anyone who understood algebra could teach it well, and we know that's not true.

It's also pretty evident that a teacher makes extensive use of procedures stored in long-term memory. Some of these procedures handle mundane tasks, for example, the procedure for passing out papers or for leading students through the Pledge of Allegiance, or for turn-taking during read-alouds. These stored procedures can also be much more complex, for example, a method for explaining what a limit of a function is or for handling a potentially dangerous student conflict in the cafeteria.

OK, so if teaching is a cognitive skill just like any other, how can you apply what I've discussed to your teaching? How can you increase (i) space in your working memory, (ii) your relevant factual knowledge, and (iii) your relevant procedural knowledge? You may recall that the cognitive principle guiding our discussion in Chapter 5 was *It is virtually impossible to become proficient at a mental task without extended practice.* Your best bet for improving your teaching is to practice teaching.

The Importance of Deliberate Practice

Until now, I have been a bit casual about how I have talked about practice. In Chapter 5, I didn't even bother to define it; I figured that you understood it to mean "repetition," and that was close enough for our purposes in that chapter. But that won't do anymore.

There are some tasks for which you reap the benefits of practice simply through repetition. That's often true for simple skills like practicing keyboarding or committing math facts to memory. But for complex skills, you might gain a lot of experience – that is, you repeat the task a lot – and yet not improve. For example, I don't think I'm a significantly better driver than I was at age 17. I'm much more experienced but during these last 40 years I haven't worked at improving. I *did* work at my driving skills when I first got behind the wheel, but after perhaps 50 hours of that, I was driving with skill that seemed adequate to me, so I stopped trying to get better (Figure 10.2).

You can see why some teachers might stop trying to improve once they are pretty good in the classroom. Indeed, a great deal of data show that teachers improve a lot during their first five years in the classroom, but after that, exactly what happens is less clear. It's a tricky research problem, because there are multiple ways to measure improvement, and different statistical techniques one might use, all of them defensible. Today most researchers think that teachers continue to improve after the first five years, but the pace of improvement is slower, and there's

FIGURE 10.2: I have a great deal of driving experience, but I have practiced driving relatively little and therefore haven't improved my driving much in the last 40 years. Source: © Daniel Willingham.

a lot of variation in how much better individual teachers get. Likely, some teachers constantly strive to improve, some stop striving once they feel they're pretty good, and many are in between.

It's easy to think indignantly, "Everyone should *always* try to improve!" But deliberate practice is hard, and it takes time and other resources that most school systems don't provide. But I am trusting that if you've read this far into the book, you are prepared to do some hard work. So let's get started.

I've just slipped in the term "deliberate practice," which has a particular meaning, so let's start there. Deliberate practice has these characteristics: (i) you pick one small feature of the skill that you know you don't do very well and try to improve it, setting a specific goal, not a vague aspiration like "get better"; (ii) as you practice, you get feedback from someone at least as knowledgeable about the skill as you are; (iii) you push yourself outside your comfort zone – you try new things; (iv) you find deliberate practice mentally demanding and, candidly, not fun; and (v) you engage in activities that contribute to the skill indirectly.*

What would that look like for teaching? Three of these five characteristics seem straightforward: you pick a fairly narrow, specific aspect of teaching you want to improve, you strive to be inventive in ways to improve it, and you expect that the process will take mental effort. The other two characteristics of deliberate practice – getting feedback and using indirect methods to improve – require some amplification.

What's tricky about feedback? Certainly, you're constantly getting very direct, real-time feedback from students via engaged or bored looks and body language. True, you can tell if a lesson is going well or poorly, but the feedback's not directive; it doesn't tell you what you might do differently. In addition, if you're new to the profession, you probably miss more of what's happening in your classroom than you think you do. You are busy *teaching* and don't have the luxury of simply *watching* what is happening in your classroom. It's hard to think about how things are going when you're in the middle of trying to make them go well! (There's working memory, making trouble again.) (See Figure 10.3.)

FIGURE 10.3: Most of us treat Scrabble as a diversion, but tournament players train hard and that includes feedback and guidance from coaches. The Nigerian national team has dominated international competition in the last five years, winning the world championship three times, a feat they credit to their coach. Source: © Getty Images/ Pius Utomi Ekpei.

FIGURE 10.4: French students learning the results of their baccalaureat. Teachers often see a self-serving bias when students learn test results; if they did well, it was because they worked hard, not because the test happened to include questions they could answer. If they do poorly, it's because the questions were tricky or unfair. Source: © Getty Images/Eric Feferberg.

It's also hard to use feedback about your own teaching because we are not impartial observers of our own behavior. Some people lack confidence and are harder on themselves than they ought to be whereas others (most of us, actually) interpret their world in ways that are favorable to themselves. Social psychologists call this the self-serving bias. When things go well, it's because we are skilled and hardworking. When things go poorly, it's because we were unlucky, or because someone else made a mistake (Figure 10.4). For these reasons, it is usually quite informative to see your class through someone else's eyes.

In addition to requiring feedback, deliberate practice usually means investing time in activities that are not the target task itself but are done for the sake of improving that task. For example, athletes of all sorts do weight and cardiovascular training to improve their endurance in their sport (Figure 10.5).

FIGURE 10.5: Chess grandmaster Fabiano Caruana's preparations for a tournament include a 5-mile run, an hour of tennis, half an hour of basketball, and at least an hour of swimming. The mental stress of high-level chess requires endurance.[1] Source: © Getty Images/Tristan Fewings.

To summarize, if you want to be a better teacher, you can't expect that improvement is a natural and unavoidable consequence of the experience you gain with passing years. You must engage in deliberate practice. There are lots of ways you could do so, of course. Here I suggest one method.

A Method for Getting and Giving Feedback

I'm going to suggest a method based on one that has been proven effective (and was developed at my home institution, University of Virginia). But I have made changes so I can't claim it's research based. It will be enough to get you started, but I encourage you to experiment with the method to figure out what works for you. I also encourage you to think carefully about a few features of this type of practice that I think are bound to be important.

First, you need to work with at least one other person. As I've said, someone else will see things in your class that you cannot, simply because she is not you and thus can be more impartial. (Of course she also has a different background and experiences than you, and that helps.) Furthermore, as anyone who has exercised knows, having a buddy helps you to stick with a difficult task.

Second, you should recognize that working on your teaching *will* be a threat to your ego. Teaching is very personal, so taking a close look at it (and inviting one or more other people to do the same) is scary. It's a good idea not to shrug off that concern ("I can take it!") but instead to put measures in place to deal with it.

Step 1: Identify Another Teacher (or Two) with Whom You Would Like to Work

Naturally it will help if this person teaches subject matter and students similar those you teach. More important, however, is that you trust each other, and that your partner is as committed to the project as you are.

Step 2: Record Yourself and Watch the Videos Alone

There is a lot of value in recording a video as you teach. As I mentioned earlier, it's difficult to watch your class while you're busy teaching it, but you can watch a video at your leisure, and you can replay important parts. An inexpensive tripod and adapter to hold your phone can be purchased online.

You should send a note home with students to let parents know that their child is being videoed, that the recordings are purely for your professional development and will not be used for any other purpose, and that they will be erased at the end of the school year. (You should check in with your principal on the issue of parental notification.)

Simply set your phone on the tripod in a place where you think it will capture most of the class and switch it on at the start of a lesson. The first few recordings you make will probably give you important information about logistical matters. You might not be able to record every type of lesson. For example, you have only one camera, so you'll be able to see only part of the classroom. Also, picking up audio is frequently difficult, so noisy participatory lessons may not work well. If you're ready to invest a bit more money, you might buy a wide-angle lens that clips onto your phone, so you can video more of the classroom, and there are mics you can add that will provide better audio quality in an echoing classroom. You can get a lot of useful tips by hopping on YouTube and searching "how to film yourself."

I suggest that you first record a lesson that you feel typically goes pretty well. It's not easy to watch yourself (and later to critique yourself), so stack the deck in your favor at first. There will be time enough later to examine the things you suspect you don't do so well.

You can expect it to take a class or two for your students to become accustomed to being videoed, although this is generally not a concern for long. Then too, it will probably take a couple of recordings for *you* to become accustomed to hearing your voice and seeing yourself move.[†]

FIGURE 10.6: Avid golfers video themselves in an effort to learn more about their strokes. Initially that may seem odd: Don't they know what they're doing? To a surprising extent, no. A golfer's stroke is so practiced that it may feel quite comfortable, even though the golfer may, for example, be arching his back in a way that he knows is bad form. Source: © Anne Carlyle Lindsay.

Once you have these practical matters settled, you can focus on content. Watch these recordings with a notepad in hand. Don't begin by judging your performance. Consider first what surprises you about the class. What do you notice about your students that you didn't already know? What do you notice about yourself? Spend time *observing*. Don't start by critiquing (Figure 10.6).

Step 3: With Your Partner, Watch Recordings of Other Teachers

Once you have grown accustomed to watching videos of yourself, it's time to include your partner. But don't watch recordings of each other yet. Observe recordings of other teachers. You can easily find videos of classrooms online.[‡]

The reason to watch other teachers first is to gain practice in constructive observation and commenting and to get this practice in a nonthreatening situation. Further, you will also get a sense of whether you and your partner are compatible for this work.

What are you looking for? It's not productive just to sit down and watch teachers and classrooms like a movie, waiting to see what will happen. You should have a concrete goal, such as observing classroom management or observing the emotional atmosphere of the classroom. Many of the videos featured on websites are there for a particular reason, so it will usually be clear why the person who posted it thought it was interesting.

Imagine what you would say to the teacher you observe. Indeed, imagine that the teacher is there in the room with you. In general, comments should have the following two properties:

1. *They should be supportive.* Being supportive doesn't mean you are there *only* to say positive things. It does mean that even when you are saying something negative, you are supporting the teacher you are observing. The point of this exercise is not to "spot the flaw," and the positive comments should outnumber the negative ones. I know that sounds corny, because when listening to positive comments a teacher can't help but think, "He is saying that only because he knows he is supposed to say something positive." Even so, positive comments remind the teacher that she *is* doing a lot of things right, and those things should be acknowledged and reinforced. (If framing things positively doesn't come to you easily, practice in your comments on social media.)

2. *They should be concrete and about the behaviors you observe, not about qualities you infer.* Thus, don't just say, "She really knows how to explain things"; instead say, "That third example really made the concept click for students." Rather than saying, "His classroom management is a mess," say, "I noticed that a lot of the students were having trouble listening when he asked them to sit down."

Step 4: With Your Partner, Watch and Comment on Each Other's Videos

You should not undertake this step until you feel quite comfortable watching recordings of other teachers with your partner. This means you should feel comfortable in what you say *and* you should feel that your partner knows how to be supportive; that is, you should feel that you wouldn't mind if your partner's comments were directed to you instead of to the unknown teacher on the video. The ground rules for commenting on the recordings of other teachers apply here as well: be supportive, be concrete, and focus on behaviors. Because this process is now interactive, there are a few additional things to think about.

The teacher whose video is being viewed should set the goal for the session. She should describe what she would like the other teacher to watch for in the session. It is vital that the viewer respect this request, even if she sees something else on the video that she thinks is important. If you present a video hoping to get some ideas about engaging students in a lesson on local government and your partner says, "Gee, I notice some real classroom-management issues here," you're going to feel ambushed, and you're not going to be motivated to continue the process.

What if your partner keeps wanting to work on trivial things and you notice that there are bigger problems that she's ignoring? If you and your partner make a habit of recording yourselves, there will likely be a time when this issue will come up naturally in the course of discussing something else. You and your partner also might consider agreeing that after viewing, say, 10 videos, each of you will suggest to the other something they might work on that hasn't come up yet.

A final point. The purpose of watching your partner teach is to help her reflect on her practice, to think about her teaching. You do that by describing what you see. Don't suggest what the teacher should do differently unless you are asked. You don't want to come off as thinking you have all the answers. If your partner wants your ideas about how to address an issue, she'll ask you, in which case you should of course offer any ideas you have. But until you're asked, remain in the mode of a careful, supportive observer, and don't slip into the role of the expert fixer, regardless of how confident you are that you have a good solution.

Step 5: Bring It Back to the Classroom and Follow Up

The purpose of recording your teaching is to increase your awareness of what is happening in your classroom and to gain a new perspective on what you are actually doing and why, and on what your students are doing and why. With that awareness will almost certainly come some resolve to make changes. Here's a method to try: Make a plan that during a specific lesson you will do one thing that addresses the issue with which you are concerned. Even if you think of three things you want to do, do just one. Keep it simple. You'll have plenty of chances to add the other two things. And of course video the lesson so you can see what happened. Don't be discouraged if it doesn't work all that well the first time. Consider whether you just need to tweak or practice this new strategy.

The program I have sketched here is rooted in the cognitive principles I have described. For example, I emphasized in Chapter 1 that the most important limitation to thinking is the capacity of working memory. That's why I recommend a video recording – because it's difficult to think deeply about your teaching while you're actually teaching. Also, because memory is based on what we think about (Chapter 3), we can't expect to remember later a complete version of what happened in a class; we remember only what we paid attention to in class. In Chapter 6 I said that experts see the world differently than novices do – they see deep structure, not surface structure – and the key reason they can see this way is that they have broad and deep experience in their field. Careful observation of a variety of classrooms will help you better recognize classroom dynamics, and careful observation of your own classroom will help you recognize the dynamics that are typical of your own teaching.

In Chapter 2 I emphasized the importance of background knowledge to effective problem solving. Background knowledge means not just subject matter knowledge; for a teacher it also means knowledge of students and how they interact with you, with each other, and with the material you teach. Careful observation, especially in partnership with another, well-informed teacher is a good method for gaining that background knowledge. Finally, Chapter 8 painted a hopeful picture of human ability – that it can be changed through sustained hard work. There is every reason to believe this is true of teaching.

Consciously Trying to Improve: Self-Management

I've said that consciously trying to improve your teaching is a crucial part of deliberate practice, and it sounds like the easiest part to implement. "Sure, I want to improve. That's why I'm here. Let's go!" But it's usually not that simple (Figure 10.7). Here are a few suggestions that might help.

First, you might plan for the extra work that will be required. In Chapter 1 I pointed out that most of us are on autopilot most of the time. Rather than think through the optimal thing to do moment to moment, we retrieve from memory what we've done in the past. Teaching is no different. It's to be expected that once you have gained sufficient experience you will teach on autopilot at least part of the time. There's nothing wrong with that, but serious work at improving your teaching means that you will be on autopilot less often. It's going to be tiring, and thinking

FIGURE 10.7: Resolving to do something difficult is easy. Following through is not. That's why, in January, gyms are crowded with exercisers following through on their solemn New Year's resolutions. But by mid-February, gyms look like this. Source: © Getty Images/Jeff Greenberg.

carefully about things you don't do as well as you'd like is emotion-ally draining. You may need a little extra support from your friends and loved ones. You may need to be more vigilant in scheduling relaxation time.

You will also spend more time on teaching. In addition to the hours spent at home grading, planning lessons, and so forth, now you will also spend more time watching videos, reviewing what you're doing well and poorly in the classroom, and planning how to do things differently than you've ever done them before. If you're going to spend an extra five hours each week (or three hours, or one hour) on teaching, where is that time going to come from? Can family or friends provide not just emotional support, but practical support in creating free time for you? If you schedule extra time for this work, you are much more likely to actually do it.

Finally, remember that you don't need to do everything at once. It's not realistic to expect to go from wherever you are now to "great" in a year or two. Because you're not trying to fix everything at once, you have to set priorities. Decide what is most important to work on, and focus on concrete, manageable steps to move you toward your goal.

Summary

From a cognitive point of view, your mind is, of course, just like that of your students. And like your students, you need factual knowl-edge, procedures, and working memory capacity to be proficient at a task. Thus, most of the implications from previous chapters apply to you as well, but in this chapter I elaborated on one: the utility of deliberate practice. Deliberate practice requires consciously trying to improve, seeking feedback, and undertaking select activities for the sake of improvement, even if they don't contribute to the skill directly. I suggested a method of gaining practice which culminates in videoing yourself as you teach and reviewing the recordings with a partner. This process allows you to see aspects of your practice that are hard to notice when your mind is occupied by teaching and offers the fresh perspective of your colleague.

Implications

The program I've laid out is time consuming, there is no doubt. I can well imagine that some teachers will think to themselves, "In an ideal world, sure – but between taking care of my kids and the house and the million other things I'm *supposed* to be doing and am not, I just don't have the time." I absolutely respect that. So start smaller. Here are a few ideas for ways you can work on your teaching that are less time consuming.

Keep a Teaching Diary

Make notes that include what you intended to do and how you thought it went. Did the lesson basically work? If not, what are your thoughts as to why it didn't? Every so often take a little time to read past entries. Look for patterns in what sorts of lessons went well and which didn't, for situations that frustrated you, for moments of teaching that really keep you going, and so on.

Lots of people start a diary but then find it difficult to stick with it. Here are a few tips that might help. First, try to find a time of day when you can write and make it a time that you're likely to be able to maintain. (For example, I'm a morning person, so I know that if I planned to write just before bed, it would never happen.) Second, try to write *something* each day, even if it's only "Today was an average day." The consistency of pulling out the diary and writing something will help make it a habit. Third, remember that this project is solely for *you*. Don't worry about the quality of the writing, don't feel guilty if you don't write much, and don't beat yourself up if you miss days, or even weeks. If you do miss some time, don't try to catch up. You'll never remember what happened, and the thought of all that work will prevent you from starting again. Finally, be honest both in your criticism and in your praise; there is no reason not to dwell on moments that make you proud. Of course, you may find uses for your diary that I've missed (Figure 10.8).

Start a Discussion Group with Fellow Teachers

Get a group of teachers together for meetings, say, monthly or semi-monthly. Unless you already know each other pretty well, I would

FIGURE 10.8: Writer David Sedaris[2] on keeping a diary: "Most of it's just whining, but every so often there'll be something I can use later: a joke, a description, a quote. It's an invaluable aid when it comes to winning arguments. 'That's not what you said on February 3, 1996,' I'll say to someone." Source: © Getty Images/Ulrich Baumgarten.

try to do this live, rather than virtually. People are more engaged when they are actually in the same room, and there are more social communication cues available in person; those will help as you're getting to know and trust one another.

There are at least two purposes to such groups. One purpose is to give and receive social support. It's a chance for teachers to grumble about problems, share their successes, and so forth. The goal is to feel connected and supported. Another purpose, not completely independent of the first, is to serve as a forum for teachers to bring up problems they are having and get ideas for solutions from the group. It is a good idea to be clear from the start about whether the purpose of your group is mostly the first function, the second, or both. If different people have different ideas about the purpose of the group, frustration is likely. If your group is very goal oriented, you can also have everyone read an article in a professional journal (for example, in *American Educator*, *Educational Leadership*, or *Phi Delta Kappan*) for discussion.

Observe Your Class

I've said that one purpose of recording your class is that teaching is so all absorbing that there's no working memory capacity remaining to really observe your students; videoing allows you to be a fly on the wall later.

Another strategy to the same end is to observe your class while someone else teaches. You might be able to do some observing while your students are working independently – by all means, try – but you're still responsible for the momentum of the class, and that will always draw your attention from observation. For that reason, the "guest star" needs to be someone you feel good about carrying that responsibility. So a likely candidate might be a fellow teacher with whom you will trade the favor. Bear in mind, there's no minimum time for this exercise.

Your goal is to observe your students' behavior. Perhaps you ask your guest teacher to conduct a teacher-centered lesson, so you can focus on the classroom dynamic that leads (or doesn't lead) to restlessness. Perhaps you want to closely observe those quiet students whose goal seems to be blending into the background – what are they thinking? And what about your more rambunctious kids? Is their dynamic different with your guest?

If the same guest teacher comes a few times and your students get to know her, you may see relationships develop. Who talks to the guest differently than they talk to you? Who shows different body language, different patterns of attention? What does the guest do in strikingly different ways than you, and how do your students react?

Or maybe you ask the guest teacher to orchestrate students working in groups, giving you a chance to observe student relationships. As with the recommendation for videos, I think it's wise to go in with a plan, rather than sitting back and watching as though you're at a movie.

Observe Children You Don't Know

What makes students in the age group you teach tick? What motivates them, how do they talk to one another, what are their passions? You probably know your students pretty well in the classroom, but would your students say they are "themselves" when they are in your classroom? Would it be useful to you to see them acting in ways that are not contrived for the classroom or when they are surrounded by a different group of children?

Find a location where you can observe children in the age group you teach. To observe preschoolers, go to a park; to watch teenagers, go to a skatepark or coffeeshop. You'll probably have to go to a different neighborhood or even a different town, because this exercise won't work if you're recognized.§ Just watch the kids. Don't go with a specific plan or agenda. Just watch. Initially, you probably will get bored. You'll think, "Right, I've seen this before." But if you keep watching, really watching, you will start to notice things you hadn't noticed before. You'll notice more subtle cues about social interactions, aspects of personality, and how students think. Allow yourself the time and space simply to observe and you will see remarkable things.

Sneak Up on It

I've said that deliberate practice often includes activities that don't directly contribute to the target skill, as when a golfer lifts weights and jogs, to build strength and stamina. How might this principle apply to teaching? An obvious example would be to improve your knowledge of your core subject matter – if you teach history, learn more history. Equally obvious: if you still feel slightly ill at ease speaking before a group, take a public speaking course, or if you lack confidence with tech, find some online tutorials relevant to the tools your school uses. But I think this principle can apply more broadly than first meets the eye.

A few years ago I met a teacher who felt she was pretty good in the classroom, but inflexible. She couldn't let herself depart from her plan, even when she saw opportunities for something really interesting to happen. So she took an improv theater class, to gain the courage to live and react more in the moment; she wanted to make herself recognize that when she let go of her plan, things still turned out okay.

If you think the visual aids you create lack verve, learn something about graphic design.

If your back is sore (or your legs, or your feet) from standing for much of the day, first invest in better shoes. Then consider yoga. (Good yoga programming can be found free online.)

If you think your lesson plans are a bit plodding and need moments of snap and pizzazz, stage magic might give you a feel for the creation and release of suspense.

If you like the idea of planning lessons as stories (see Chapter 3), but story structure doesn't make a lot of sense to you, take a course in writing short-form fiction.

If you'd like to give your students more autonomy but still worry about losing control, study leadership and how to empower people with responsibility.

And I think everyone should take a course in cognitive psychology, of course!

Notes

*The theory of deliberate practice was developed by Anders Ericsson, and in his conception, it applies to domains in which experts largely agree on the sequence of training. Thus, if you want to learn piano, or ballet, everyone agrees on what should be learned first, what should be learned second, and so on. That does not apply to teaching; people don't even agree on what expert teaching looks like, much less the exact training regimen to get there. Nevertheless, I think these four principles are broadly supported and apply to improving classroom practice.

†My father started to go bald at about age 40. He lost hair mostly on the back of his head and it wasn't very noticeable from the front, but by the time he was 55 the bald spot was pretty sizable. At that time he saw a photograph of a crowd of people, including himself with his back to the camera. He pointed to himself and said, "Who is that bald-headed gentleman?" It's not easy seeing what the camera sees.

‡In the first edition of this book I listed a couple of good repositories of classroom videos. As I prepared the second edition, neither site still served that function; one had become a Thai language site for viewing online movies. So I'm leaving you to search on your own.

§The wife of a friend of mine teaches seventh grade. My friend told me that walking our small downtown with her is like being accompanied by a celebrity – everyone knows her, and even the cool kids greet her and are excited to get a greeting in return. He also mentioned that she's not reluctant to use her authority. "She puts on that teacher voice and tells kids who are misbehaving to knock it off, and they always do."

Further Reading

Less Technical

James Clear has a useful "Beginner's Guide to Deliberate Practice" on his website. Search "James Clear deliberate practice."

There's a great three-minute video in which Dylan Wiliam draws the distinction between ego-involving and task-involving feedback, very relevant for the video viewing I suggest you do. Search YouTube for "Dylan Wiliam: Feedback on Learning."

Deans for Impact, a nonprofit devoted to projects in teacher education (and with which I have worked) has published a very useful 14-page booklet about improving one's teaching via deliberate practice. Search "Deans for Impact Practice with Purpose."

More Technical

Early, D. M., Maxwell, K. L., Ponder, B. D., & Pan, Y. (2017). Improving teacher-child inter-actions: a randomized controlled trial of Making the Most of Classroom Interactions and My Teaching Partner professional development models. *Early Childhood Research Quarterly*, 38(1), 57–70. This article reports research showing that My Teaching Partner improves teaching. My Teaching Partner asks teachers to video themselves teaching and to discuss the recording with an expert coach. The technique provides the backbone for the method I describe in this chapter.

Ericsson, K.A., & Harwell, K. (2019). Deliberate practice and proposed limits on the effects of practice on the acquisition of expert performance: why the original definition matters and recommendations for future research. *Frontiers in Psychology*, 10, 2396. A recent review of the literature on deliberate practice, written by the researcher who first characterized it. (Fair warning, not all researchers take as extreme a view of the power of practice.)

Feldon, D. F. (2007). Cognitive load and classroom teaching: the double-edged sword of automaticity. *Educational Psychologist*, 42(3), 123–137. This article examines the role of automaticity in teaching practice, and the positive and negative consequences of its development.

Keller, M. M., Neumann, K., & Fischer, H. E. (2017). The impact of physics teachers' pedagogical content knowledge and motivation on students' achievement and inter-est. *Journal of Research in Science Teaching*, 54(5), 586–614. Field research showing the importance of pedagogical content knowledge to student achievement in high school science classes. For comparable findings in mathematics see Campbell, P. F., Nishio, M., Smith, T. M., et al. (2014). The relationship between teachers' mathemat-ical content and pedagogical knowledge, teachers' perceptions, and student achieve-ment. *Journal for Research in Mathematics Education* 45 (4): 419–459.

Mezulis, A. H., Abramson, L.Y., Hyde, J.S., & Hankin, B.L. (2004). Is there a universal positivity bias in attributions? A meta-analytic review of individual, developmental, and cultural differences in the self-serving attributional bias. *Psychological Bulletin*, 130, 711–747. Integrative review on the human tendency to interpret ambiguous events in ways that favor us. For example, I may figure that your class misbehaves because your classroom management is lousy, but if my class misbehaves, it's because they are bad kids. This is why it's useful to work on your teaching with a buddy.

Papay, J. P., & Kraft, M. A. (2015). Productivity returns to experience in the teacher labor market: methodological challenges and new evidence on long-term career improve-ment. *Journal of Public Economics*, 130, 105–119. In the first edition of this book I cited studies indicating that teachers improved in their practice a lot in the first few years, but not thereafter. This article (and others following it) used more sophisticated analytic techniques to show that improvement continues much longer than that.

Schneider, M., & Preckel, F. (2017). Variables associated with achievement in higher educa-tion: a systematic review of meta-analyses. *Psychological Bulletin*, 143(6), 565–600. Many many studies over the past 100 years verify the importance of feedback for learning. This study examined common characteristics of successful college teachers and observed that one was the effective use of feedback.

Discussion Questions

1. In Chapter 4 I discussed the difficulty of understanding abstract ideas in the first place, and that, once they are understood, it's hard to recognize them again later because they can appear with a different surface structure. In Chapter 6 I said that the ability to recognize those abstract ideas is one of the hallmarks of expertise. These facts seem to point all the more urgently to the importance of observing classrooms. It's *experience* that gives you that sixth sense that a small-group discussion is on the verge of a breakthrough, or that a moody child is on the verge of a tantrum. How often are you able to observe other teachers? If the answer is "seldom" or "never," what are the obstacles? Given the apparent usefulness of observation, can you think outside the box to make it possible?

2. As I mentioned in the footnotes, the original framing of deliberate practice suggests that it applies to domains (e.g., learning to play violin) in which there is a widely agreed upon *sequence* to the skills to be learned. Do you think teachers could develop such a sequence, however rough? Here's a thought to get you started: a very common complaint among first-year teachers is that they were not taught enough about classroom management in their teacher education programs. Arguably, that skill should have been first in the sequence. What do you think?

3. Many schools have one or two ineffectual teachers who give no sign that they care about improving. Everyone knows who they are, and naturally everyone feels sorry that their students have a year that's not all it could be. (And no one feels this more acutely than the teacher who teaches those students the following year.) This chapter has made it clear that improvement is not easy; what can be done to persuade those bootless teachers to buckle up and try to get better? What do they see as the obstacles and how can they be removed or overcome?

4. How much mentoring do first-year teachers get in your school? Does anyone observe their classes? (Here I mean observe for the sake of improving their practice, not evaluation.) I could imagine arguments for and against observing first-year teachers. On the one hand, we might think first-year teachers need more observation – why not provide guidance as soon as possible? On the other hand, teaching is hard enough in your first year, and observation will only add to the stress. What's your take? And should the process of observation be different for beginning teachers compared to those with more experience?

5. In some countries (especially the United States), complaints about professional development abound; those who lead professional development sessions are out of touch, they claim research backing when it seems suspect, and more. Relevant to this chapter, professional development is often a one-day affair. Someone comes in and tells teachers, "you ought to do x, y, and z," and leaves. What's missing is (i) someone with experience in x, y, and z observing you while you try to do x, y, and z to offer guidance; (ii) any opportunity for you to try x, y, and z and reflect on what it meant to your students and your practice. An obvious remedy would be for this work to be folded into the professional development itself. If that's not possible, what might you and fellow teachers do to ensure some practice and feedback for professional development sessions, or for the days and weeks following such sessions?

Conclusion

Reynolds Price, the well-known author, was one of the few celebrities on the faculty of Duke University when I studied there in the early 1980s. He strode about the campus with a long-stepped gait, often wearing an enormous, bright red scarf. He seemed not unaware that he was watched.

When I took a creative writing seminar with Price, he showed the somewhat forbidding air we students expected from an artist, as well as polished manners and a stock of stories about the famous people he had met. We didn't just respect him, we revered him. For all that, he was quite gracious and took each of us seriously, although it was probably not possible for anyone to take us as seriously as we took ourselves.

Imagine our surprise when Price once told us that any writer should proceed on the assumption that what the reader *really* wants to do is drop his book and turn on the television, or get a beer, or play golf. It was as though he had lit a stink bomb at a swank party. Watch television? Drink a beer? We thought we were writing for a sophisticated audience, for the literate; it sounded as though Price was telling us to pander. Later in the semester I understood that he was just making explicit a principle that should have been obvious: If your writing is not interesting, why should anyone read it?

Years later I see these words through the lens of cognitive psychology rather than literature. Reading is a mental act that literally changes the thought processes of the reader. Thus every piece of prose or poetry is a proposal: "Let me take you on a mental journey. Follow and trust me. The path may sometimes be rocky or steep, but I promise a rewarding adventure." The reader may accept your invitation but the decision-making process does not stop there. At every step your audience may conclude that the way is too difficult or that the scenery is dull and end the mental trip. Thus the writer must keep in the forefront of her mind whether the reader is being adequately rewarded for her time and effort. As the ratio of effort to reward increases, so does the likelihood that the writer will find herself alone on the path.

I think this metaphor applies also to teaching. A teacher tries to guide the thoughts of the student down a particular pathway, or perhaps to explore a broader swath of new terrain. It may be novel country even for the teacher, and their journeys occur side by side. Always the teacher encourages the student to continue, not to lose heart when he encounters obstacles, to use the experience of previous journeys to smooth the way, and to appreciate the beauty and awe that the scenery might afford. As the author must convince the reader not to drop the book, so too must the teacher persuade the student not to discontinue the journey. Teaching is an act of persuasion.*

So how do you persuade the student to follow you? The first answer you might think of is that we follow people whom we respect and who inspire us. True enough. If you have students' respect, they will try to pay attention both to please you and because they trust you; if you think something is worth knowing, they are ready to believe you. The problem is that students (and teachers) have only limited control over their own minds.

Although we like to think that we decide what to pay attention to, our minds have their own wishes and desires when it comes to the focus of attention. For example, you may sit down to read something – say, a report – that you know will be dull but that you nevertheless want to read carefully. Despite your best intentions, you find yourself thinking about something else, with your eyes merely passing over the words. Similarly, most of us have had a teacher whom we liked but did not think was especially effective; he was disorganized, or a little dull, even if also kind and earnest. I said in Chapter 1 that interesting-sounding content doesn't guarantee attention. (Remember my story about the sex talk from my seventh-grade teacher?) The student's desire to understand or to please the teacher is no guarantee of sustained attention.

So how can a teacher maximize the chances that students will follow her? Another of my college writing instructors answered that question for me when she made this claim: "Most of writing is anticipating how your reader will react." To properly guide the reader on this mental journey, you must know where each sentence will lead him. Will he find it interesting, confusing, poetic, or offensive? How a reader reacts depends not just on what you write but also on who the reader is. The simple sentence "Teaching is like writing" will generate different thoughts in a preschool teacher and a sales clerk. To anticipate your reader's reaction, you must know his personality, his tastes, his biases, and his background knowledge. We have all heard the advice "Know your audience." My professor explained why this is true for writing, and I believe it is no less true for teaching.

Thus, to ensure that your students follow you, you must keep them interested; to ensure their interest, you must anticipate their reactions; and to anticipate their reactions, you must know them. "Know your students" is a fair summary of the content of this book. This maxim sounds suspiciously like *bubbe* psychology. If you weren't aware that you should know your students (and I'm sure you were), your grandmother could have told you it was a good idea. Can cognitive science do no better than that?

What cognitive science can offer is elaboration that puts flesh on the bare-bones slogan. There are particular things you should know about your students, and other things you can safely ignore. There are also actions you can take with that knowledge, and other actions that sound plausible but may well backfire. Table C.1 summarizes the principle of each chapter in this book, the type of knowledge you need to deploy that principle, and what I take to be the most important classroom implication.

TABLE C.1: The principles of the mind discussed in this book, along with the knowledge needed to deploy them, and the most important implication of each.

Chapter	Cognitive principle	Required knowledge about students	Most important classroom implication
1	People are naturally curious, but they are not naturally good thinkers.	What is just beyond what my students know and can do?	Think of to-be-learned material as answers, and take the time necessary to explain to students the questions.
2	Factual knowledge precedes skill.	What do my students know?	It is not possible to think well on a topic in the absence of factual knowledge about the topic.
3	Memory is the residue of thought.	What will students think during this lesson?	The best barometer for every lesson plan is "Of what will it make the students think?"
4	We understand new things in the context of things we already know.	What do students already know that will be a toehold on understanding this new material?	Always make deep knowledge your goal, spoken and unspoken, but recognize that shallow knowledge will come first.
5	Proficiency requires practice.	How can I get students to practice without boredom?	Think carefully about which material students need at their fingertips, and practice it over time.

6	Cognition is fundamentally different early and late in training.	What is the difference between my students and an expert?	Strive for deep understanding in your students, not the creation of new knowledge.
7	Children are more alike than different in terms of learning.	Knowledge of students' learning styles is not necessary.	Think of lesson content, not student differences, driving decisions about how to teach.
8	Intelligence can be changed through sustained hard work.	What do my students believe about intelligence?	Always talk about successes and failures in terms of process, not ability.
9	Technology changes everything . . . but not the way you think.	The changes to complex cognition brought about by tech are hard to predict.	Don't assume you know how new tech will work out in the classroom.
10	Teaching, like any complex cognitive skill, must be practiced to be improved.	What aspects of my teaching work well for my students, and what parts need improvement?	Improvement requires more than experience; it also requires conscious effort and feedback.

Cognitive scientists do know more than these 10 principles. These were selected because they meet four criteria:

1. As described in the book's introduction, each of these principles is true *all* of the time, whether the person is in the laboratory or the classroom, alone or in a group. The complexity of the mind means that its properties often change, depending on the context. These 10 principles are always applicable.

2. Each principle is based on a great deal of data, not only on one or two studies. If any of these principles is wrong, something close to it is right. I don't anticipate that in 10 years I will

write a third edition of this book in which a chapter is deleted because new data have overturned the conclusion.

3. Using or ignoring the principal can have a sizable impact on student performance. Cognitive scientists know lots of other things about the mind that suggest classroom applications, but applying these principles would yield only a modest effect, so it is not clear that it would be worth the effort.

4. In identifying a principle it had to be fairly clear to me that someone would know what to do with it. For example, "Attention is necessary for learning" didn't make the cut even though it meets the other three criteria, because it provides teachers with no direction for what they might do that they aren't already doing.

I have claimed that these principles can make a real difference, but that claim is not meant to imply that applying them is easy. ("Just apply my secret tips and boom! You're a great teacher!") All of the principles listed in Table C.1 must be leavened with good sense, and any of them can be taken too far or twisted out of shape. What then is the role of cognitive science in educational practice if it cannot offer firm prescriptions?

Education is similar to other fields of study in that scientific findings are useful but not decisive. An architect will use principles of physics in designing an office building, but she will also be guided by aesthetic principles and by her budget. Similarly, knowledge of cognitive science can be helpful in planning what you teach and how, but it is not the whole story.

Not the whole story – but I see two ways that cognitive science can be useful to teachers. First, knowledge of cognitive science can help teachers balance conflicting concerns. Classrooms are, after all, not just cognitive places. They are also emotional places, social places, motivational places, and more. These diverse elements prompt different concerns for the teacher, and they sometimes conflict, that is, the best practice cognitively may be poor practice motivationally. Knowing the principles of cognitive science presented here can help a teacher as she balances the different, sometimes conflicting concerns of the classroom.

Second, I see principles of cognitive science as useful boundaries to educational practice. Principles of physics do not prescribe for a civil engineer exactly how to build a bridge, but they let him predict how it is likely to perform if he builds it. Similarly, cognitive scientific principles do not prescribe how to teach, but they can help you predict how much your students are likely to learn. If you follow these principles, you maximize the chances that your students will flourish.

Education is the passing on of the accumulated wisdom of generations to children, and we passionately believe in its importance because we know that it holds the promise of a better life for each child, and for us all, collectively. It would be a shame indeed if we did not use the accumulated wisdom of science to inform the methods by which we educate children. That has been the purpose of *Why Don't Students Like School?* Education makes better minds, and knowledge of the mind can make better education.

Notes

*I believe Price would have agreed that his advice applies to teaching, about which he later wrote this: "If your method reaches only the attentive student, then you must either invent new methods or call yourself a failure." Price, R. (2001). *Feasting of the Heart*. New York: Scribners, 81.

Glossary

Abstract knowledge Knowledge that could apply to many situations and is described independent of any particular situation. Categories are usually abstract; the idea "dog" can be defined independently of any particular dog. Problem solutions too may be abstract: knowing how to solve a long-division problem is independent of any particular numbers you might divide.

Automatic/Automaticity A process is automatic if it requires few or no attentional resources. It also may happen even if you don't intend for it to happen if the right trigger is in the environment.

Autopilot A common language term, not a technical term. That feeling that you're doing something complex but aren't really having to think about it. Driving is the classic example; you stop at red lights, put on your blinker when you turn, check your mirrors when you change lanes, all the while scarcely thinking about it.

Background knowledge Knowledge of the world. It could be on any topic—that the sky is blue, that San Marino is near the Adriatic, and so on. Background knowledge (on the relevant topic) is essential to reading comprehension and to critical thinking.

Chunking The process of combining smaller units of knowledge (e.g., the letters "b," "e," and "d" into a single unit "bed"). Chunking is an important method of working around the space limitation of working memory. Note that chunking requires information from long-term memory; seeing the letters "b," "e," and "d" and recognizing that they can be grouped into the word "bed" requires having the word bed in long-term memory.

Cognitive ability Capacity for or success in certain types of thought. Basically amounts to how well you do something, for example, think with words or with numbers. Contrasts with **cognitive style**.

Cognitive style A bias or tendency to think in a particular way, for example, in words or in visual mental images. Basically amounts to how you like to do something. One style is not superior to another, but you're supposed to think more successfully if you use your preferred style than if you are forced to use a nonpreferred one.

Concrete knowledge Contrasting with abstract knowledge, concrete knowledge deals with specifics. You may learn that several objects are "dogs," so you know *those particular objects* are dogs – you wouldn't recognize a new dog because you don't have the abstract idea of "dog" in memory.

Confirmation bias Once we hold a belief, we unconsciously interpret ambiguous evidence as being consistent with our belief, and if we seek evidence for it, we search for evidence that supports it, rather than evidence that refutes it.

Cramming Loading all of your practice (or studying) to the time just before you will be tested.

Cue Something in the environment that prompts recall of a memory or a thought that prompts recall of a memory.

Deep knowledge Knowledge characterized by deep understanding *and* concrete examples *and* how the two fit together. People with deep knowledge can extend their knowledge to new examples and can consider hypothetical, "what if" questions about it. Contrast with **rote knowledge** and **shallow knowledge**.

Deliberate practice Requires that you select one small element of a complex task for improvement. You seek feedback on how you're doing and try new things in an effort to improve. Deliberate practice is understood to be effortful, as it requires considerable attention.

Digital immigrant A person who did not grow up using digital devices, that is, born before the mid-1980s. They were proposed to be uncomfortable using such devices, with the analogy of someone who is not a native speaker of a language. In addition, it was proposed that persistent use of digital devices actually changes cognitive processing and biases. Contrast with **digital native**.

Digital native A person who grew up using digital devices. The term was popularized in 2001 and referred to anyone born in the mid-1980s or after. Because of their frequent use of digital devices, it was suggested that these people not only were comfortable using them but thought differently. Contrast with **digital immigrant**.

Discount rate The relative value placed on a good or experience in the near future versus the more distant future. A reward that you might get in the near future have greater value than the same reward that you might get in the more distant future. The reward value drops steeply as you move forward in time and is steeper the younger you are. (Elsewhere referred to as delay discounting, temporal discounting, time discounting, or time preference.)

Distributed practice The method of spacing out bouts of studying or practice. Works best when one sleeps between study sessions. Spaced practice is a synonym. Contrast with **cramming**.

Fixed mindset The belief that talents (including intelligence) are mostly a matter of genetic inheritance and that individuals are mostly powerless to change whatever talent Nature has given them in a domain.

Flynn effect A significant increase in the average intelligence quotient across time, measured in a representative sample of a country's population. These increases have been observed in many countries. It's important because the country's gene pool could not change quickly enough to account for the increase. Thus, the Flynn Effect is evidence of the importance of the environment to intelligence.

Fourth-grade slump A phenomenon observed in the reading achievement of children from low-income families. They read at grade level until third or fourth grade, then seemingly overnight, they are behind their peers. This happens when reading tests change from emphasizing mostly decoding (appropriate for early grades, obviously) to setting a higher bar for student comprehension as children reach the point that most decode fairly well. Children from low-income homes have a disproportionate problem with comprehension because they have fewer opportunities to pick up factual knowledge at home.

g (general intelligence) General intelligence is not specified in cognitive terms. It's really a pattern of data. It refers to the fact that performance on virtually all measures of mental ability correlate. The correlations are by no means identical across tests, but they are always positive, which is interpreted as reflecting a general mental ability that contributes very broadly.

Grit Passion and perseverance for long-term goals. People who talk about grit in the context of education sometimes focus on perseverance and forget passion – you're supposed to feel strongly about the work!

Growth mindset The belief that talents (including intelligence) can be developed through hard work, effective strategies, and helpful feedback. Contrast with fixed mindset.

GWAS Acronym for genome-wide association study. These studies search for relationships between genetic regions and traits, including behavioral traits. These studies differ from previously used techniques because they can examine all genetic regions simultaneously, rather than examining a small part of the genome (selected by some hypothesis).

Intelligence Most psychologists would agree that intelligence refers to the ability to understand complex ideas, to use different forms of reasoning, to overcome obstacles by engaging thought, and to learn from experience.

Learning style See **cognitive style**.

Long-term memory The mind's storehouse for factual knowledge as well as procedural memory (how to do things). It's not easy to get information into long-term memory, but once there it will likely stick around, potentially forever.

Metacognition Thinking about thinking. This might mean planning problem solving in stages, or remembering a strategy you were taught for what to do when you don't understand a difficult passage of text, or deciding how to study for a quiz.

Mnemonic Any of a group of memory tricks that are most helpful when the to-be-learned content is not meaningful.

Multiple intelligences A particular theory of intelligence proposed by Howard Gardner, suggesting that there are eight largely independent intelligences. Most psychologists agree that intelligence is multifaceted (that is, not a single thing) but they disagree with the list of intelligences Gardner proposes.

Multitasking Commonly thought of as "doing two things at once," but when we feel we are doing two tasks at once we are actually rapidly switching between them.

Overlearning Continuing to practice or study after it seems that you've mastered the content or skill. You don't seem to improve, but the continued practice protects against forgetting.

Pedagogical content knowledge Knowledge not just of the material to be taught, but knowledge relevant to *how* to teach it. Thus, content knowledge for spelling is the spelling of words. Pedagogical content knowledge for the teaching of spelling includes ways to help students remember spelling, knowledge of what sorts of words students find easy or difficult, knowing good ways to assess spelling knowledge, and so on.

Practice Repetition, but without some of the elements that make for deliberate practice.

Procedural memory Memory for how to do things, for example, what to do when a pot boils over on a stove or how to find the best route between two points on a paper map.

Rote knowledge Things that one memorizes with little or no understanding of meaning, as when children learn to sing their country's national anthem but are really just saying the words. Contrast with **shallow knowledge** and **deep knowledge**.

Self-serving bias The tendency to believe that when something positive happens, it's due to our own positive traits (our character, our abilities, or hard work) but when there's a negative outcome it's due to external factors (for example, bad luck or someone else's incompetence).

Shallow knowledge Shallow knowledge has meaning associated with it – the student does understand – but the meaning is limited. The understanding of meaning is concrete, and it's limited to a small set of examples. Contrast with **rote knowledge** and **deep knowledge**.

Social proof Social proof is our tendency to believe things because others believe them. It may seem foolish, but we can't evaluate the evidence for every candidate belief we encounter, so if most of the people we know believe something is true, we're usually willing to accept that it is true.

Spacing The method of distributing bouts of studying or practice. Works best when one sleeps between study sessions. **Distributed practice** is a synonym. Contrast with **cramming**.

Stories Stories have these characteristics: they are populated by strong characters, the events described are driven by a central conflict that concerns one or more characters, complications arise as the characters struggle to resolve the conflict, and the events described are causally linked. Memory is facilitated when to-be-learned content is presented in a story structure.

Transfer The successful application of old knowledge to a new problem.

Working memory The mental space in which you briefly hold information and that also serves as the staging ground of thought. Working memory is usually thought of as synonymous with consciousness, and its space is limited. Overwhelming working memory is a common reason people get confused.

Notes

Chapter One

1. Roitfeld, C. (2016). Icons: In bed with Kim and Kanye. *Harper's Bazaar* (28 July). https://www.harpersbazaar.com/fashion/photography/a16784/kanye-west-kim-kardashian-interview/ (accessed 24 July 2020).
2. Duncker, K. (1945). On problem-solving. *Psychological Monographs* 5: 113.
3. Townsend, D. J., and Bever, T. G. (2001). *Sentence Comprehension: The Integration of Habits and Rules*, 2. Cambridge, MA: MIT Press.
4. Simon, H. A. *Sciences of the Artificial*, 3e, 94. Cambridge, MA: MIT Press.
5. Aristotle. (2009). *The Nicomachean Ethics* (trans. D. Ross; ed. L. Brown), 137. Oxford, UK: Oxford University Press.

Chapter Two

1. In Everett's preface to his English translation of Deschanel, A. P. (1898). *Elementary Treatise on Natural Philosophy*. New York: Appleton.
2. Virginia Department of Education. Released Tests and Item Sets. http://www.doe.virginia.gov/testing/sol/released_tests/index.shtml (accessed 17 July 2020).
3. Yip, K. Y., Ho, K. O., Yu, K. Y., et al. (2019). Measuring magnetic field texture in correlated electron systems under extreme conditions. *Science* 366(6471): 1355-1359.
4. Melville, H. (1902; 1851) *Moby-Dick*, 135. New York: Scribners.
5. Recht, D. R. and Leslie, L. (1988). Effect of prior knowledge on good and poor readers' memory of text. *Journal of Educational Psychology* 80: 16–20.
6. Bransford, J. D., and Johnson, M. K. (1972). Contextual prerequisites for understanding: some investigations of comprehension and recall. *Journal of Verbal Learning and Verbal Behavior* 11: 717–726.
7. Wason, P. C. (1968). Reasoning about a rule. *Quarterly Journal of Experimental Psychology* 20: 273–281.

8. Griggs, R. A., and Cox, J. R. (1982). The elusive thematic-materials effect in Wason's selection task. *British Journal of Psychology* 73: 407–420.

9. Van Overschelde, J. P., and Healy, A. F. (2001). Learning of nondomain facts in high- and low-knowledge domains. *Journal of Experimental Psychology: Learning, Memory, and Cognition* 27: 1160–1171.

10. Bischoff-Grethe, A., Goedert, K. M., Willingham, D. T., and Grafton, S. T. (2004). Neural substrates of response-based sequence learning using fMRI. *Journal of Cognitive Neuroscience* 16: 127–138.

11. Willingham, D. T., and Lovette, G. (2014). Can reading comprehension be taught? *Teachers College Record* www.tcrecord.org, ID Number: 17701.

Chapter Three

1. I'm not trying to be funny. College student really do remember jokes and asides best. Kintsch, W., and Bates, E. Recognition memory for statements from a classroom lecture. *Journal of Experimental Psychology: Human Learning and Memory* 3: 150–159.

2. Dinges, D. F., Whitehouse, W. G., Orne, E. C., et al. (1992). Evaluating hypnotic memory enhancement (hypermnesia and reminiscence) using multitrial forced recall. *Journal of Experimental Psychology: Learning, Memory, and Cognition* 18: 1139–1147.

3. Nickerson, R. S., and Adams, M. J. (1979). Long-term memory for a common object. *Cognitive Psychology* 11: 287–307.

4. Hyde, T. S., and Jenkins, J. J. (1973). Recall for words as a function of semantic, graphic, and syntactic orienting tasks. *Journal of Verbal Learning and Verbal Behavior* 12: 471–480.

5. Barclay, J. R., Bransford, J. D., Franks, J. J., et al. (1974). Comprehension and semantic flexibility. *Journal of Verbal Learning and Verbal Behavior* 13: 471–481.

6. Allyn, B. (2020, 23 January). Fidget spinners, packing, note-taking: staying awake in the senate chamber. *National Public Radio.* https://www.npr.org/2020/01/23/799071421/fidget-spinners-pacing-note-taking-staying-awake-in-the-senate-chamber (accessed 17 July 2020).

Chapter Four

1. Searle, J. (1980). Minds, brains and programs. *Behavioral and Brain Sciences* 3: 417–457.

2. Gick, M. L., and Holyoak, K. J. (1980). Analogical problem solving. *Cognitive Psychology* 12: 306–355.

3. Thorndike, E. L. (1923). The influence of first-year Latin upon ability to read English. *School and Society* 17: 165–168.

Chapter Five

1. Rosinski, R. R., Golinkoff, R. M., and Kukish, K. S. (1975). Automatic semantic processing in a picture-word interference task. *Child Development* 46 (1): 247–253.
2. Willingham, D. T. (2017). *The Reading Mind: A Cognitive Approach to Understanding How the Mind Reads.* San Francisco, CA: Jossey-Bass.
3. Whitehead, A. N. (1911). *An Introduction to Mathematics*, 61. New York: Holt.
4. Ellis, J. A., Semb, G. B., and Cole, B. (1998). Very long-term memory for information taught in school. *Contemporary Educational Psychology* 23: 419–433.
5. Bahrick, H. P., and Hall, L. K. (1991). Lifetime maintenance of high school mathematics content. *Journal of Experimental Psychology: General* 120: 20–33.
6. Green, E. A., Rao, J. M., and Rothschild, D. (2019). A sharp test of the portability of expertise. *Management Science* 65 (6): 2820–2831.

Chapter Six

1. Kaplow, L. (Writer), and O'Fallon, P. (Director). (2004, November 23). Paternity [television broadcast]. House, MD. (D. Shore and B. Singer, Executive producers). New York: Fox.
2. Chase, W. G., and Simon, H. A. (1973). Perception in chess. *Cognitive Psychology* 4: 55–81.
3. Chi, M. T. H., Feltovich, P. J., and Glaser, R. (1981). Categorization and representation of physics problems by experts and novices. *Cognitive Science* 5: 121–152.
4. Chi, Feltovich, & Glaser (1981), 146.
5. https://www.carnegiehall.org/Visit/Carnegie-Hall-FAQs (accessed 19 July 2020).
6. Ericsson, K. A., Krampe, R. T., and Tesch-Römer, C. (1993). The role of deliberate practice in the acquisition of expert performance. *Psychological Review* 100: 363–400.
7. Simon, H., and Chase, W. (1973). Skill in chess. *American Scientist* 61: 394–403.
8. Celebrating Jazz Pianist Hank Jones. (2005, June 20). Interview on Fresh Air. http://www.npr.org/templates/story/story.php?storyId=4710791 (accessed 29 July 2020)
9. Salzman, M. (1987). *Iron and Silk*, 98. New York: Knopf.
10. Cronbach, L. J. (1954). *Educational Psychology*, 14. New York: Harcourt, Brace.
11. Emerson, R. W. (1883). *Works of Ralph Waldo Emerson*, 478. London: Routledge.

Chapter Seven

1. Kraemer, D. J., Rosenberg, L. M., and Thompson-Schill, S. L. (2009). The neural correlates of visual and verbal cognitive styles. *Journal of Neuroscience* 29 (12): 3792–3798.

2. Tolstoy, L. N. (1899). *What Is Art?*, 124 (trans. A. Maud). New York: Thomas Crowell.
3. Wilson, E. O. (2013). *Letters to a Young Scientist*, 33. New York: Norton.
4. Mineo, L. (2018). "The greatest gift you can have is a good education, one that isn't strictly professional." *Harvard Gazette* (9 May). https://news.harvard.edu/gazette/story/2018/05/harvard-scholar-howard-gardner-reflects-on-his-life-and-work/ (accessed 19 July 2020).
5. Armstrong, T. (2000). *Multiple Intelligences in the Classroom*, 2e. Alexandria, VA: Association for Supervision and Curriculum Development.
6. Gardner, H. (2013). Howard Gardner: Multiple intelligences are not learning styles. *Washington Post* (16 October) https://www.washingtonpost.com/news/answer-sheet/wp/2013/10/16/howard-gardner-multiple-intelligences-are-not-learning-styles/ (accessed 21 August 2020).

Chapter Eight

1. Kovacs, K., and Conway, A. R. (2019). What is IQ? Life beyond "general intelligence". *Current Directions in Psychological Science* 28 (2): 189–194.
2. Zushi, Y. (2017). In praise of Keanu Reeves, the nicest of meatheads. *New Statesman* (24 February). https://www.newstatesman.com/culture/film/2017/02/praise-keanu-reeves-nicest-meatheads (accessed 19 July 2020).
3. Savage, J.E., Jansen, P.R., Stringer, S., et al. (2018). Genome-wide association meta-analysis in 269,867 individuals identifies new genetic and functional links to intelligence. *Nature Genetics* 50: 912–919.
4. Selzam, S., Ritchie, S. J., Pingault, J. B., et al. (2019). Comparing within- and between-family polygenic score prediction. *American Journal of Human Genetics* 105 (2): 351–363.
5. Dickens, W.T. (2008). Cognitive ability. In: *The New Palgrave Dictionary of Economics* (ed. Palgrave Macmillan). London: Palgrave Macmillan. doi: https://doi.org/10.1057/978-1-349-95121-5 (accessed 13 July 2020).
6. Duyme, M., Dumaret, A., and Tomkiewicz, S. (1999). How can we boost IQs of "dull" children? A late adoption study. *Proceedings of the National Academy of Sciences* 96: 8790–8794.
7. Nisbett, R. E., Aronson, J., Blair, C., et al. (2012). Intelligence: new findings and theoretical developments. *American Psychologist* 67 (2): 130–159.
8. Flynn, J. R. (1987). Massive IQ gains in 14 nations: what IQ tests really measure. *Psychological Bulletin* 101: 171–191.
9. Blackwell, L. S., Trzesniewski, K. H., and Dweck, C. S. (2007). Implicit theories of intelligence predict achievement across an adolescent transition: a longitudinal study and an intervention. *Child Development* 78 (1): 246–263.
10. Organisation for Economic Cooperation and Development. (2019). *PISA 2018 Results (Volume III): What School Life Means for Students' Lives*, PISA. Paris: OECD Publishing. doi: https://doi.org/10.1787/acd78851-en (accessed 19 July 2020). See also Sisk, V. F., Burgoyne, A. P., Sun, J., et al. (2018).

To what extent and under which circumstances are growth mind-sets important to academic achievement? Two meta-analyses. *Psychological Science* 29 (4): 549–571.

11. Yeager, D. S. Hanselman, P., Walton, G. M., et al. (2019). A national experiment reveals where a growth mindset improves achievement. *Nature* 573 (7774): 364–369.

12. Rege, M., Hanselman, P., Solli, I. F., et al. (accepted for publication). How can we inspire nations of learners? Investigating growth mindset and challenge-seeking in two countries. *American Psychologist*.

13. Yeager, D., Walton, G., and Cohen, G. L. (2013). Addressing achievement gaps with psychological interventions. *Phi Delta Kappan* 94 (5): 62–65.

14. Sisk, V. F., Burgoyne, A. P., Sun, J., et al. (2018). To what extent and under which circumstances are growth mind-sets important to academic achievement? Two meta-analyses. *Psychological Science* 29 (4): 549–571.

15. Dweck, C. (2015). Carol Dweck revisits the growth mindset. *Education Week* 35 (5): 20–24.

Chapter Nine

1. Prensky, M. (2001). Digital natives, digital immigrants. *On the Horizon* 9(5): 1–6.

2. Kennedy, G., Judd, T., Churchward, A., and Gray, K. (2008). First year students' experiences with technology: are they really digital natives? *Australasian Journal of Educational Technology.* 24(1): 108–122.

3. Valtonen, T., Pontinen, S., Kukkonen, J., et al. (2011). Confronting the technological pedagogical knowledge of Finnish Net Generation student teachers. *Technology, Pedagogy and Education* 20(1): 3–18.

4. Rideout, V., and Robb, M. B. (2019). *The Common Sense census: Media use by tweens and teens, 2019.* San Francisco, CA: Common Sense Media. https://www.commonsensemedia.org/sites/default/files/uploads/research/2019-census-8-to-18-key-findings-updated.pdf (accessed 19 July 2020).

5. Rogers, R. D., and Monsell, S. (1995). Costs of a predictable switch between simple cognitive tasks. *Journal of Experimental Psychology: General* 124(2): 207–231.

6. Warschauer, M. (2005). Going one-to-one. *Educational Leadership* 63(4): 34–38.

7. Yau, J.C., and Reich, S.M. (2017). Are the qualities of adolescents' offline friendships present in digital interactions? *Adolescent Research Review* 3: 339–355.

8. Singer, N. (2017). How Google conquered the American classroom. *New York Times* (May 14): p. A1.

9. Twenge, J.M. 2017. *IGen.* New York: Simon and Schuster.

10. Iyengar, S. (2018). US trends in arts attendance and literary reading: 2002–2017. National Endowment for the Arts. https://www.arts.gov/impact/research/publications/us-trends-arts-attendance-and-literary-reading-2002-2017 (accessed 19 July 2020).

11. Scholastic. (2019). *Kids and family reading report*, 7e. https://www.scholastic
    .com/readingreport (accessed 19 July 2020).
12. Twenge, J.M. (2017). *IGen*. New York: Simon and Schuster.
13. Data for the American Time Use Survey are available from the Bureau of
    Labor Statistics, https://www.bls.gov/tus/ (accessed 19 July 2020).
14. Casey, B. J. (2019). Arrested development or adaptive? The adolescent and self
    control. Kavli Keynote address presented at the International Convention of
    Psychological Science. Paris, France (7 March). https://www.youtube.com/
    watch?v=1xCmPwXxyvA&feature=emb_logo (accessed 19 July 2020).

Chapter Ten

1. Kumar, A. (2020). The grandmaster diet: How to lose weight while
   barely moving. https://www.espn.com/espn/story/_/id/27593253/why-
   grandmasters-magnus-carlsen-fabiano-caruana-lose-weight-playing-chess
   (accessed 27 July 2020).
2. New Yorker (2009). Ask the Author Live: David Sedaris. (14 August). https://
   www.newyorker.com/books/ask-the-author/ask-the-author-live-david-
   sedaris (accessed 28 July 2020).

Index

Page numbers followed by *f* and *t* refer to figures and tables, respectively.